# A SENSE OF PLACE

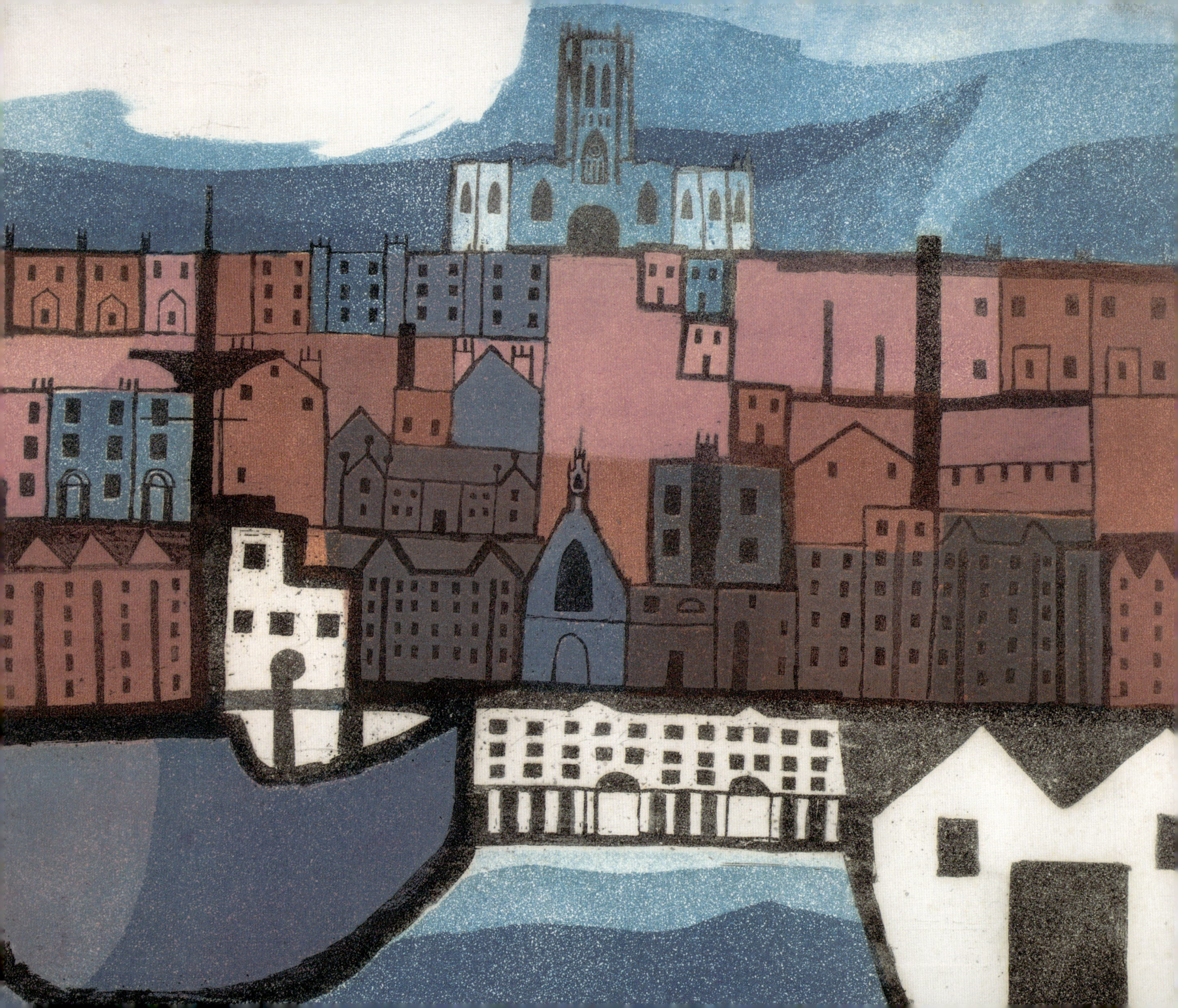

# A SENSE OF PLACE
## THE ART OF Helena Markson

Emma Mason

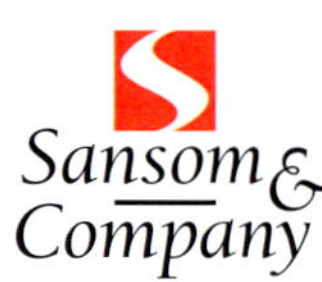

First published in 2016 by
Bread and Butter Press
3 Cornfield Terrace
Eastbourne
East Sussex BN21 4NN

www.breadandbutterpress.co.uk


Publishing services by Sansom & Co
a publishing imprint of Redcliffe Press Ltd

www.sansomandcompany.co.uk





ISBN: 978-0-9955037-0-0

*British Library Cataloguing–in-Publication Data*
A catalogue record for this book is available from the British Library



Design and typesetting by Design Deluxe, Bath

# CONTENTS

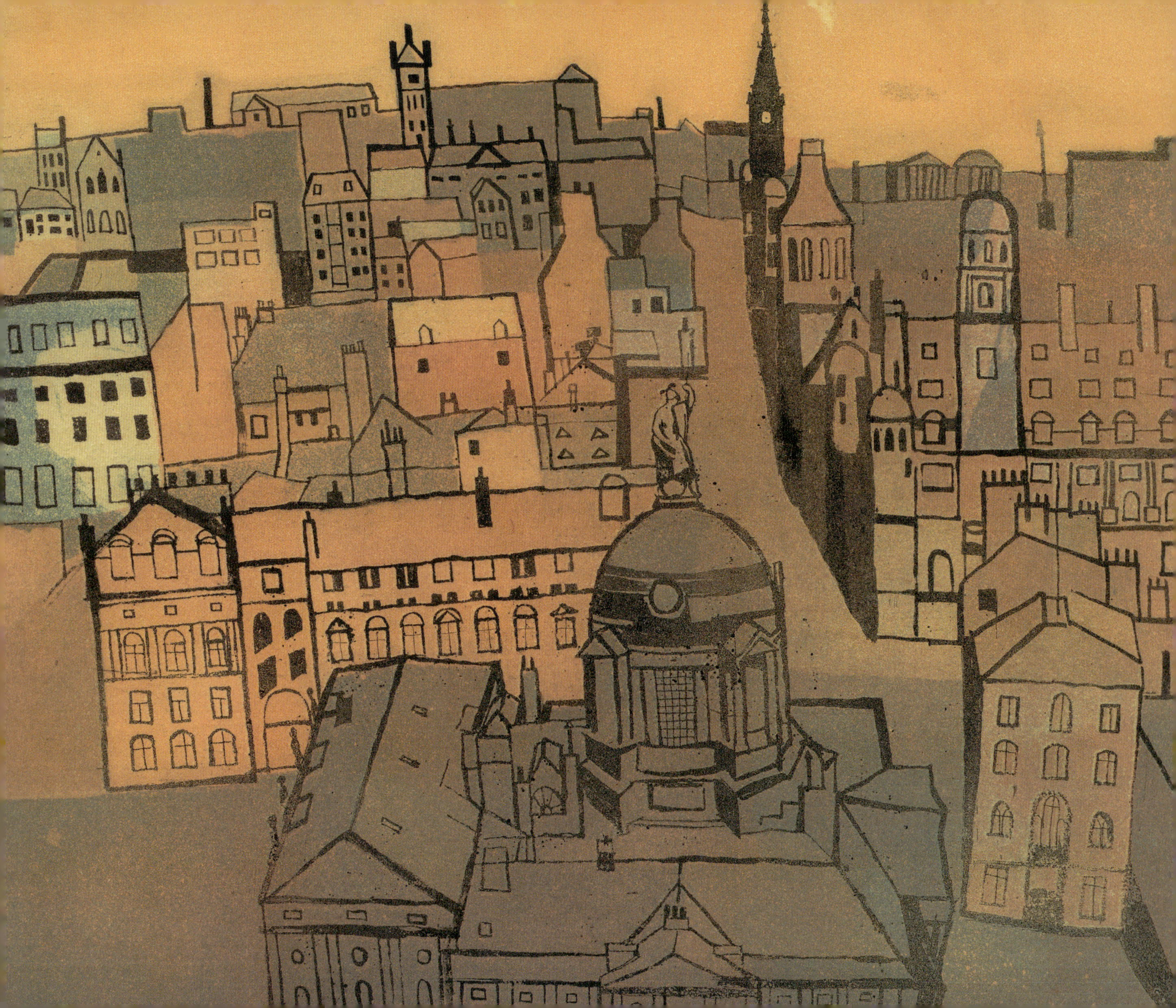

Helena Markson (1934–2012), printmaker and teacher, was an important influence on the story of modern printmaking both in the UK and in Israel. She spent her life teaching printmaking and creating her own beautiful prints, mostly etching and aquatint, which were inspired by the world around her. She exhibited her work in many of the important print exhibitions in London in the 1950s and 1960s and she was a co-director of the first open-access Fine Art Printmaking Workshop in London. In Israel she set up the fine art print studios at the University of Haifa and she is considered a pioneer of modern printmaking in Israel. It was in 2012 that Helena's sister Irene contacted our gallery to explain that Helena had died quite suddenly earlier that year and that she would like us to see Helena's prints.

Our gallery specialises in original prints by printmakers working from the post-war years to the present and so we were very interested to see Helena's work. My husband Richard and I travelled up to Essex to visit Helena's former home to view her archive. It was wonderful to see Helena's prints, which covered a period of over fifty years. As well as the prints, which had been carefully stored, Helena had kept meticulous records and notes. It is through these records that I was able to learn more about her life and work. When Helena's family suggested that I write a book about Helena I was delighted. Helena's contribution to printmaking deserves greater recognition and I hope that this book brings her story and her prints to a wider audience. I would particularly like to thank Helena's sister Irene for her trust and support.

# EARLY LIFE

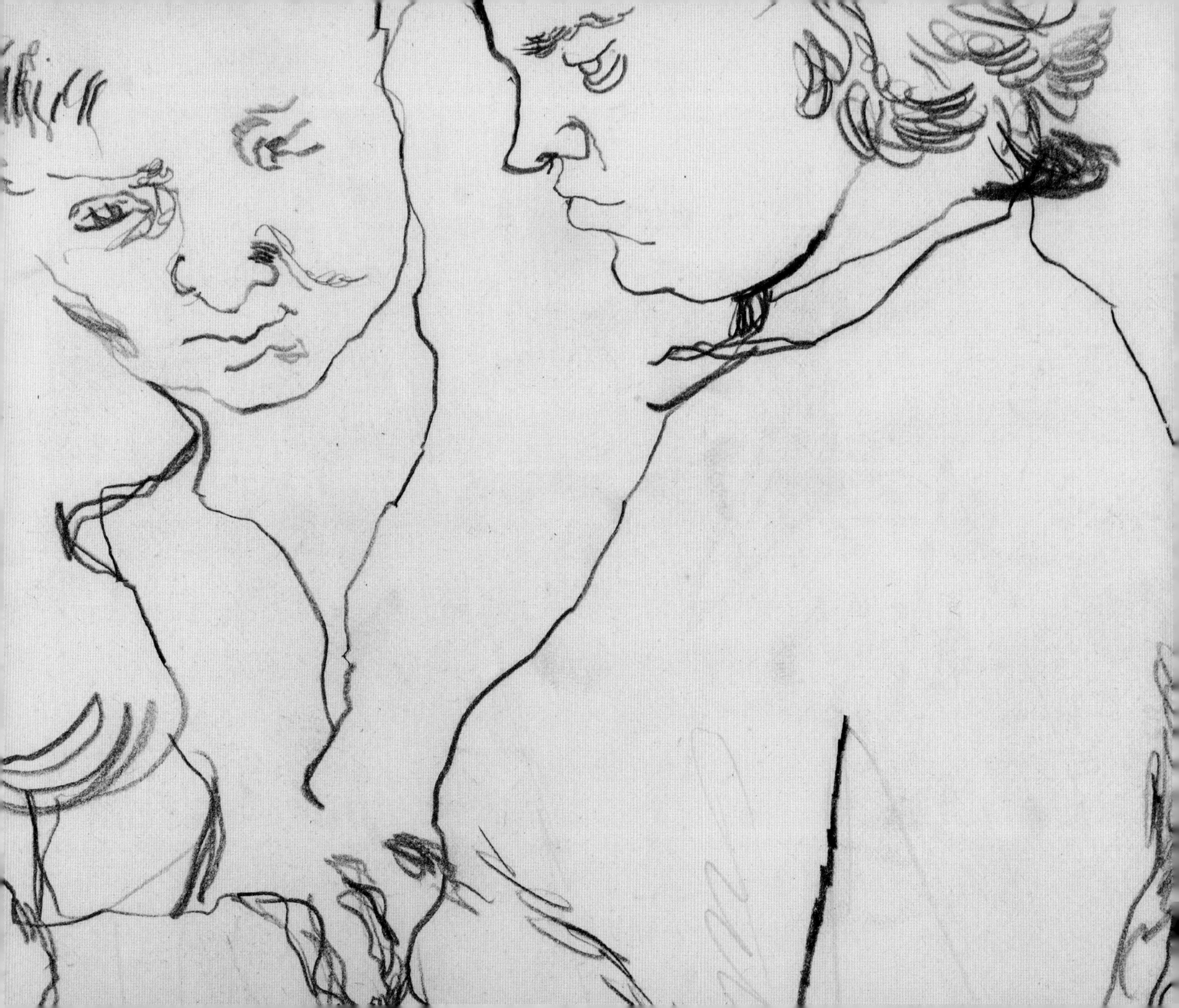

HELENA MARKSON was born in London in 1934. Her parents were Simon and Bertha Markson. Her father Simon had grown up in Birmingham with family which could be traced in England to the early 1800s. Bertha's family were Londoners who arrived in England from Lithuania in the early 1900s. Both families were entrepreneurial and established comfortable lifestyles. Helena's father was in the retail clothes business and her mother was at home running the house and taking care of their children. Helena was the middle child of three, with an older sister Irene and younger brother Edward.

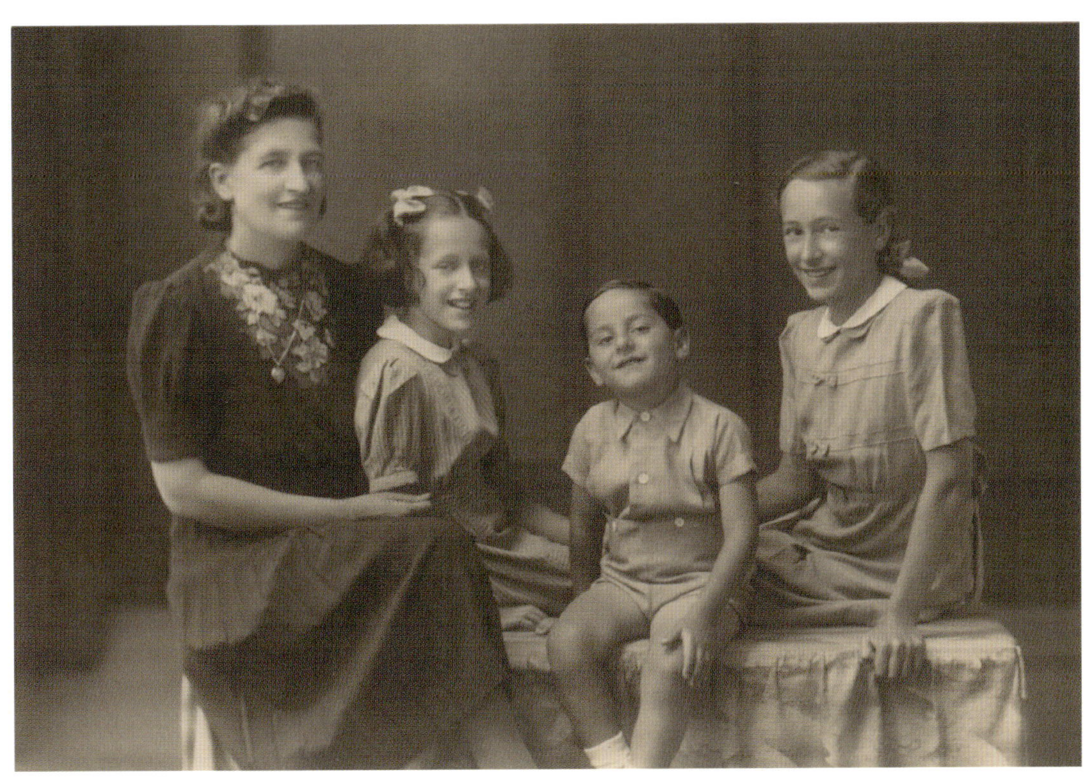

Helena's mother and children (Helena second left)

Helena spent her early childhood in London but when she was nearly five years old, just before the outbreak of the Second World War, the family decided to leave London for a safer town and moved to the small cathedral town of Salisbury in Wiltshire. Simon and Bertha both enjoyed and stressed the creative and dramatic arts and all three children were encouraged to take part in the arts. Helena reflected those interests, and as a child enjoyed ballet, music and art lessons. She excelled in each of these, learning the piano, taking dance classes and discovering what she saw as a gift at an early age in drawing images of family and the buildings around her. She had a happy childhood with family and friends and in later life spoke fondly about Salisbury:

*'I grew up in Salisbury where the beautiful and interesting architecture was always in my view.'[1]*

After leaving school aged sixteen she attended the local art school, Salisbury School of Art, where she was to study for two years from 1950–2. Here she first discovered the delights of printmaking. It was to become a lifelong passion.

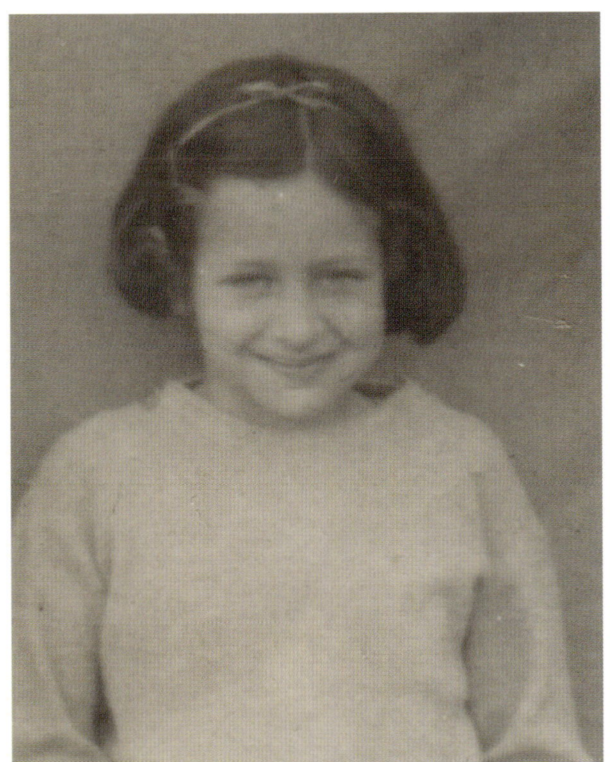

Helena aged 6 years

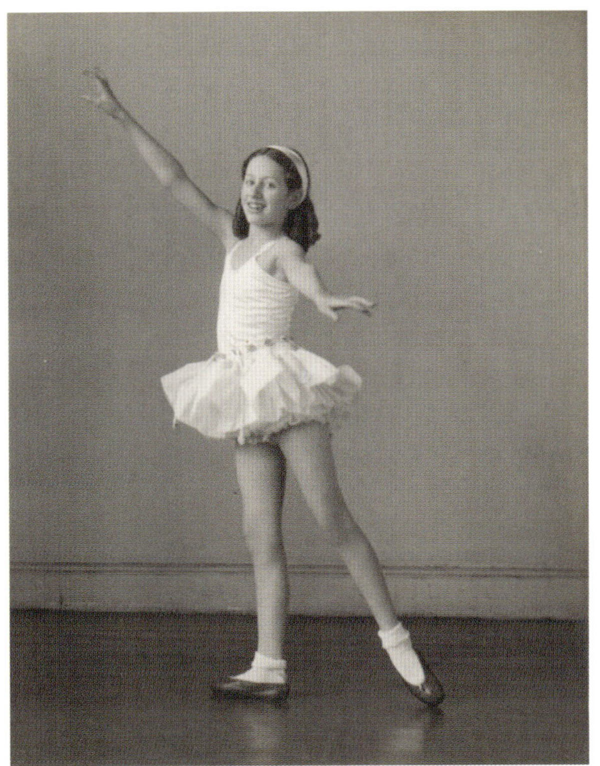

Helena at ballet class

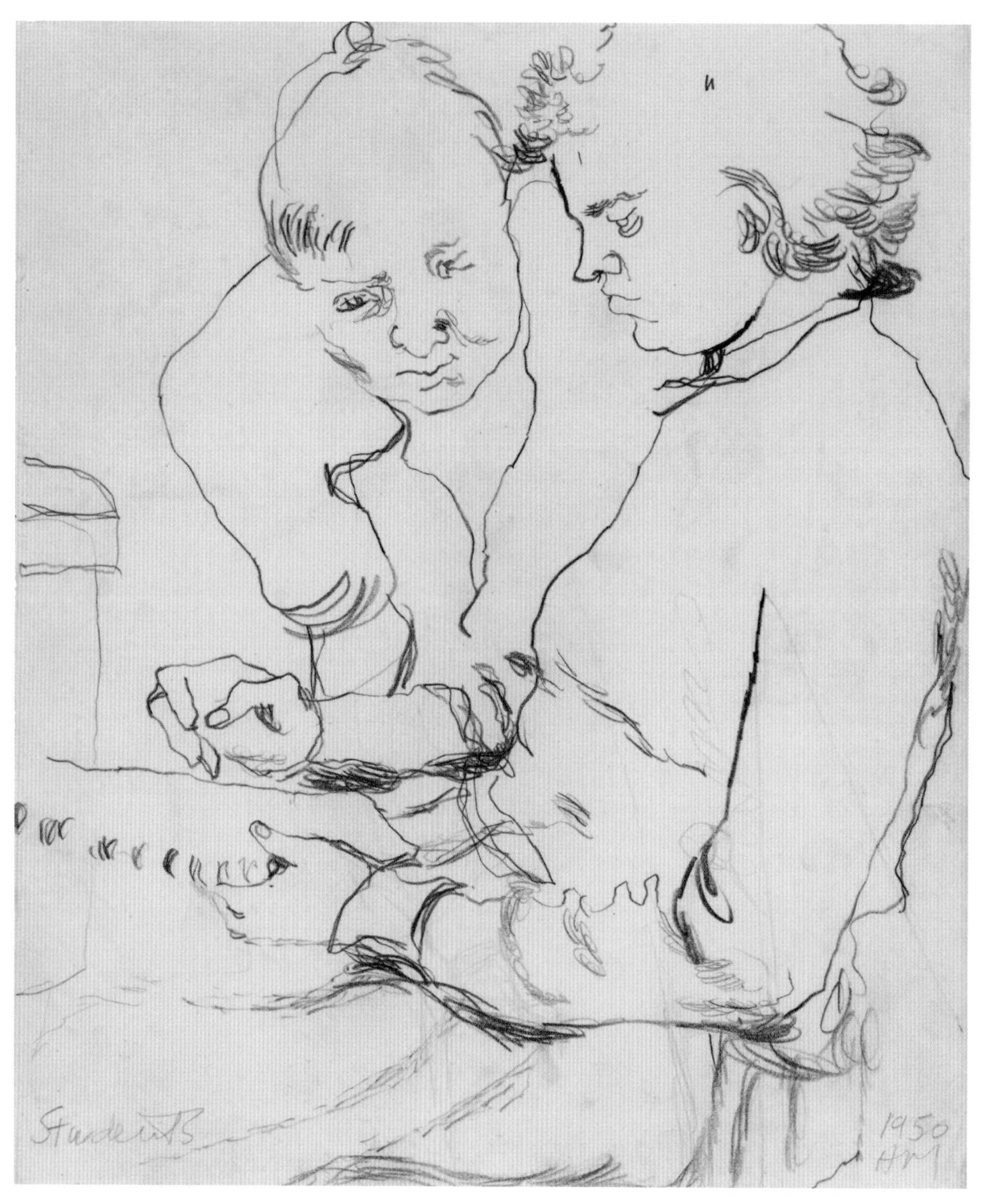

Sketch of art class from Helena's student sketchbook    1950 pencil 27cm x 22cm

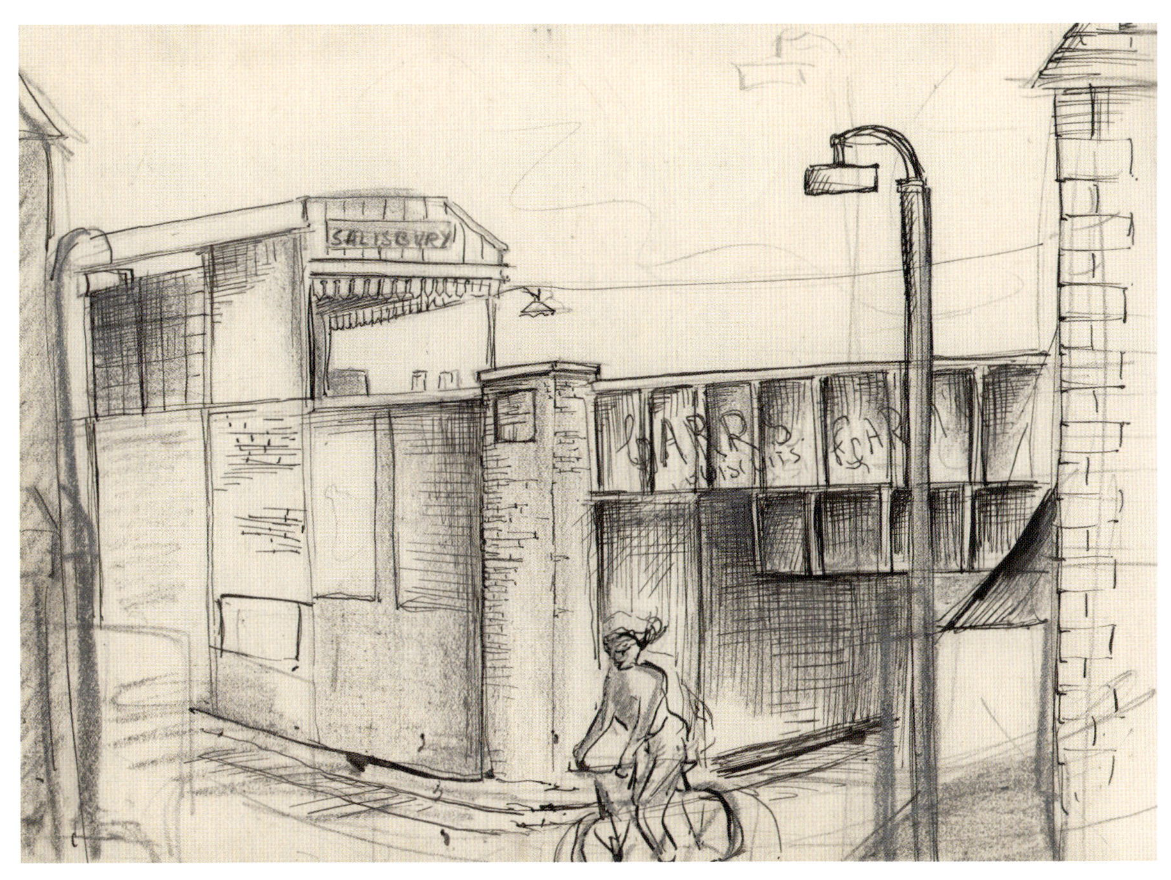

Sketch of Salisbury from Helena's student sketchbook   c.1950 pencil 20cm x 25cm

# LONDON LIFE

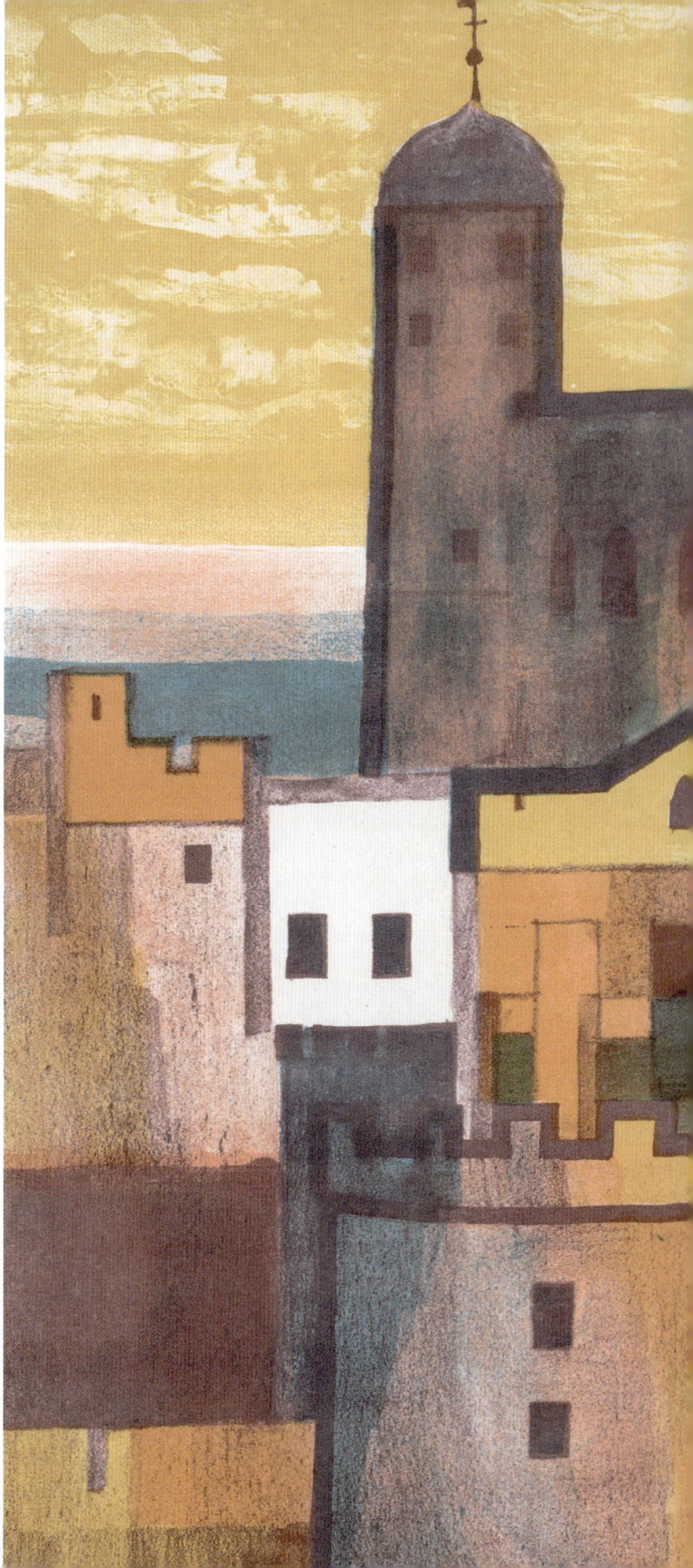

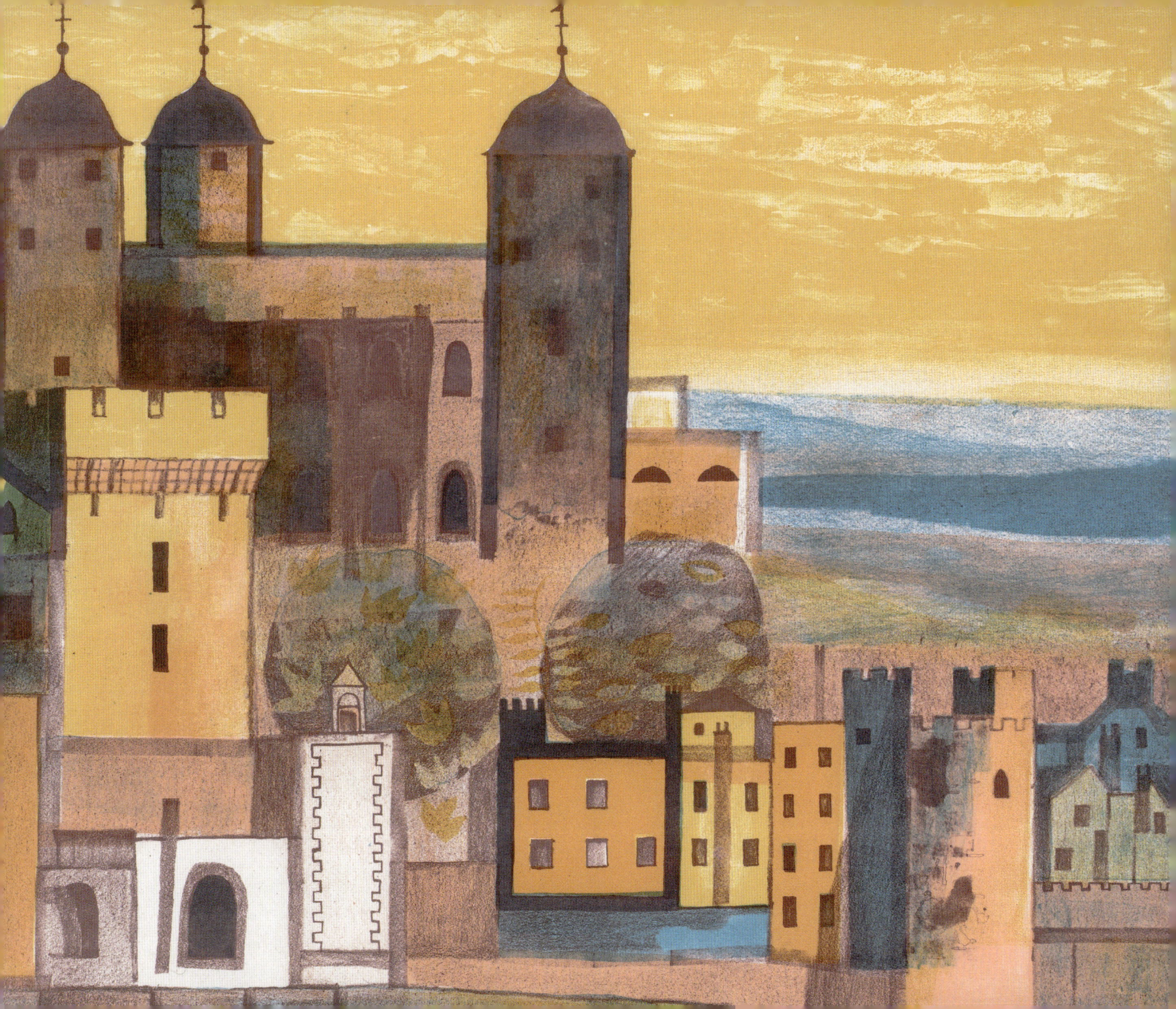

After studying at Salisbury School of Art, Helena gained a place at the Central School of Arts and Crafts, in London, from 1952–6. Her specialised studies were in printmaking, mural painting and illustration. She was taught etching and aquatint under painter and printmaker Merlyn Evans (1910–73) who was a very important influence. He had studied printmaking in Paris in 1934–6 under Stanley William Hayter. Evans was a skilled and inspiring teacher and with him Helena explored line etching and sugar-lift aquatint to deep etch. She learnt about the spontaneous nature of the aquatint process and how to use colour on separate plates, all of which she was to use extensively in her printmaking. Recognising her talent, Evans encouraged Helena. A few years later, in 1960, Evans wrote a reference for Helena who was applying for a teaching post:

*'Miss Helena Markson, whilst a student of etching in my class, showed originality and talent and was particularly successful in etching in colour, using several plates …
I think very highly of her as a draughtsman, designer and colourist and have pleasure in recommending her for a teaching post.'*[2]

Whilst at the Central School of Arts and Crafts she gained her National Diploma in Design (NDD) and her Central School Diploma (CSD). She also won two special awards, the William Atkinson Award, and the Queen's Scholarship, which at the time was given for the most outstanding woman student.

Throughout this time Helena lived in north London, first in Hampstead before moving to a flat in Stoke Newington's High Street. She liked being in the heart of a large urban environment and she became very familiar with the city, its streets and buildings, and people, all images and subjects that were to influence her work. From early on Helena was drawn to making images of the environment around her, the places she lived, as can been seen in her early prints such as *The High Street* and *Stoke Newington in the Rain*.

Following art school Helena stayed in London. She began to work full time on her printmaking and to build a body of work to establish herself as artist and printmaker. She needed access to a print studio and through the Central School of Arts and Crafts she heard about a studio in London where she could work with access to printing presses for etching and lithography. This was the print studio established a few years earlier by printmaker Birgit Skiöld.

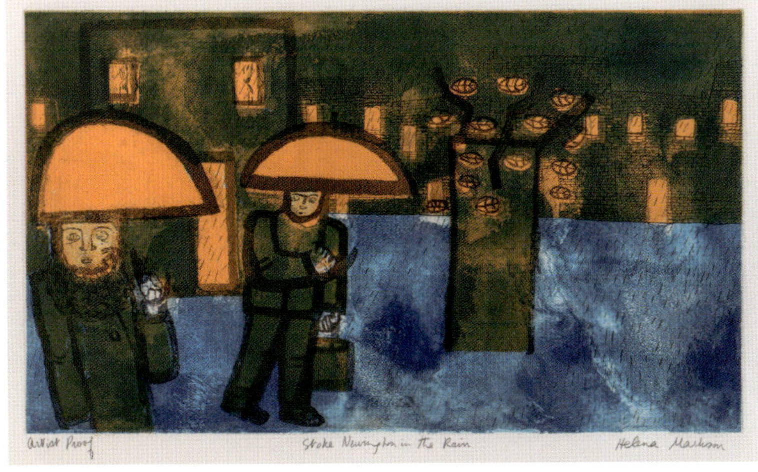


*Stoke Newington in the Rain*   c.1954 etching and aquatint 30cm x 52cm

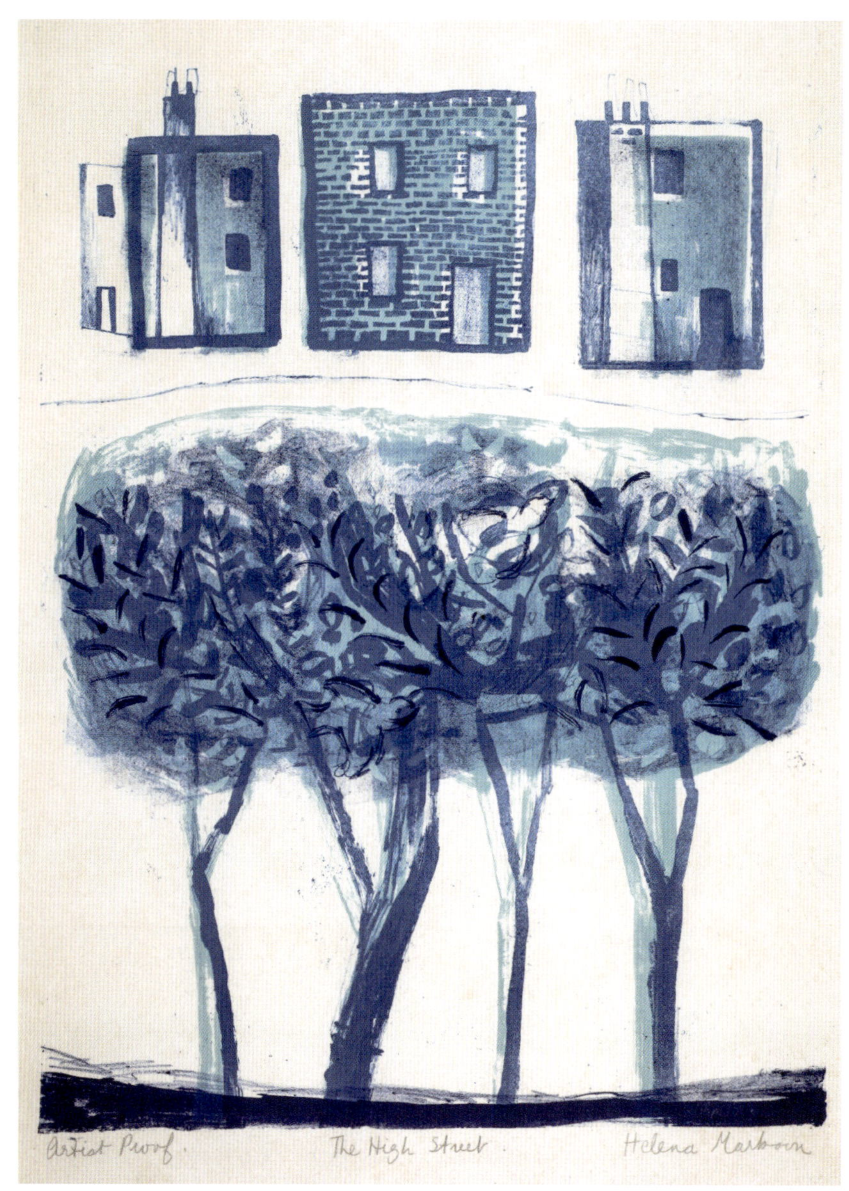



*The High Street*   c.1955 lithograph 48cm x 36cm

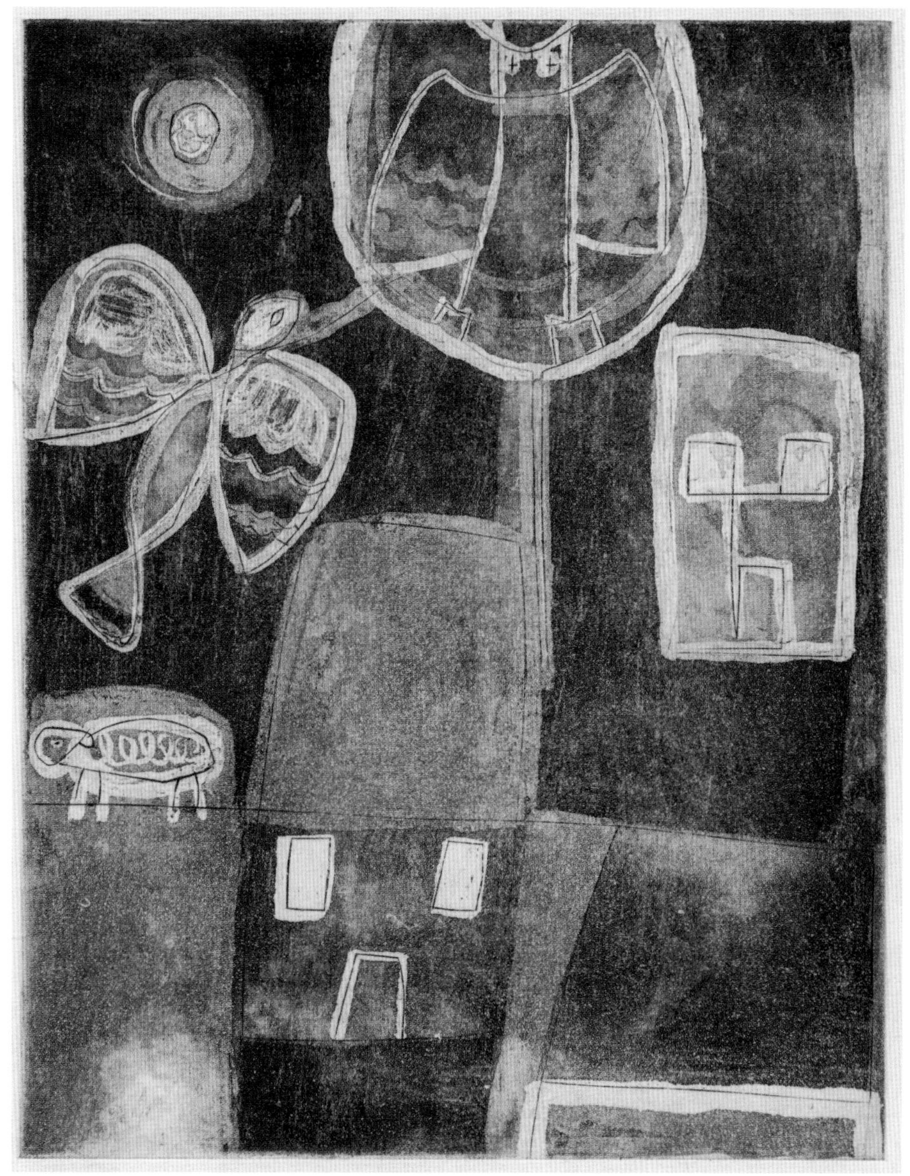

*Owl House*   c.1958 etching 18cm x 14cm

Born in Stockholm in 1923, Birgit Skiöld came to
London in 1948 to study at the Anglo-French Art
Centre in St John's Wood, where she met Francis Bacon
and Edouardo Paolozzi. Whilst in London she became
interested in printmaking and she enrolled at Regent Street
Polytechnic (now University of Westminster) where she
studied lithography with Henry Trivick and etching with
Richard Beer. Beer recalls Skiöld as being talented and very
determined, someone who wanted to be successful in their
chosen field and someone who made a strong and positive
impression on those around her.

Following studies in Paris, Skiöld returned to London
in 1954. She lived at 76 Charlotte Street in central
London and set up a studio in a basement a short distance
away in George Street, Marylebone. She had acquired
the lithographic press and stones that belonged to
Vanessa Bell (of Omega Workshop, Fitzroy Square and
Bloomsbury Group) which had more recently been used by
artist and illustrator, Edward Ardizzone. With her press in
place she and fellow students made prints but Skiöld soon
saw the need for a different kind of studio and identified the
need for open-access printmaking facilities. By open-access
she meant a print studio that was open for use by anyone
with prior experience in printmaking so there was no need
for a teacher or technician.

With her vision and ambition Birgit Skiöld founded the Fine
Art Printmaking Workshop in London in 1956. It became
known simply as The Print Workshop and was also often
referred to by the artists as the 'Basement'. This is the
studio that Helena used in the early years after completing
her studies at Central School of Arts and Crafts. It was the
first open-access professional print workshop in England,
a non-commercial open studio, where artists could work
independently producing etchings and lithographs. Skiöld
found a permanent home for the workshop in the basement
of the artist Adrian Heath's house at 28 Charlotte Street,
London. Adrian Heath and his wife Corinne were benevolent
landlords and charged only a small rent. In return Heath was
able to use the print facilities. The presses were moved into
the workshop in May 1958. The Print Workshop provided
a professional and welcoming place where artists found a
busy centre for avant-garde ideas, and a dedicated space
for print culture. Artists paid a nominal charge for use of
the workshop and were provided with the basic essentials.
They paid for their own ink and paper.

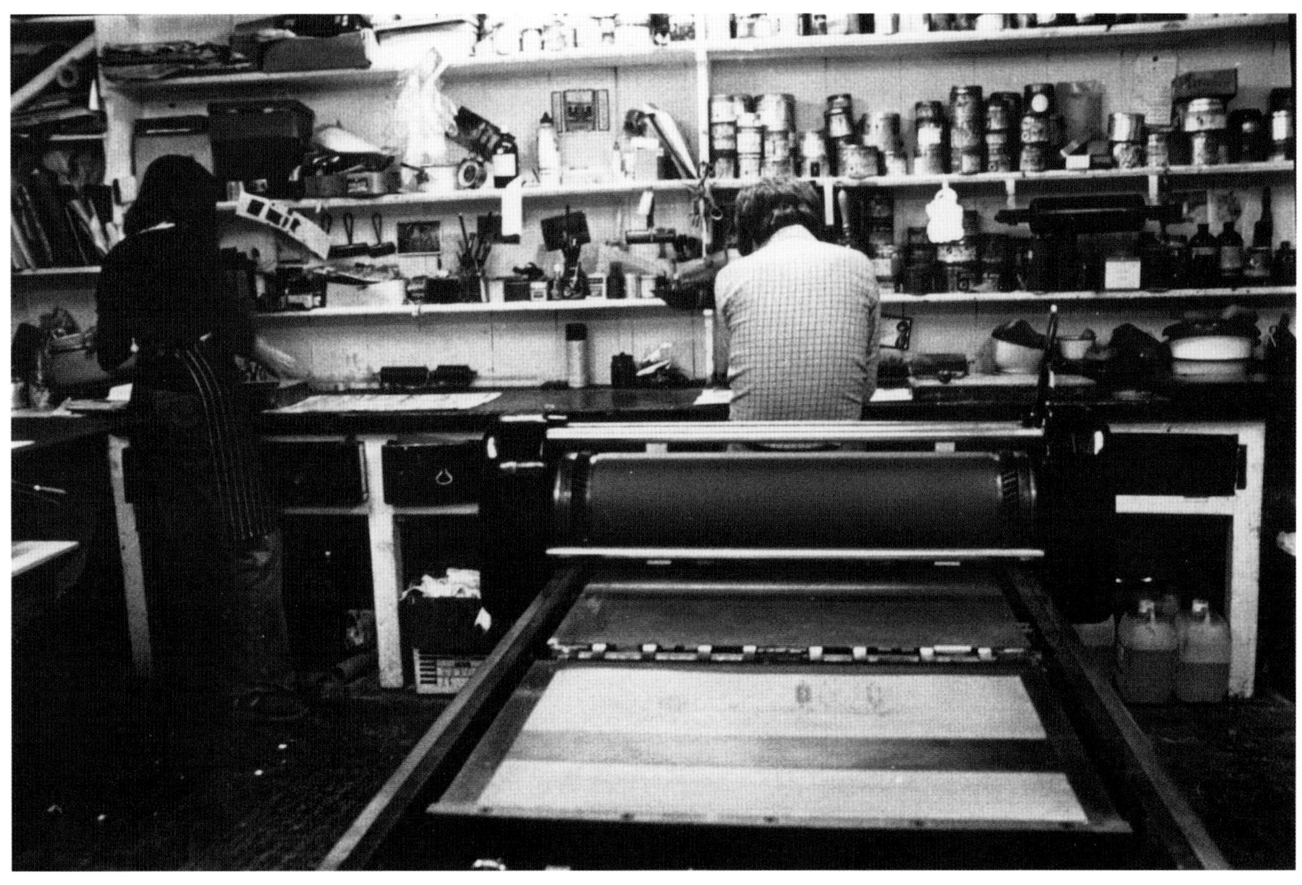

The Print Workshop, Charlotte Street c.1963

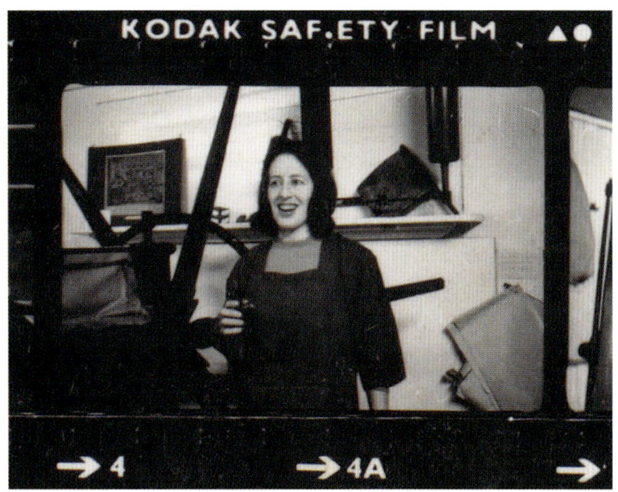


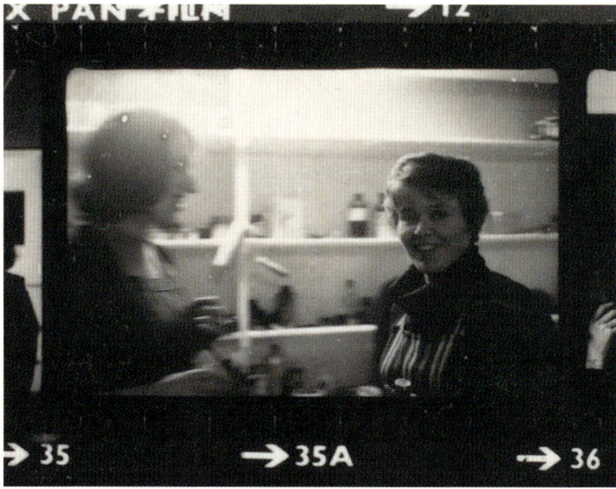


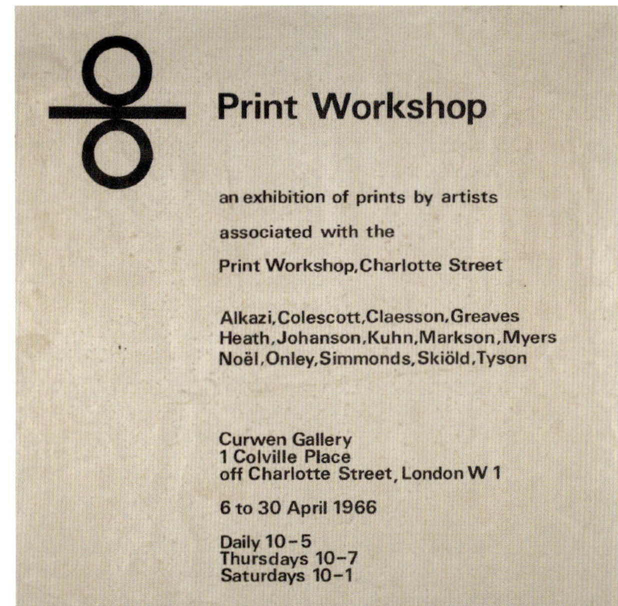


Helena at The Print Workshop c.1963

Helena and Birgit Skiold at The Print Workshop c.1963

Birgit Skiöld's motivation to open such a workshop was in part influenced by English artist William Hayter's famous Atelier 17 studio, which had reopened in Paris in 1950, after a period in New York during and after the war. William Hayter had collaborated on printmaking with Picasso, Miro and Kandinsky in Paris, and Pollock and Rothko in New York. It was an inspiring story with a strong link to Helena's approach to printmaking with the influence on her of her teacher Merlyn Evans who had studied in Paris under Hayter at his Atelier 17 studio.

It was into this exciting new environment that Helena Markson arrived in 1959, keen, ready to create her work. Initially Helena was one of many artists and printmakers who used the print studio. After a couple of years she became more involved and helped with the daily running of the workshop. In 1963 Helena became a co-director of the Fine Art Printmaking Workshop, working alongside Birgit Skiöld. Helena worked there until 1966 and gained enormous experience in running a workshop, which was to be very useful in her later career. The workshop itself continued very successfully for many more years, run by Skiöld until her untimely death in 1982. It became a destination of choice for artists and printmakers with Michael Ayrton, Jim Dine, David Hockney and Victor Pasmore all using the facilities. The workshop at Charlotte Street is an important part of the story of printmaking in post-war Britain.

*'In England, outside the art-school system, there is nowhere for a painter to make etchings, engravings and lithographs except a small, friendly, but difficult-to-find, basement in Charlotte Street. Here is a highly professional workshop, presided over by an enterprising expatriate Swede, Birgit Skiöld, who is helped by another print-maker Helena Markson. It was started in 1957 with the assistance of Adrian Heath and the encouragement of Robert Erskine, and has provided a kindly and useful refuge for print-makers of many nationalities who have come to London to work, benefit from interchange of ideas and gather technical information.'*[3]

Whilst she was working at the print workshop Helena also found time for her own work and became fully absorbed in printmaking. She was still living in London, in Stoke Newington and became increasingly aware of the buildings and the city around her. Early prints show her response to the city with her etching *Canonbury* from 1957 and then a more abstracted view in the etching *House Landscape* from 1959. These early prints bring together a strong sense of place in her work. Just as Salisbury had influenced her as a young student, now London images were part of her work.

In 1957 Helena showed prints in her first important group exhibition, 'British Graphic Art' held at the St George's Gallery at 7 Cork Street, London. The exhibition showed thirty-two prints by British artists working during the previous twelve months. There were prints by Helena's former tutor Merlyn Evans as well as work by artists such as Terry Frost, Anthony Gross, Michael Rothenstein, Julian Trevelyan, Patrick Heron, Bernard Cheese and Michael Ayrton. Amongst the names was Helena Markson, the only female artist to exhibit work in the exhibition, which at the time was quite an achievement. Helena exhibited *Limehouse*, an aquatint and etching based on the Limehouse district of London.

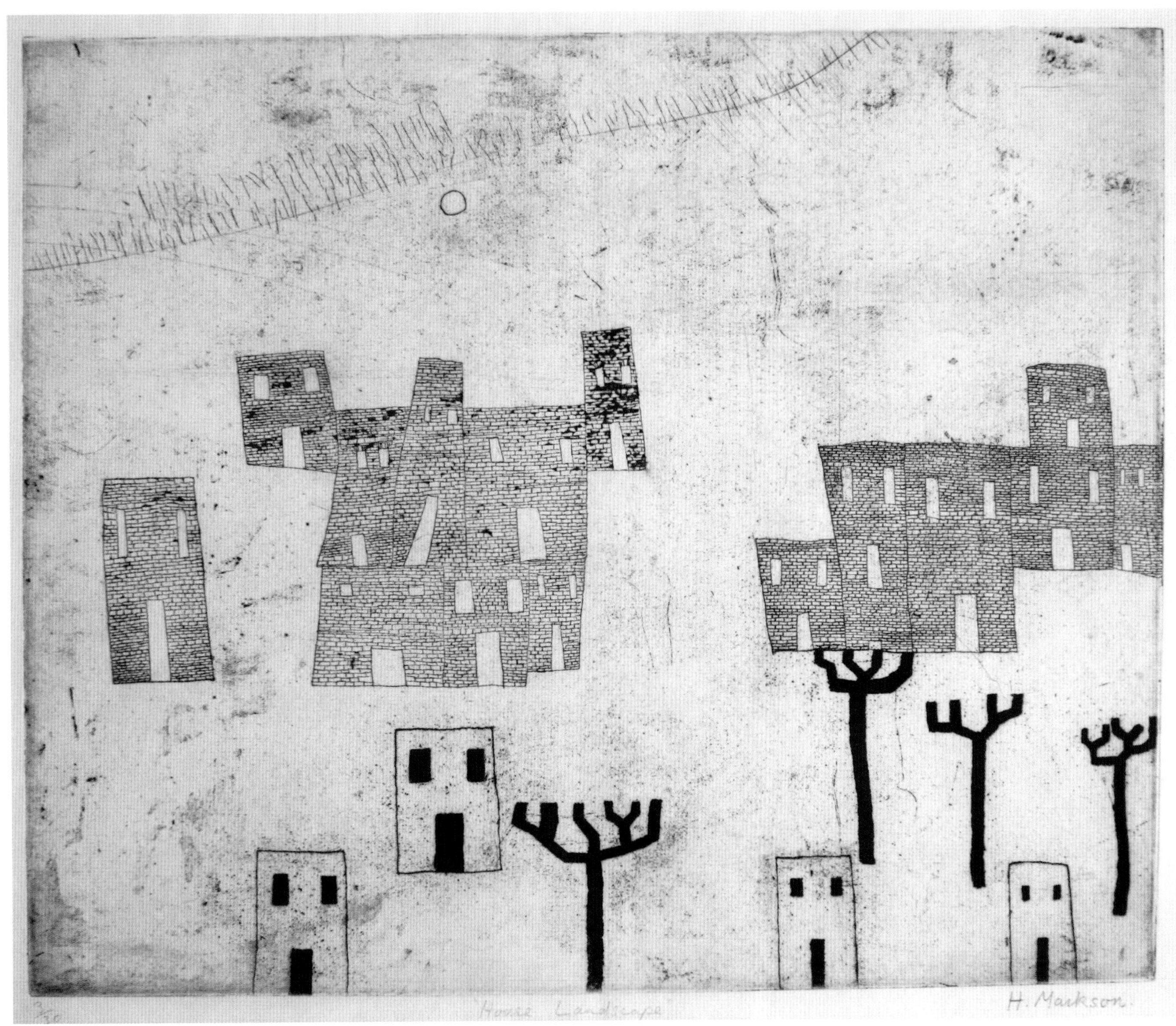

*House Landscape*    1959 etching and aquatint 37cm x 44cm

The catalogue for the exhibition included four small strips of film with transparency images of each of the thirty-two exhibited prints. Fortunately Helena kept all her exhibition catalogues and it is wonderful to see them and the small filmstrips which when held up to the light today still reveal some wonderful images of prints from the time.

In order to explain printmaking techniques the St George's Gallery also produced a short film 'Artists Proof' which showed six artists demonstrating six different print processes; Merlyn Evans – aquatint, John Coplans – silkscreen, Alistair Grant – lithography, Anthony Gross – etching, Anthony Harrison – engraving and Roland Jarvis – woodcut. The catalogue and film were the idea of Robert Erskine who had founded the St George's Gallery in 1954. Erskine was committed to promoting print and graphic art and he believed part of his role was to demystify the print process to the public. St George's Gallery was the first gallery in London to specialise in prints; they were recognised as pioneers in exhibiting prints. Erskine was to be influential in encouraging others in the field, such as Stanley Jones who set up the Curwen Press, and he was also a generous supporter of Birgit Skiöld's vision for her print workshop. They were to organise several exhibitions of prints by artists from the Print Workshop over the coming years.

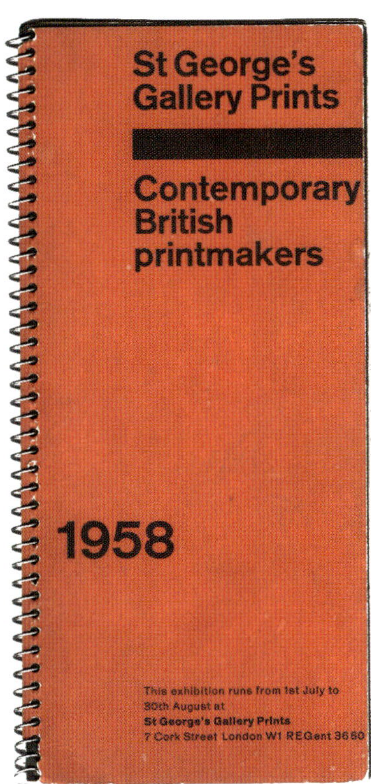


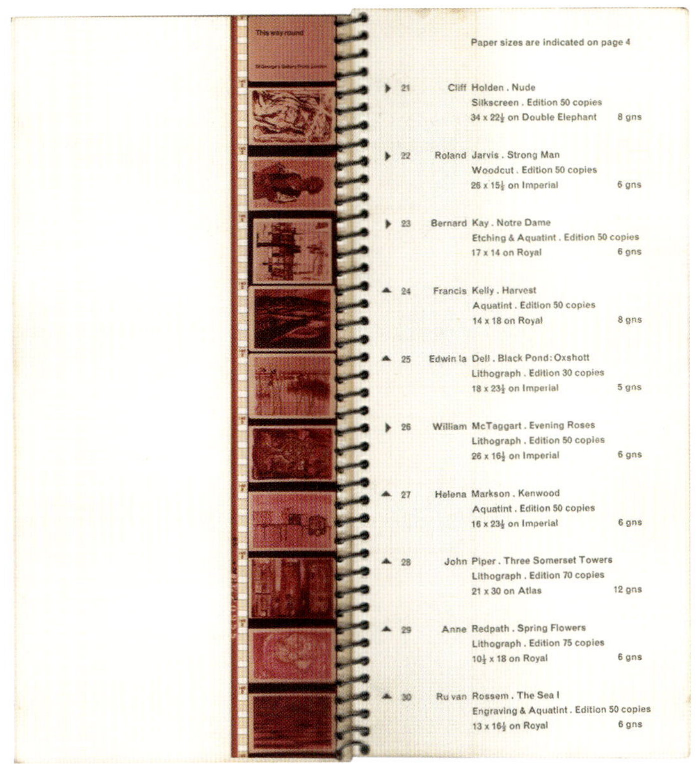


St George's Gallery Catalogue

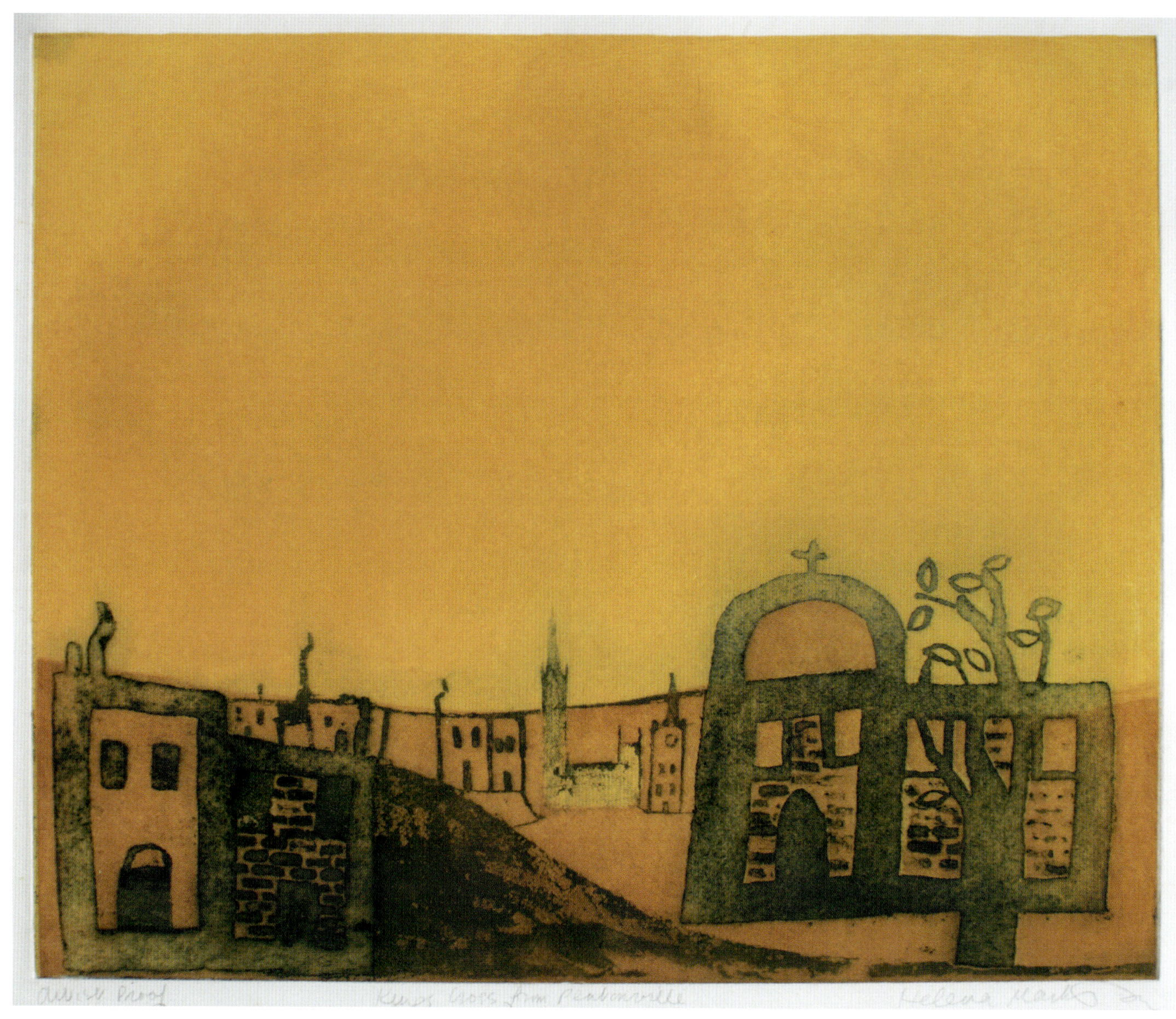

*Kings Cross from Pentonville*   c.1957 etching and aquatint 40cm x 47cm

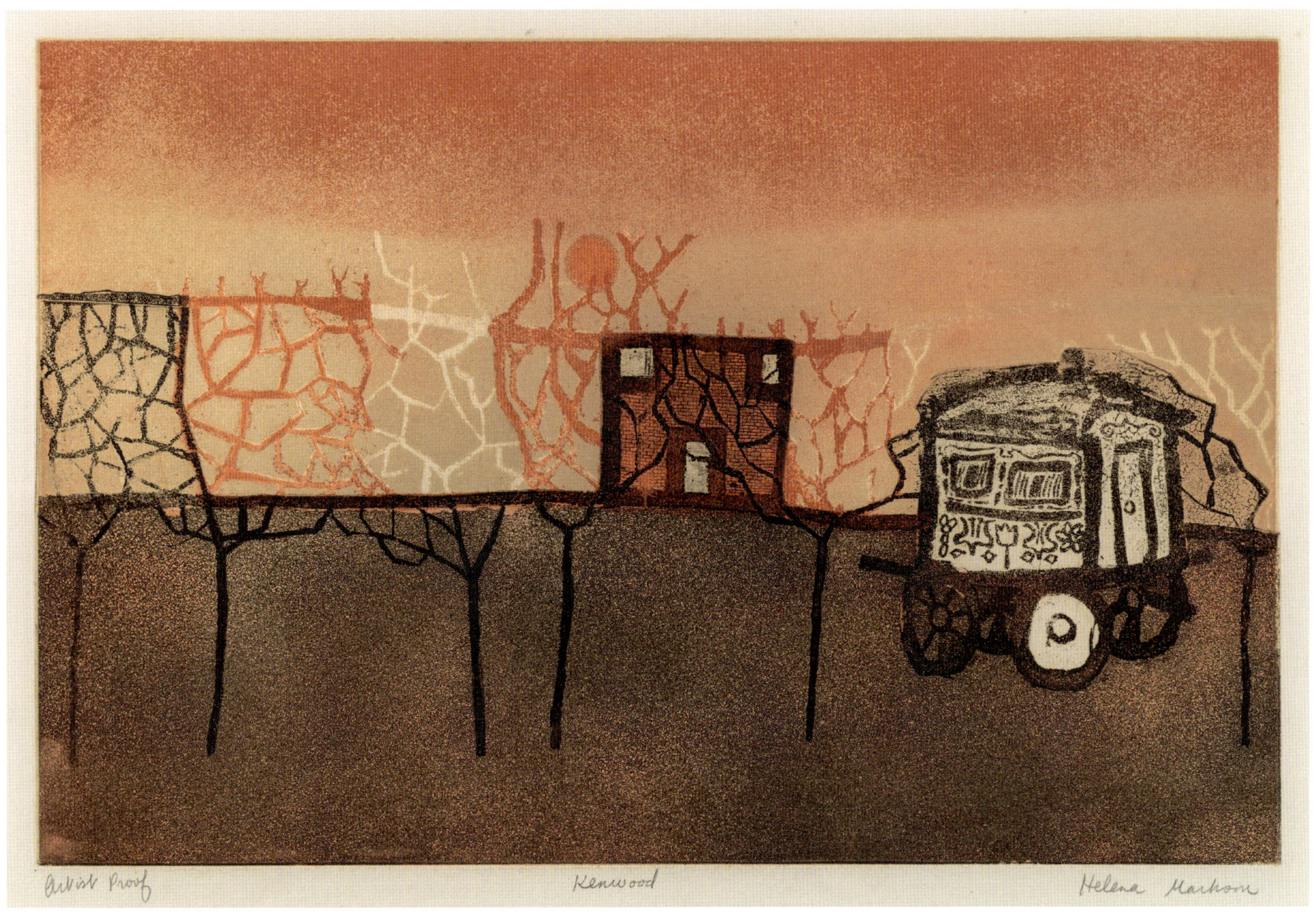


*Kenwood*    1958 etching and aquatint 40cm x 60cm

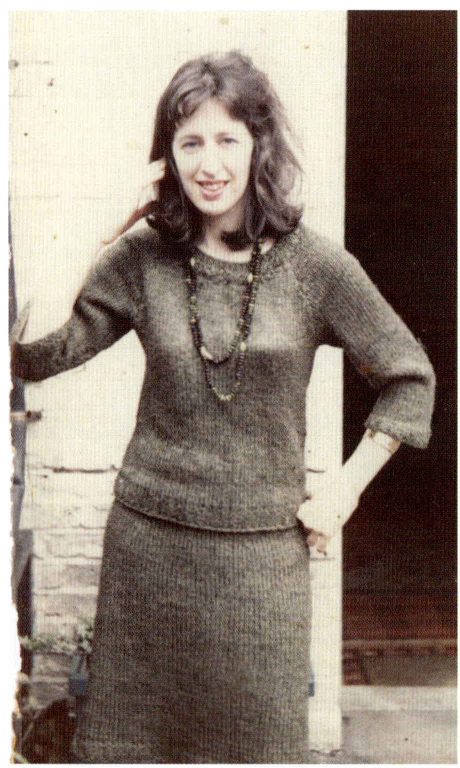

Helena c.1962



In 1958 St George's Gallery held an exhibition of 'Contemporary British Printmakers' involving many printmakers from Birgit Skiöld's Print Workshop, including prints by Helena Markson who exhibited an aquatint, *Kenwood*. The catalogue again included a filmstrip with images of the prints and another film by Robert Erskine, this time called *Linocuts* showing the artist Michael Rothenstein at work.

Through these exhibitions Helena was starting to gain more recognition for her printmaking and her prints were becoming sought after. With increased confidence she took part in more exhibitions.

In 1959, the Print Workshop held its first group show: 'Etchings and Lithographs: 16 studio artists at Print Workshop'. The exhibitors included Tag Ahmed, Richard Beer, Kathan Brown, Richard Fozard, Adrian Heath, Stanley Jones, Helena Markson, Richard Platt, Birgit Skiöld, James Tiley, Ian Tyson and John Watson.

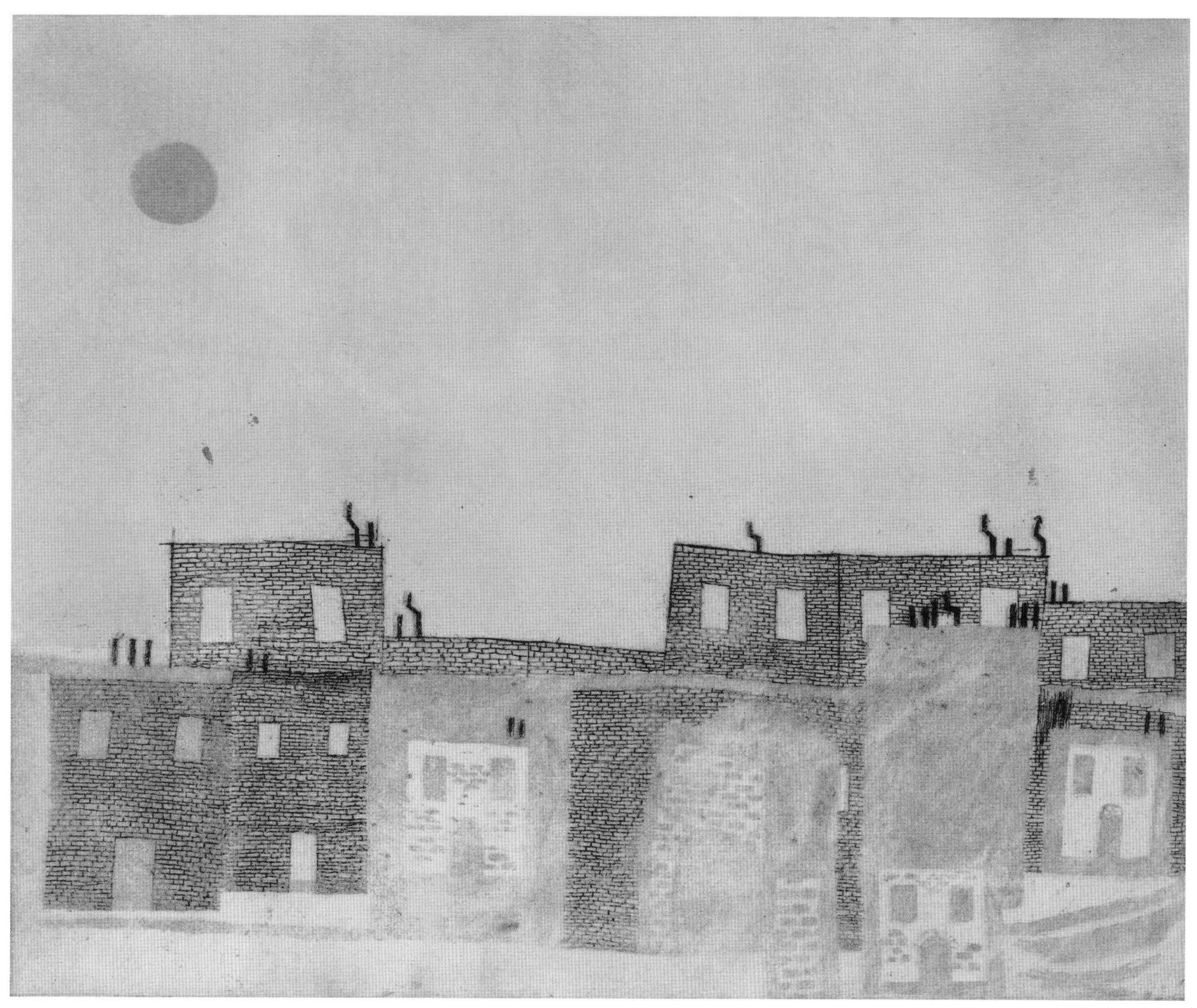

*Limehouse*    1957 etching and aquatint 40cm x 48cm

In the spring of the same year an important exhibition
'The Graven Image' was held at the Whitechapel Art Gallery
in London and Helena was invited to take part. She
exhibited *Limehouse*, her etching from 1957. This was
exhibited alongside prints by leading artists of the time
such as William Scott, Ceri Richards, Barbara Hepworth,
John Piper, Edward Bawden and Stanley William Hayter.
Helena wrote in her notes from the time how she felt that the
exhibition marked the beginning of a renaissance in the fine
art print in England, something that Robert Erskine noted,
writing in his wonderful introduction to the catalogue:

*'This exhibition takes place today because it is an
exhibition of a movement that is gaining momentum.
Ten years ago there would have been very little material
to exhibit. In ten years' time there will be infinitely more
prints to choose from and ten times as many artists
making them. By then it may perhaps be possible to draw
conclusions as to the relative prominence of certain styles
and manners in present-day printmaking in this country.
Today it would be foolish to draw such conclusions,
as we are too near the beginning; the umbrella is
only half open. All we can say is that the revival of
printmaking in its contemporary form is a matter of
justifiable pride to us as it has attained its adulthood
in a remarkably short time.'[4]*

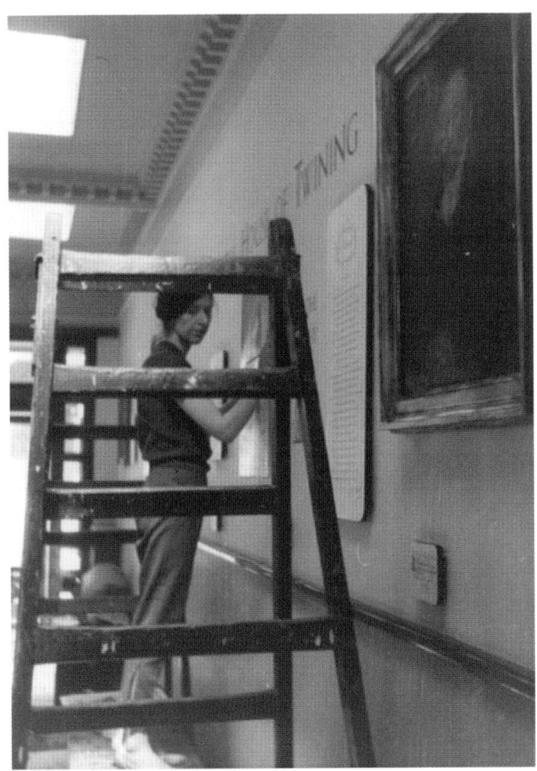

Helena at Twinings head office 1962

Reading such catalogues and looking back at these exhibitions we can start to understand the excitement around printmaking at this time and appreciate how enthused Helena must surely have felt to be part of this movement.

Like many printmakers at the time, in addition to working at the print workshop Helena decided to teach. In 1965 she took a teaching job at the Byam Shaw School of Drawing and Painting where she taught lithography and etching. Then she taught at St Martin's School of Art and at Chelsea College of Art where in addition to etching and lithography she taught illustration. Helena enjoyed teaching and it was something she would return to throughout her working life.

In 1962 she was offered a commission by Twinings to design a mural based on 'The History of the House of Twining' to go in the entrance to their head office in the Strand, London. Her art school studies in mural decoration proved useful and she combined painting and calligraphy in her design. It was a prestigious commission she took pride in. Although Helena enjoyed these commissions she chose to give her time primarily to printmaking and teaching.

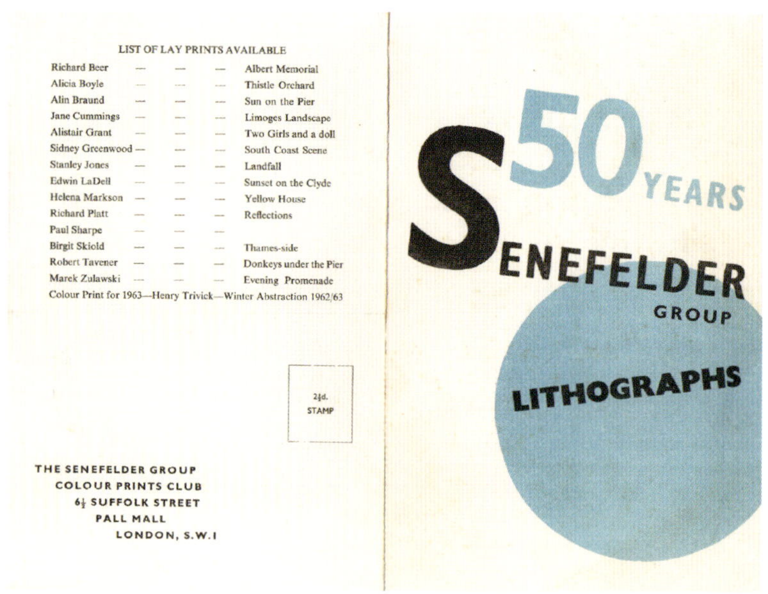

In the late 1950s Helena joined the Senefelder Group which enabled her to work and exhibit with other printmakers. Formed in 1910 the Senefelder Group of Artist Lithographers, as it became known, was named after Alois Senefelder who discovered the process of lithography in 1798 when working in Bavaria. The group worked to promote the art of lithography and held regular exhibitions at which Helena exhibited lithographs such as *Canonbury*, *Leith Hill*, *Clissold Church* and *Yellow House*.

One of the first Senefelder Group exhibitions Helena exhibited at was held in 1959 at the Crafts Centre in London. A review describes her work:

*'Quiet beauty of brick walls, houses and washing lines is turned by Helena Markson into a simple, effective composition in her* Canonbury.'[5]

Senefelder Prints Club Catalogue
Senefelder Catalogue 1967

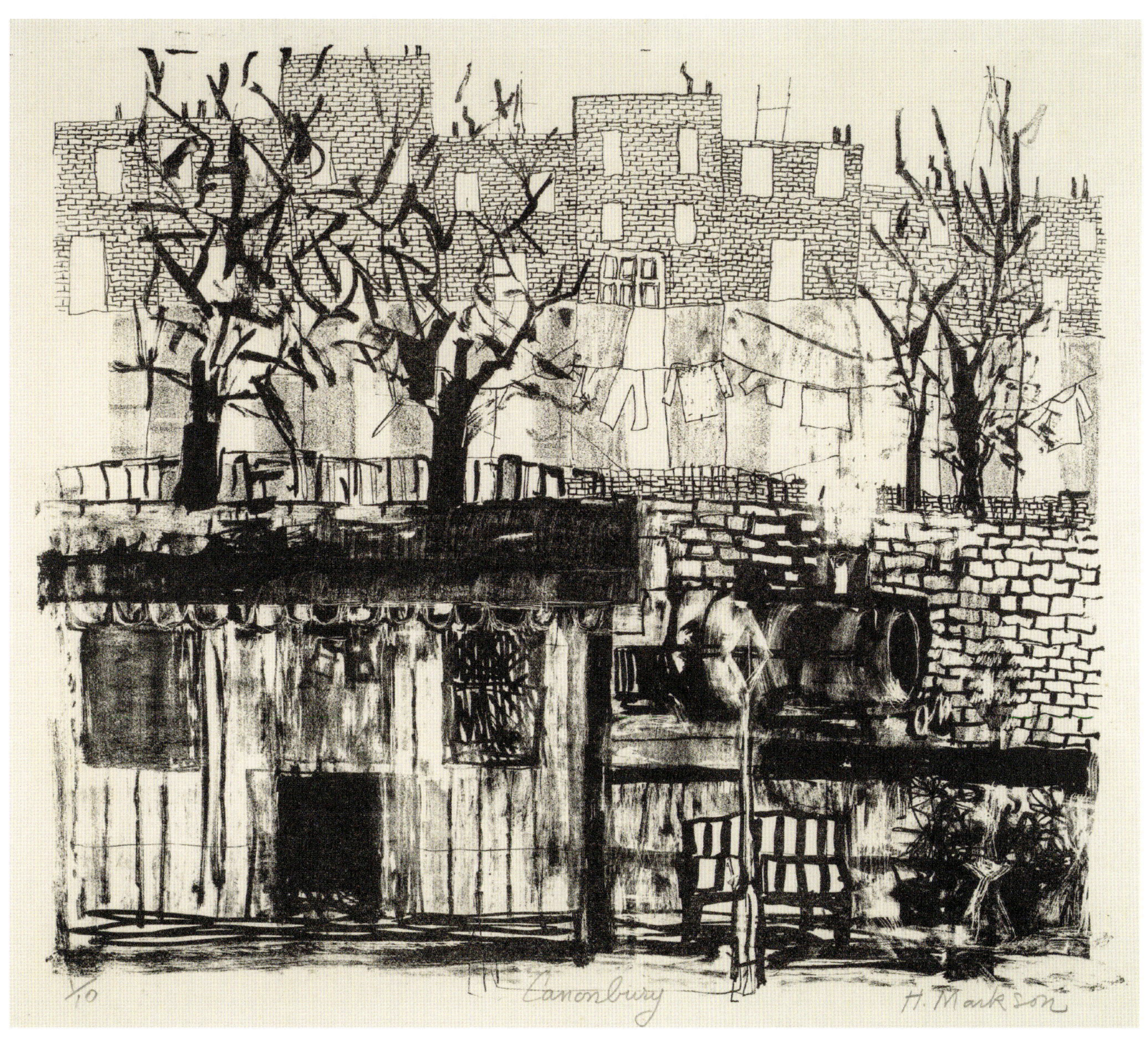

*Canonbury*    1957 lithograph 31cm x 35cm

In 1961 the Group held an important exhibition 'Colour Lithographs' at Leeds City Art Gallery with exhibiting artists including Adrian Heath and Birgit Skiöld of the Charlotte Street Print Workshop as well as other important artists such as John Piper, Charles Keeping, Robert Tavener and Stanley Jones. Helena also took part in the Senefelder Colour Prints Club where, for two guineas, the public could choose one lithograph a year, chosen from a selection of prints by different artists. The Senefelder Print Club generously offered to send the lithographs on approval for the customer to then choose which to keep. The print that Helena listed as available to the Prints Club was *The Yellow House* which had been praised when exhibited:

*'The most charming print in the exhibition was by Helena Markson,* The Yellow House, *which was completely captivating with its uninhibited colour and the unpremeditated vigour of its application, and quite unselfconscious and without artifice.'[6]*

It was through exhibiting at one of the Senefelder exhibitions that she was offered perhaps her most important commission. Graeme Shankland, architect and city planner for Liverpool in the early 1960s, was drawn to her work with its intuitive response to buildings and places. He invited her to produce a series of prints illustrating the changing urban landscape of Liverpool.

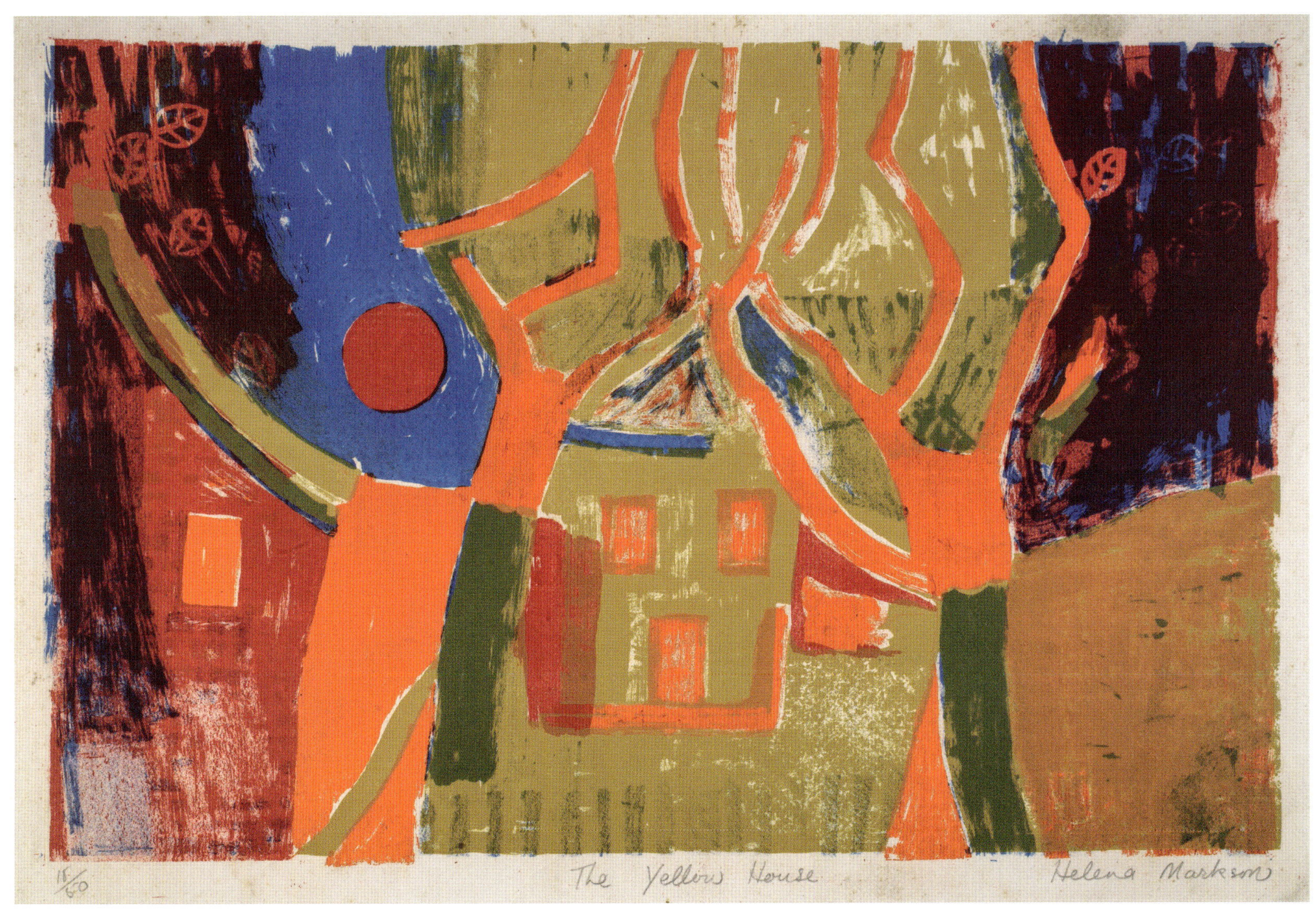

*The Yellow House*   c.1960 lithograph 30cm x 45cm

The fact that Shankland noticed Markson's work was not altogether surprising, as other architects had also been impressed by her work. In 1962 the architecture magazine *Keystone* had a feature titled 'Helena Markson – Prints of London' with the opening lines:

*'The work of artists whose imagination is triggered off by an interest in buildings and townscape is automatically interesting to architects.'*[7]

The article continues by describing Helena's work:

*'She is developing a personal language full of wit, fantasy and a richly individual colour sense out of the bricks, mortar and backyard streets of North East London in general and of Stoke Newington in particular. Miss Markson draws North East London with sympathy. This is no introspective revelling in decay: the drawings are unpretentious and are humane in spite of the almost total absence of figures. It does not seem too fanciful to suspect that this is because the buildings, trees, park benches, garden sheds, are themselves the real* dramatis personae *of these pictures. After all these are some of the most familiar objects of our lives and carry a vast train of human association'.*[8]

With an eye to the future the article concludes that Helena Markson would be a great asset to any team of architects and that this 'modest and gifted artist' deserves a commission. We do not know if Shankland had read this article but he was certainly in agreement with it and saw the potential in Helena's work.

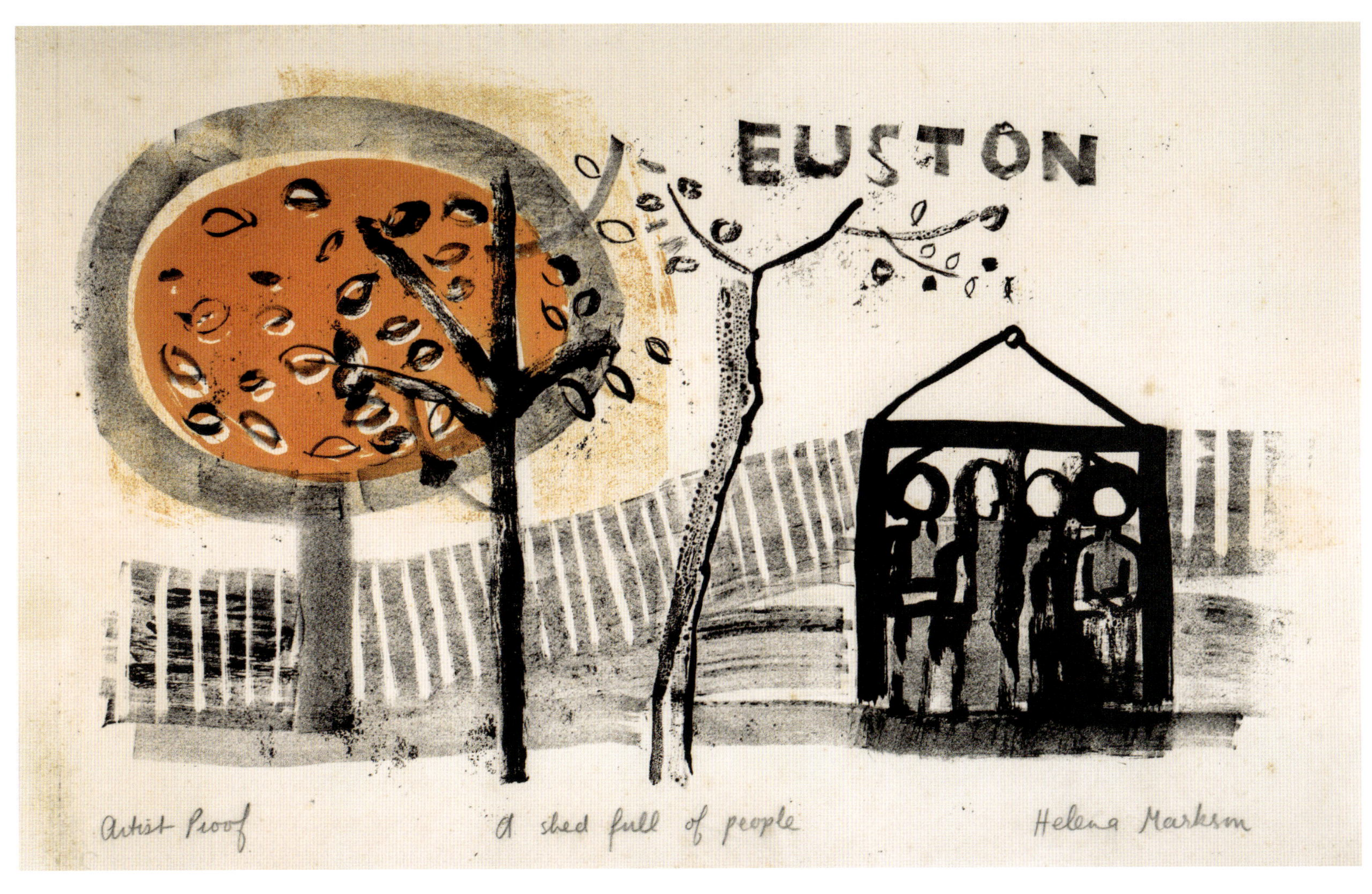



*A Shed full of people*   c.1958 etching and aquatint 35cm x 48cm

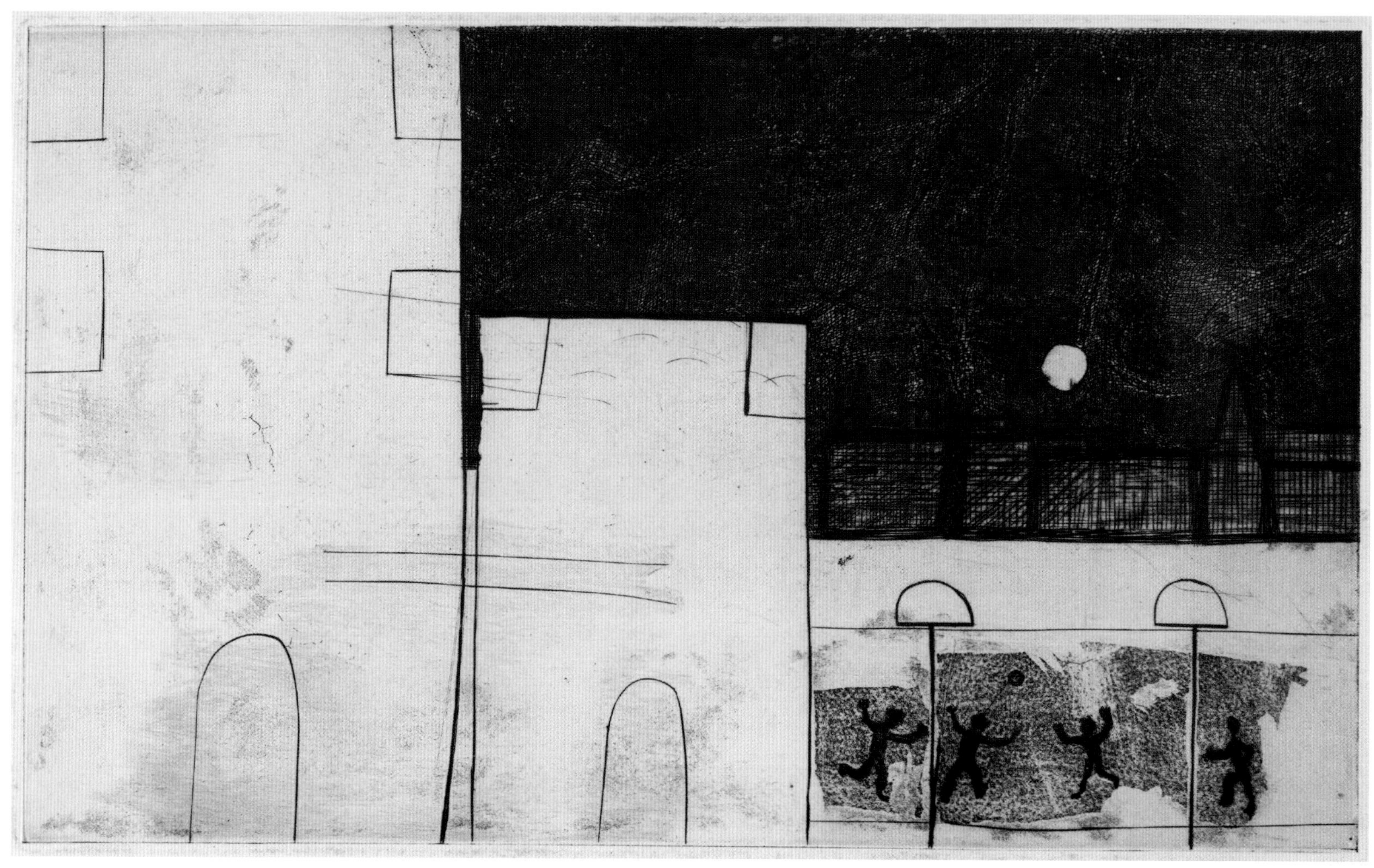

*Playground*   c.1956 etching 16cm x 26cm

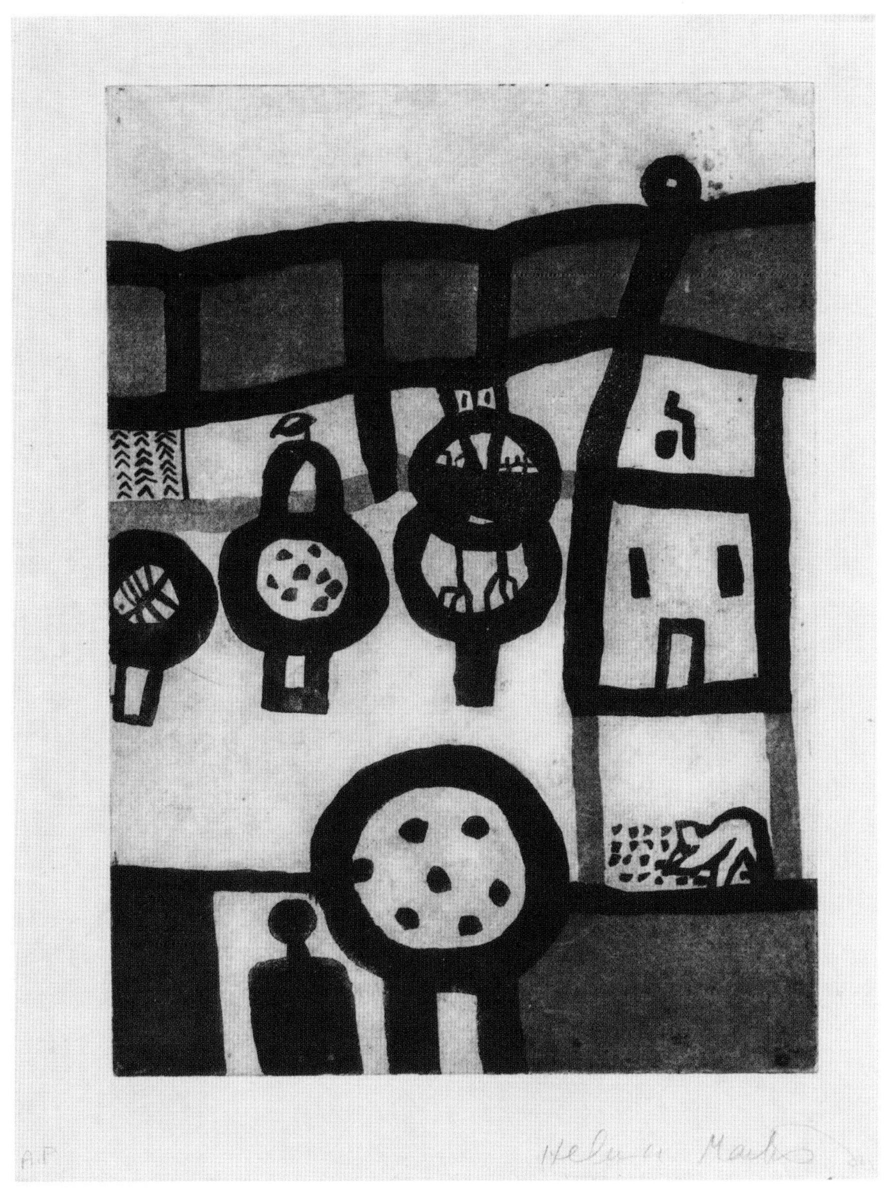

Untitled    1950s etching and aquatint 34cm x 24cm



*Keystone* magazine cover

# LIVERPOOL AND THE LIVERPOOL SERIES

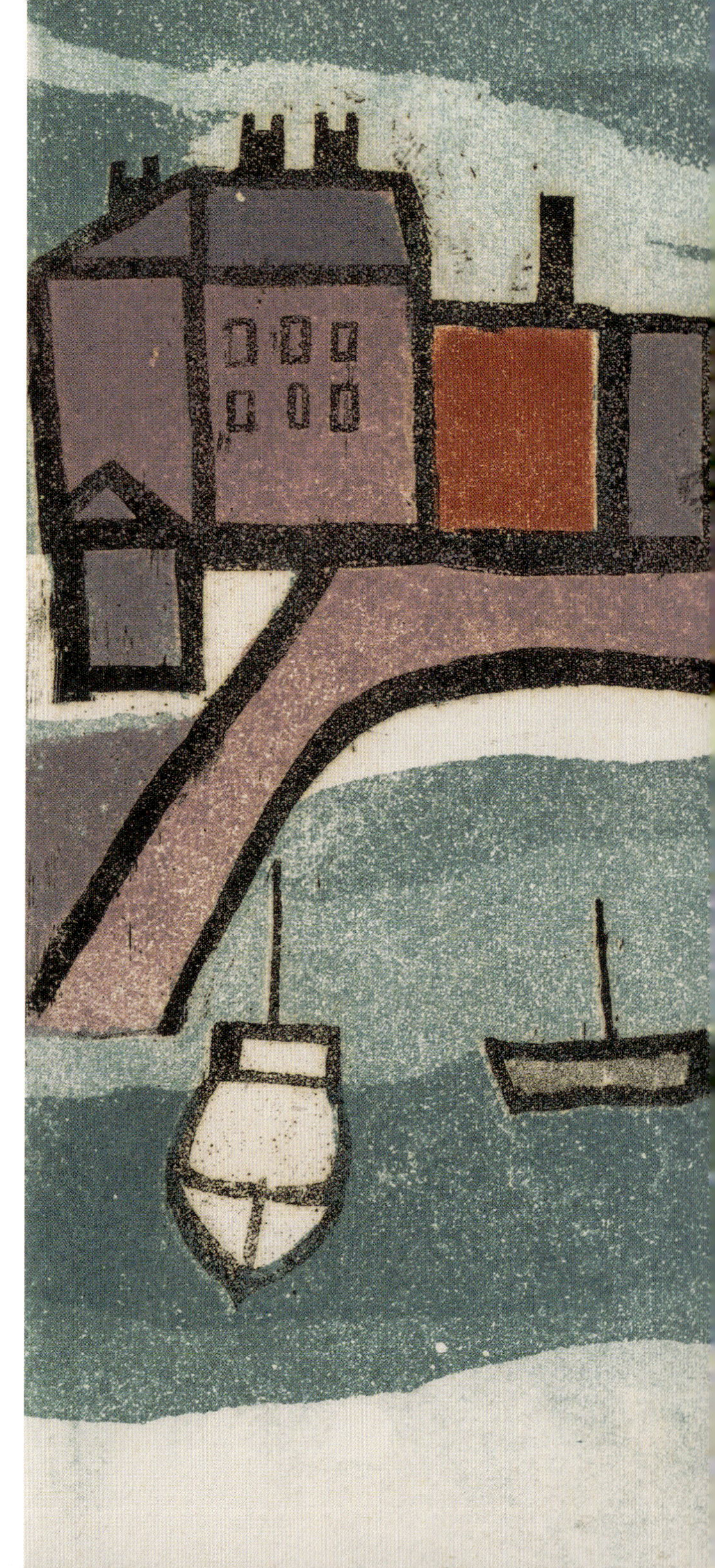

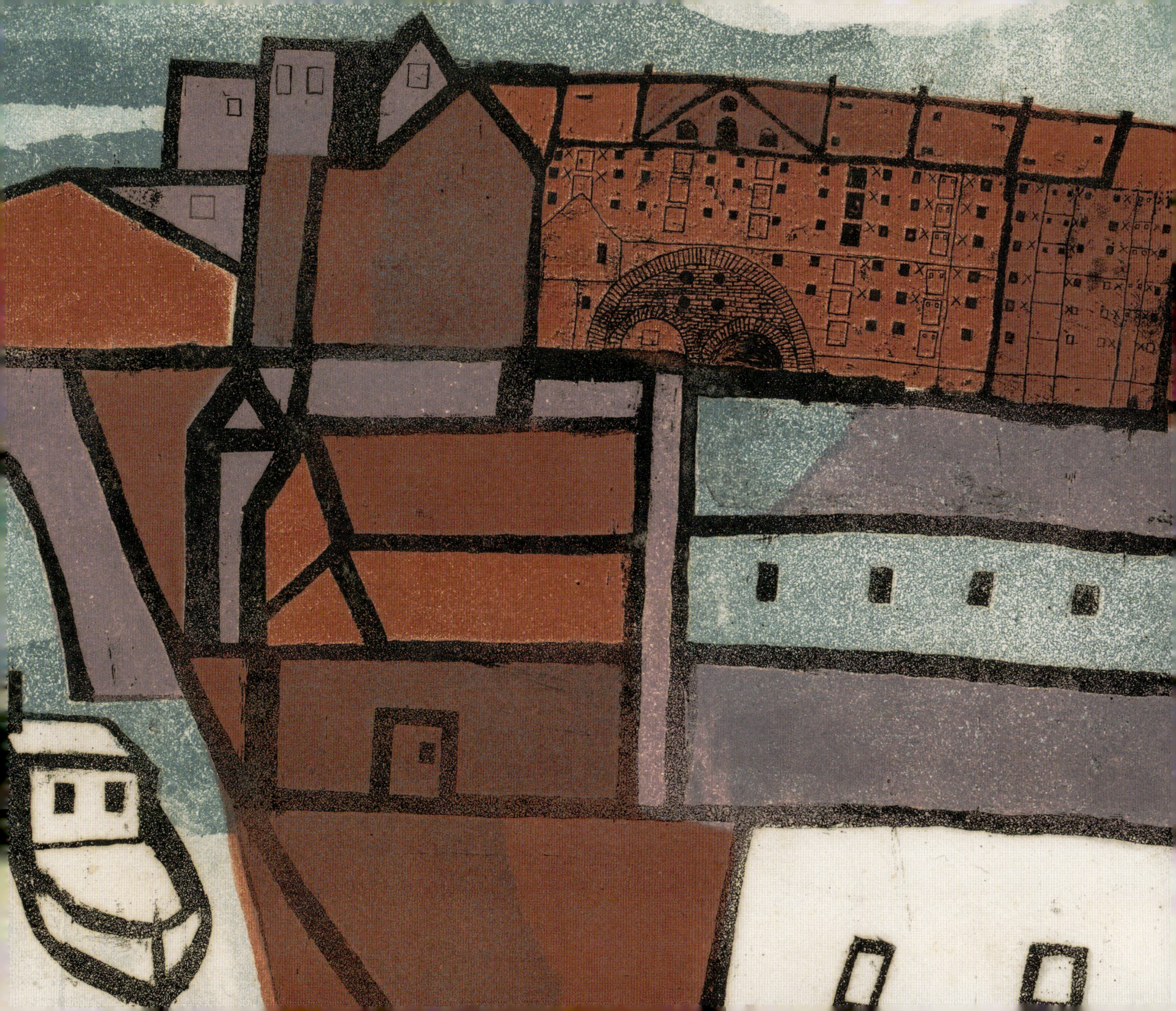

Graeme Shankland was a leading architect in post-war Britain. He was a strong character and well known for his Communist beliefs. He worked as an architect in the Planning Division of the London County Council designing many housing schemes and he was involved in plans for the design of the South Bank Centre. In 1961 he was appointed City Planner in Liverpool and in the following years became heavily involved in bold plans for the urban renewal of Liverpool. Shankland later established his own architectural practice, joined by Oliver Cox, a former fellow architect from the London County Council and together they ran Shankland Cox.

Shankland suggested to Helena that she produce a series of prints, which would record the changing cityscape of Liverpool. Although initially Helena felt somewhat intimidated she was encouraged by Shankland's faith in her:

*'… I was able to respond in a positive way. Some buildings were about to be pulled down after all. I believe he thought I might contribute something to capture visually the sense of the place – for me this confidence was hugely encouraging.'[9]*



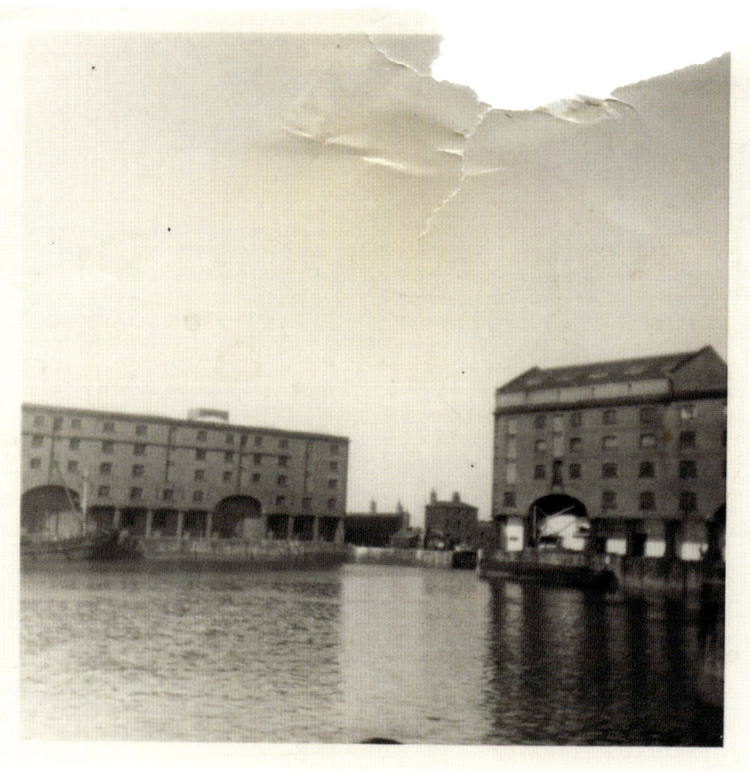

Photos of Liverpool taken by Helena

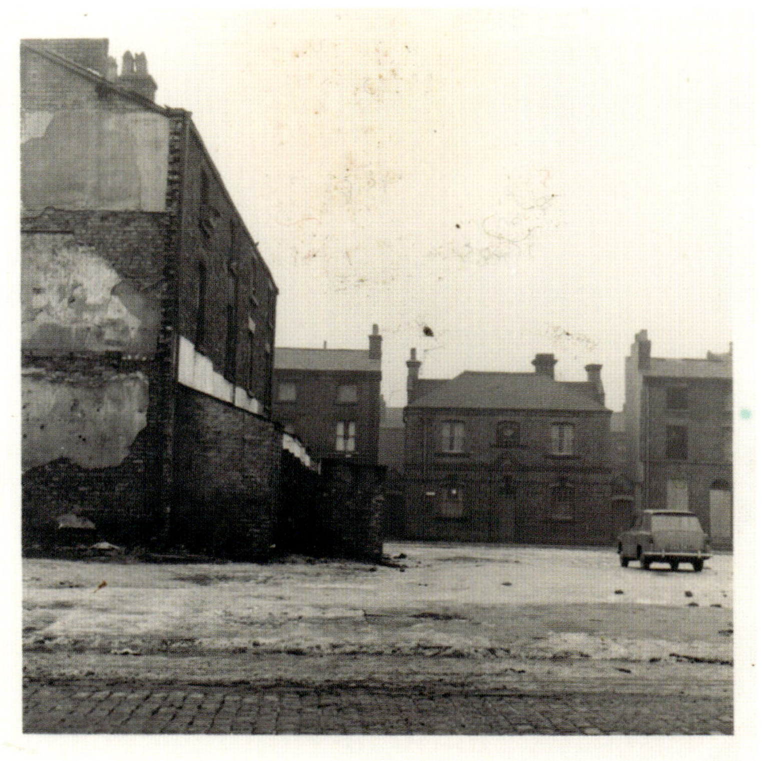 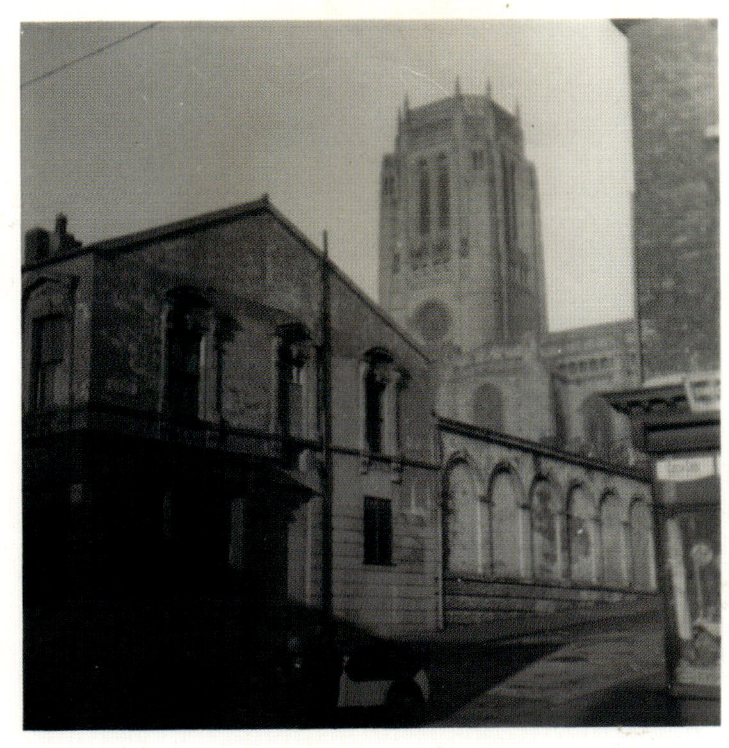

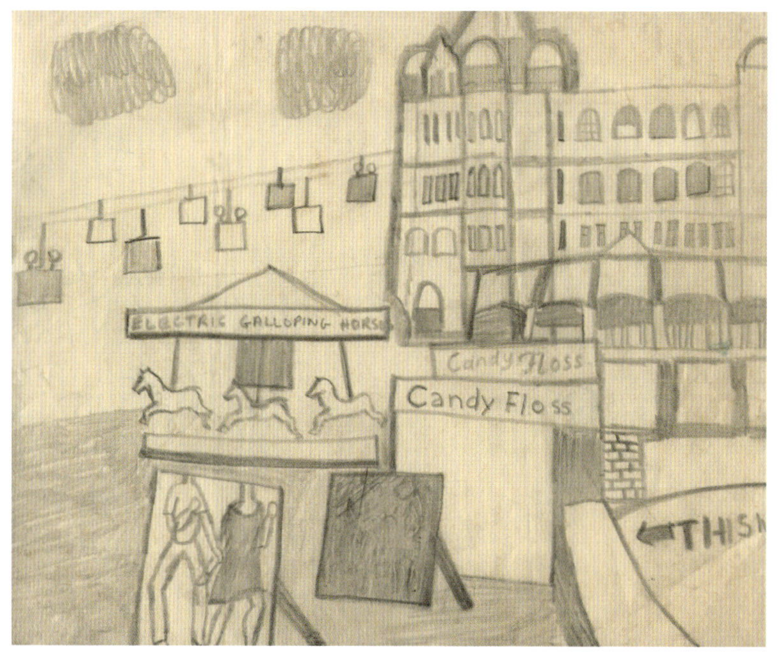



Drawing for *New Brighton Fair*    1964 pencil 25cm x 32cm

Helena made several trips to Liverpool over a three-year period, sketching and photographing different areas of the city. She recalled how she became more and more involved in the project, losing her initial lack of confidence. In later years Helena reminisced about her work for the Liverpool Series:

*'Liverpool is a unique city with its great contrasts of activities and array of architecture. The historical context was both enlightening and stimulating where for me the buildings became the* persona *in human terms as expressed in the images – "dramatis personae".'[10]*

*'I became very connected to the city, the projects of renewal and my personal relationship as an artist with the subject and the challenge to express ideas visually. The medium of etching aquatint contributed to the growth of ideas. I may not have always succeeded in what I aimed to do, but I am happy with most images and hopeful that there is truth there.'[11]*

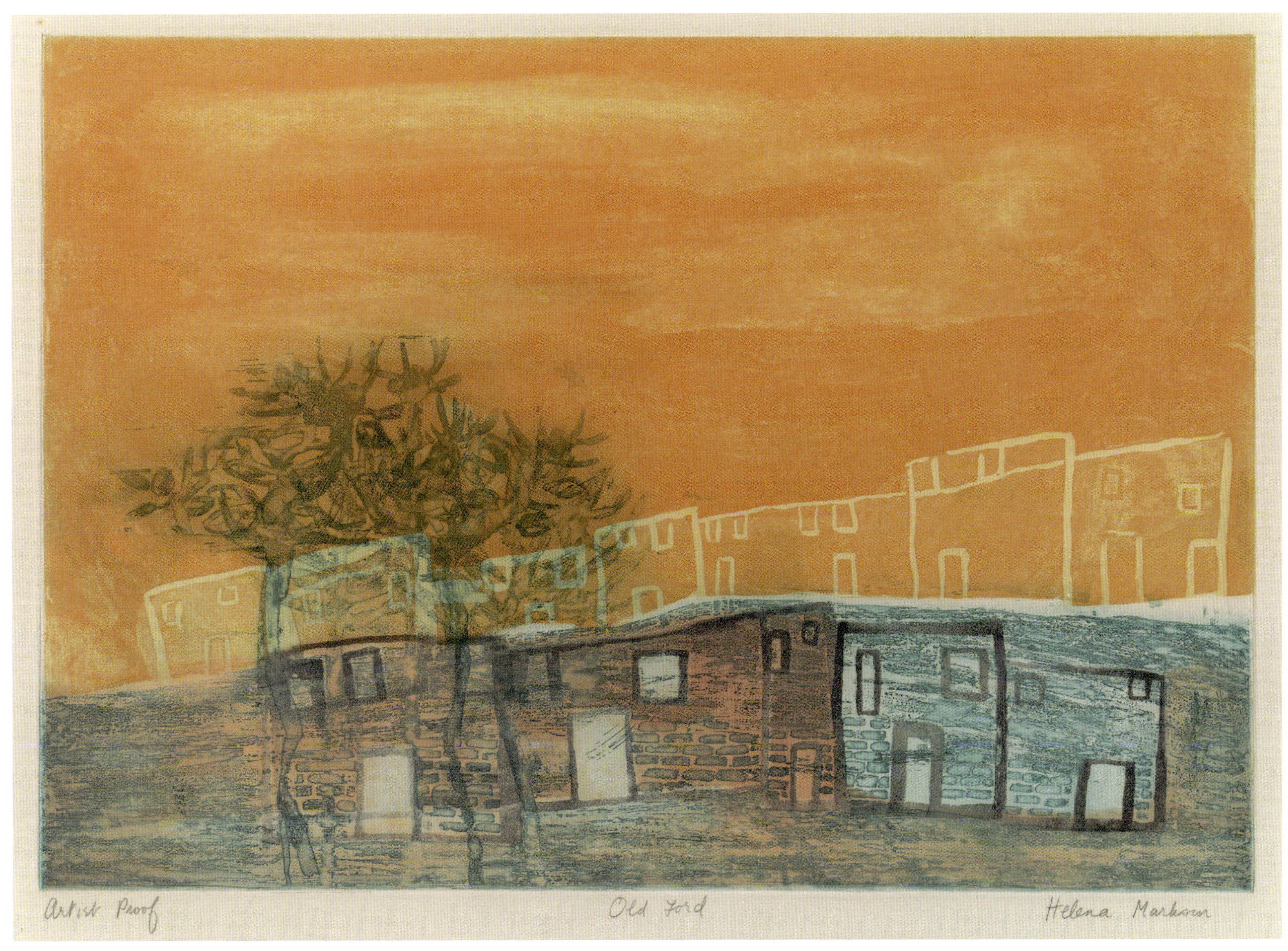


*Old Ford*   c.1966 etching and aquatint 40cm x 57cm

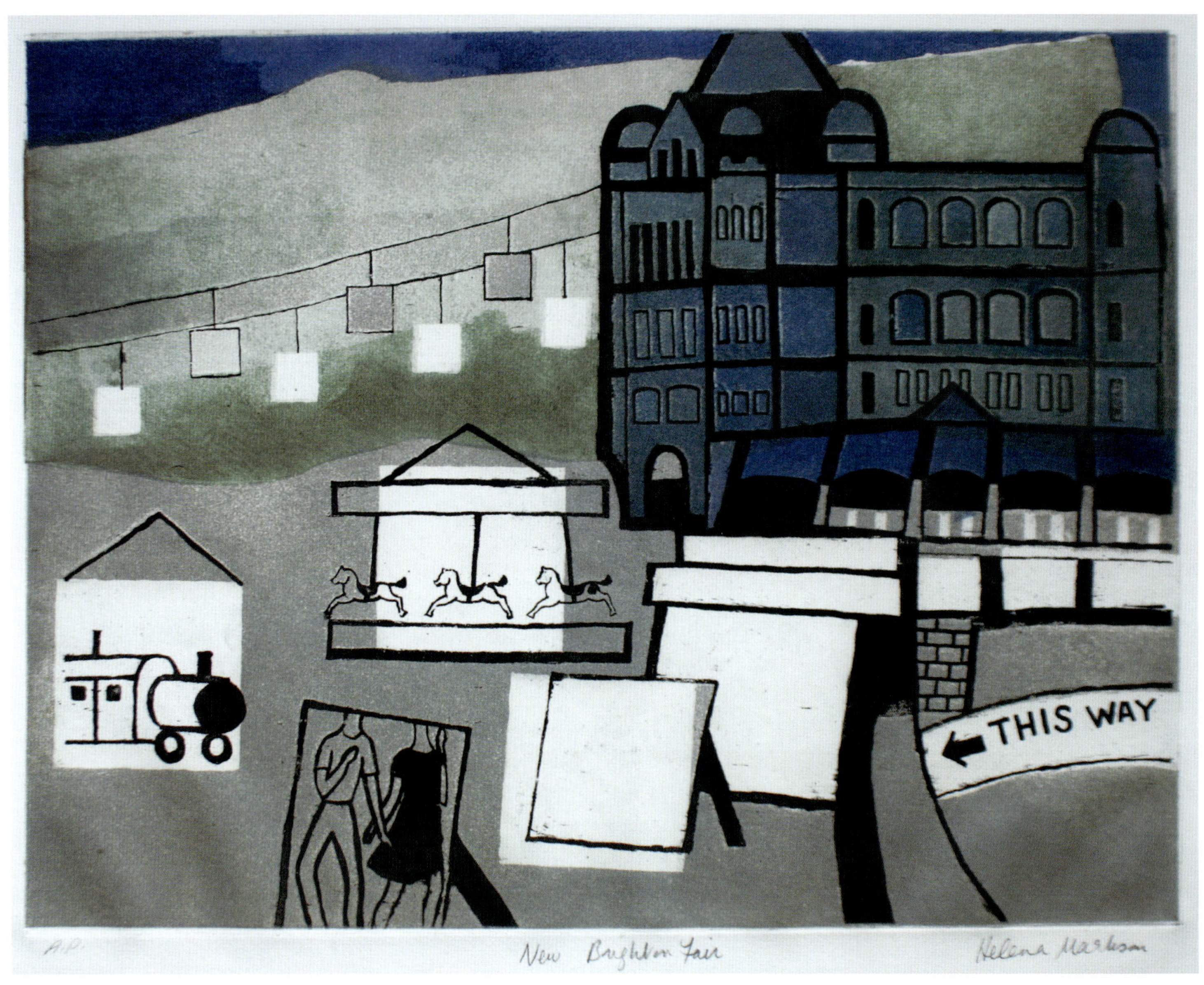


*New Brighton Fair*    1967–68 etching and aquatint 42cm x 55cm

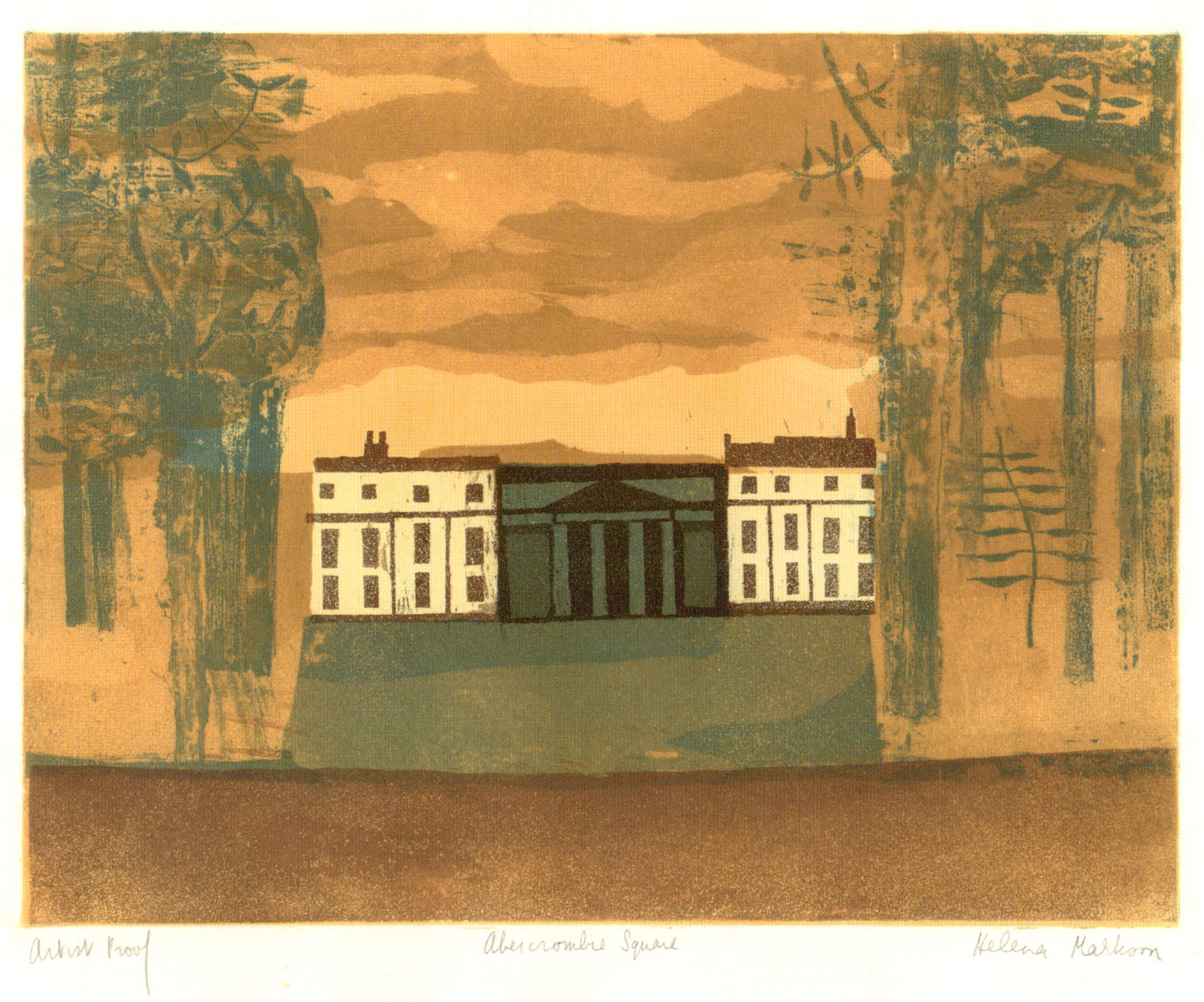


*Abercombie Square*    1967–8 etching and aquatint 42cm x 55cm

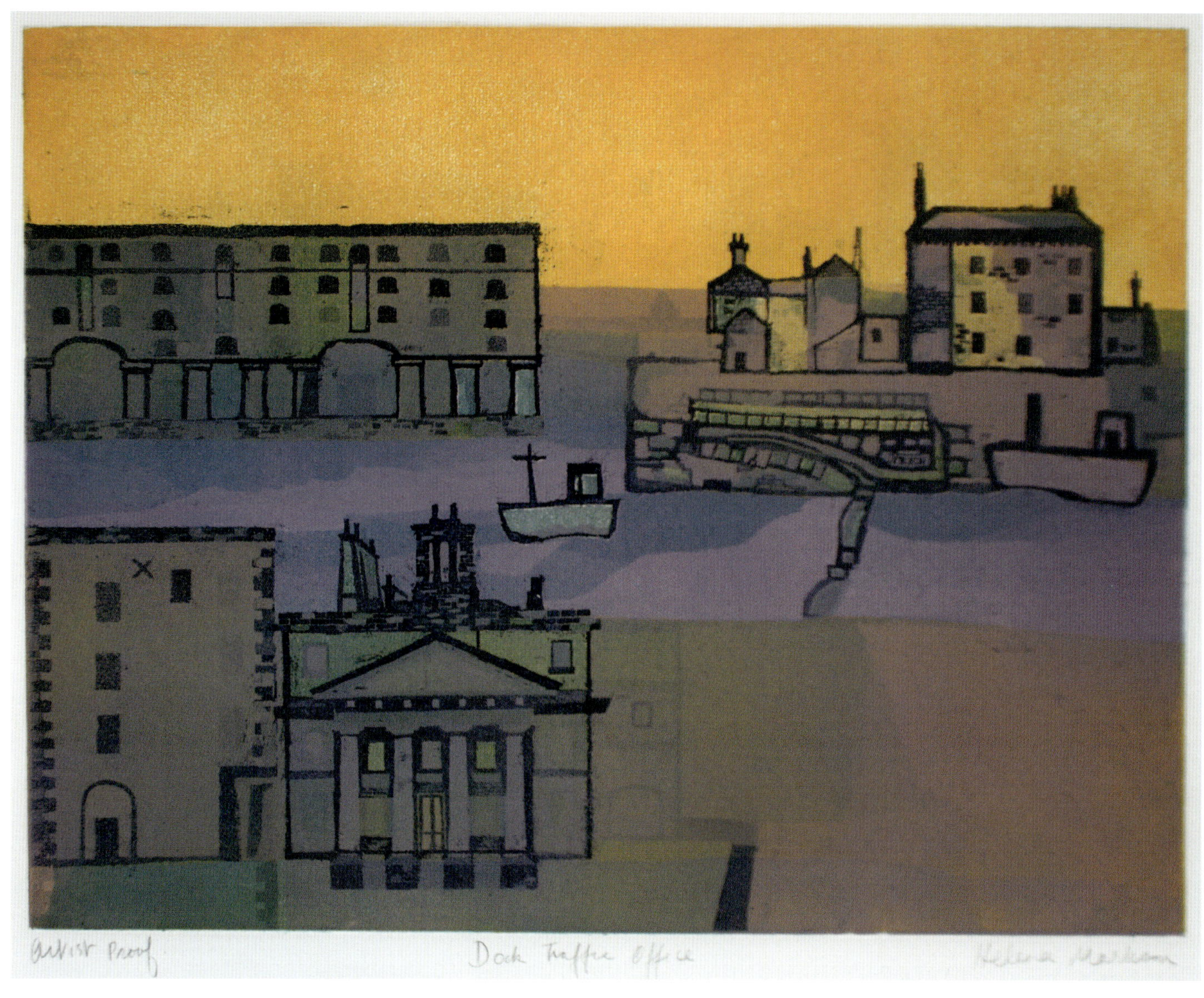



*Dock Traffic Office*    1966–67 etching and aquatint 43cm x 55cm

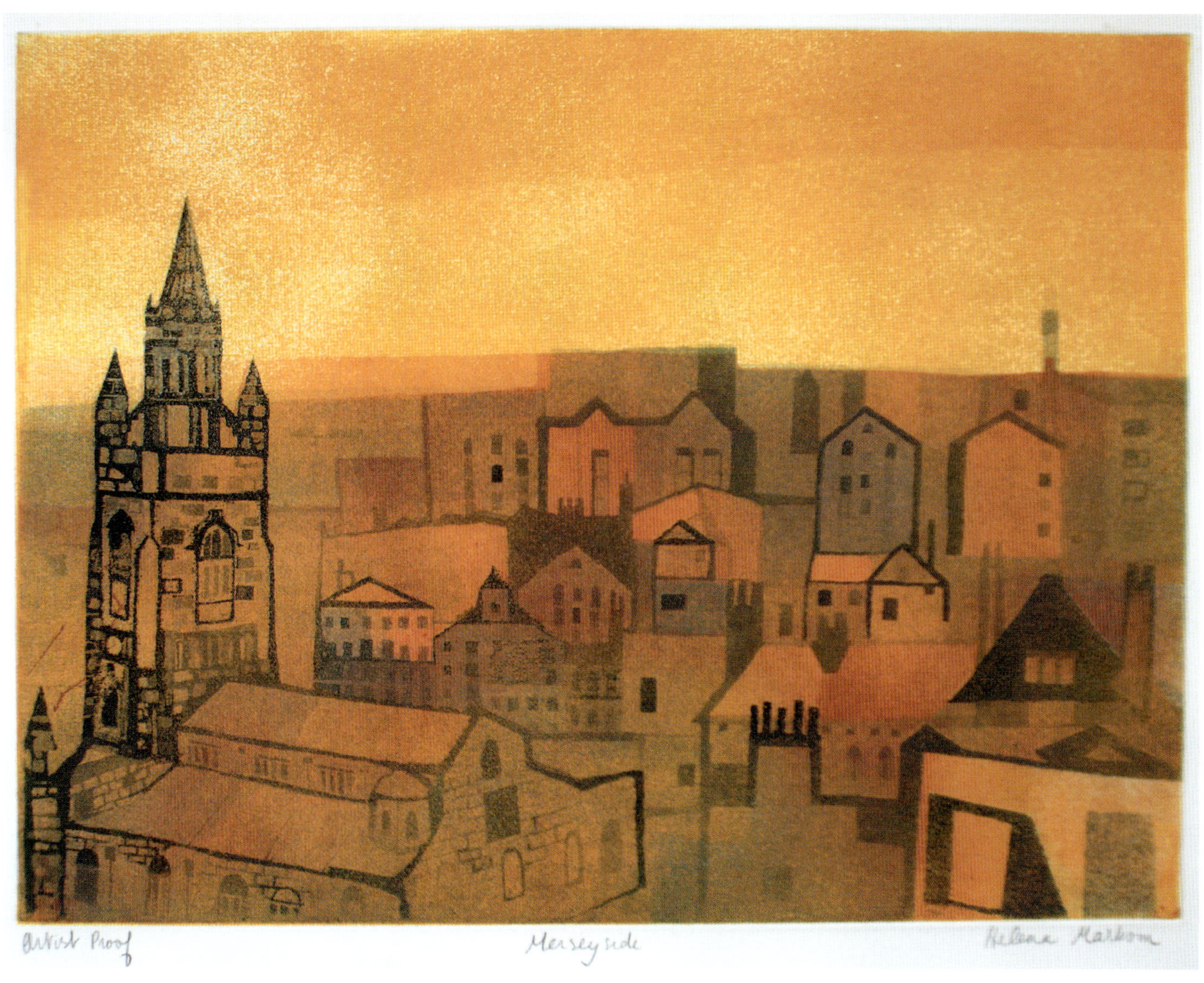


*Merseyside*    1967–68 etching and aquatint 42cm x 55cm

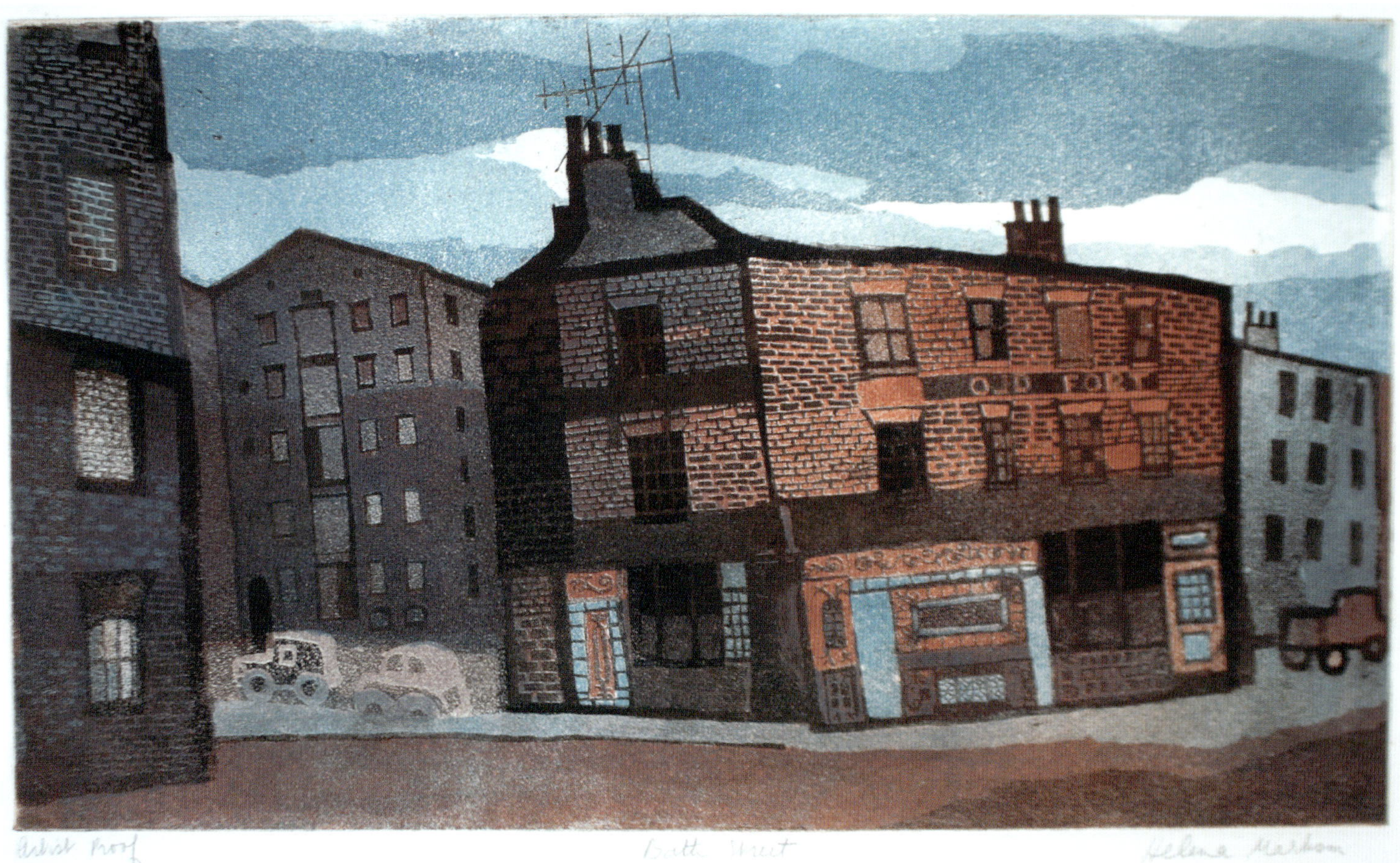



*Bath Street*    1966–67 etching and aquatint 35cm x 59cm

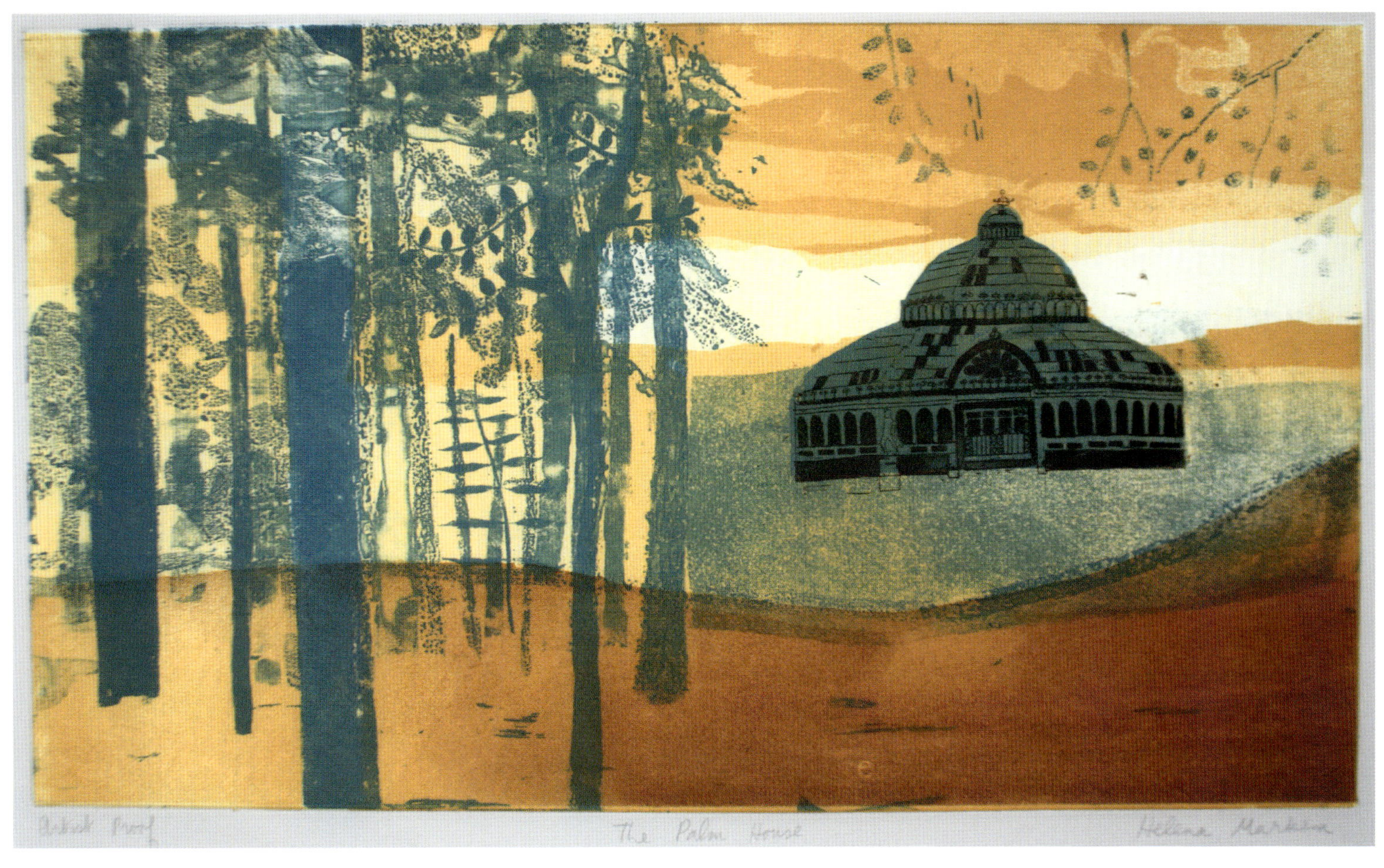



*The Palm House*    1967–68 etching and aquatint 35cm x 60cm

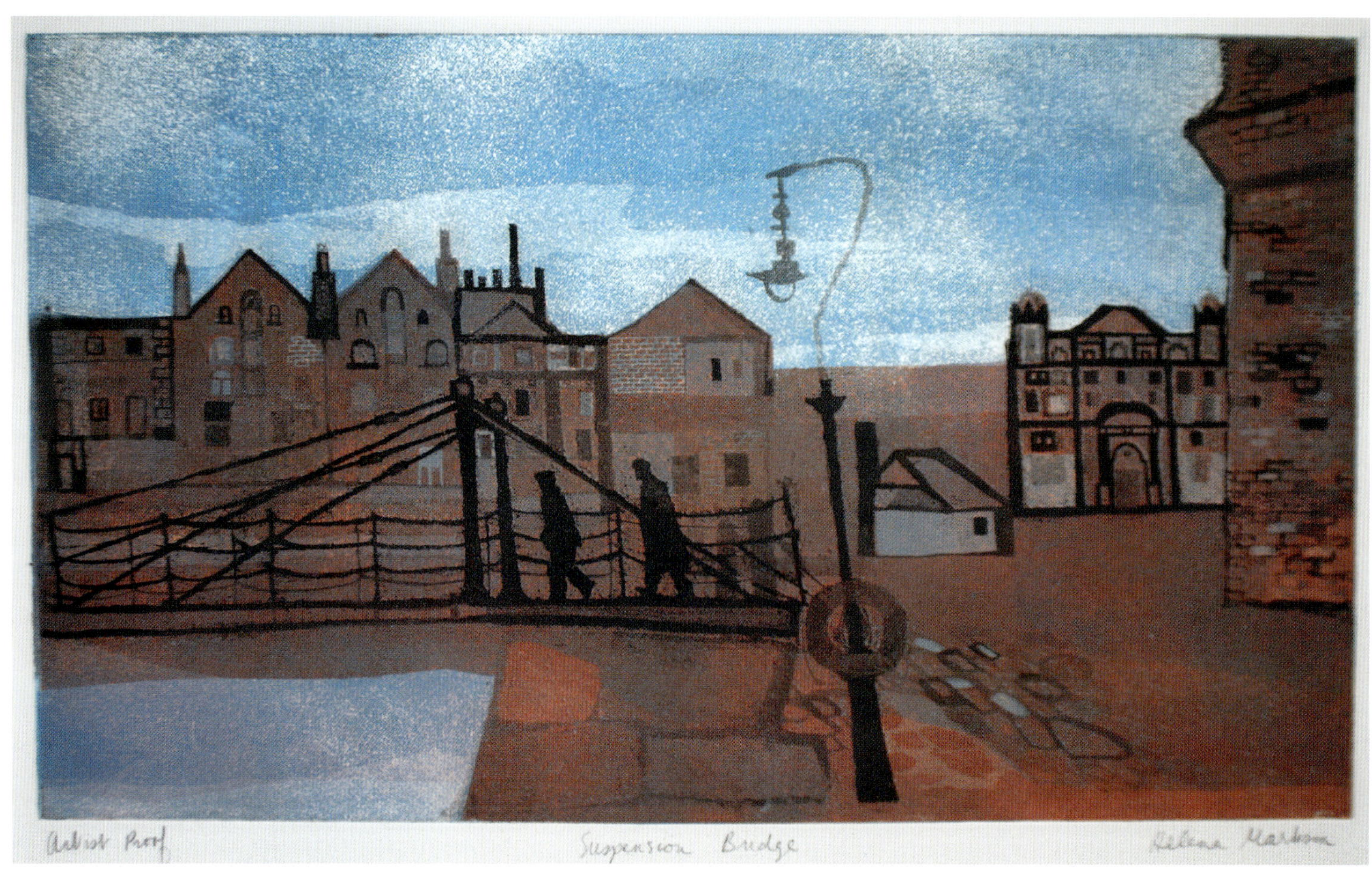


*Suspension Bridge*   1966–67 etching and aquatint 35cm x 60cm

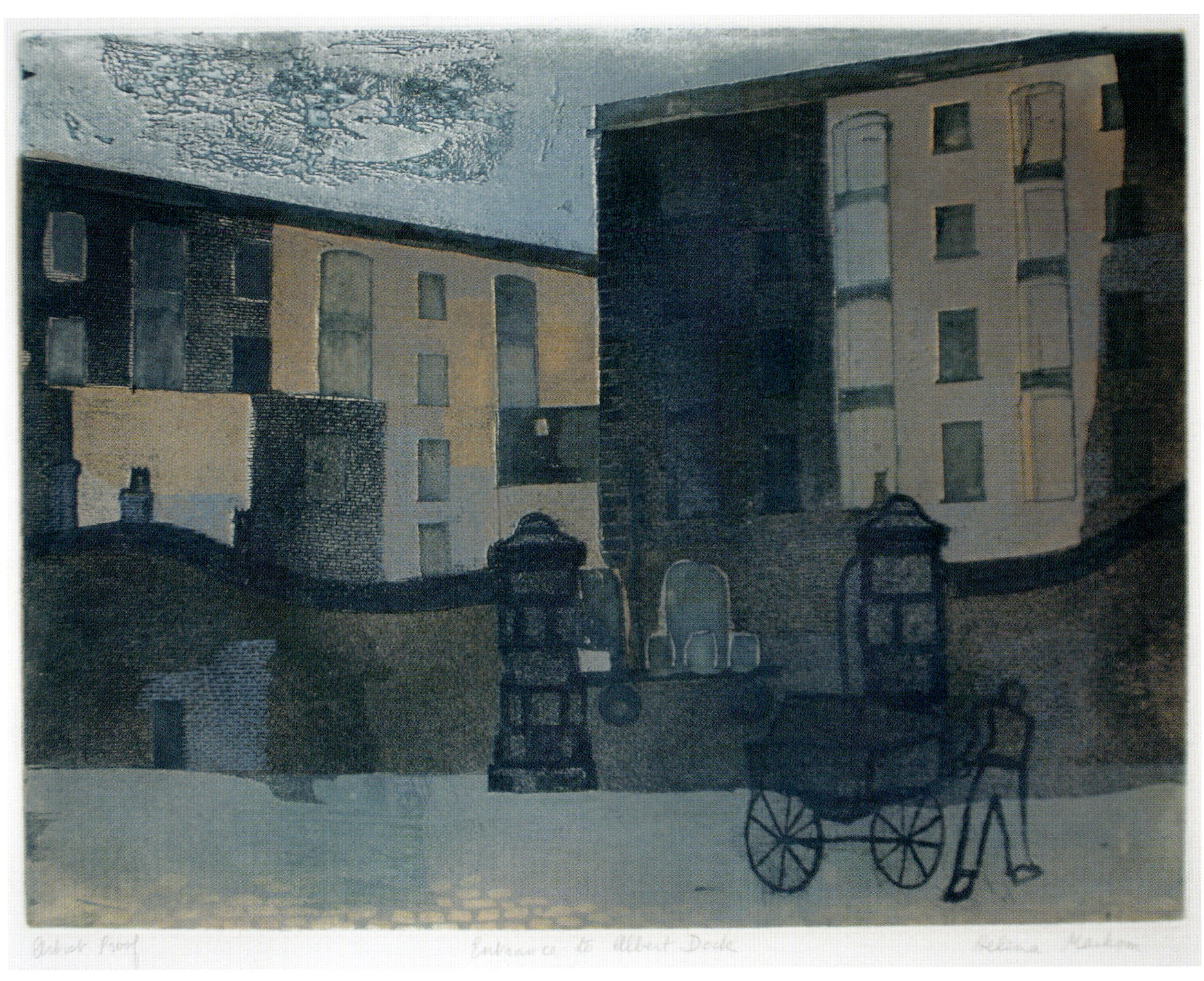

*Entrance to Albert Dock*    1966–67 etching and aquatint 43cm x 54.5cm

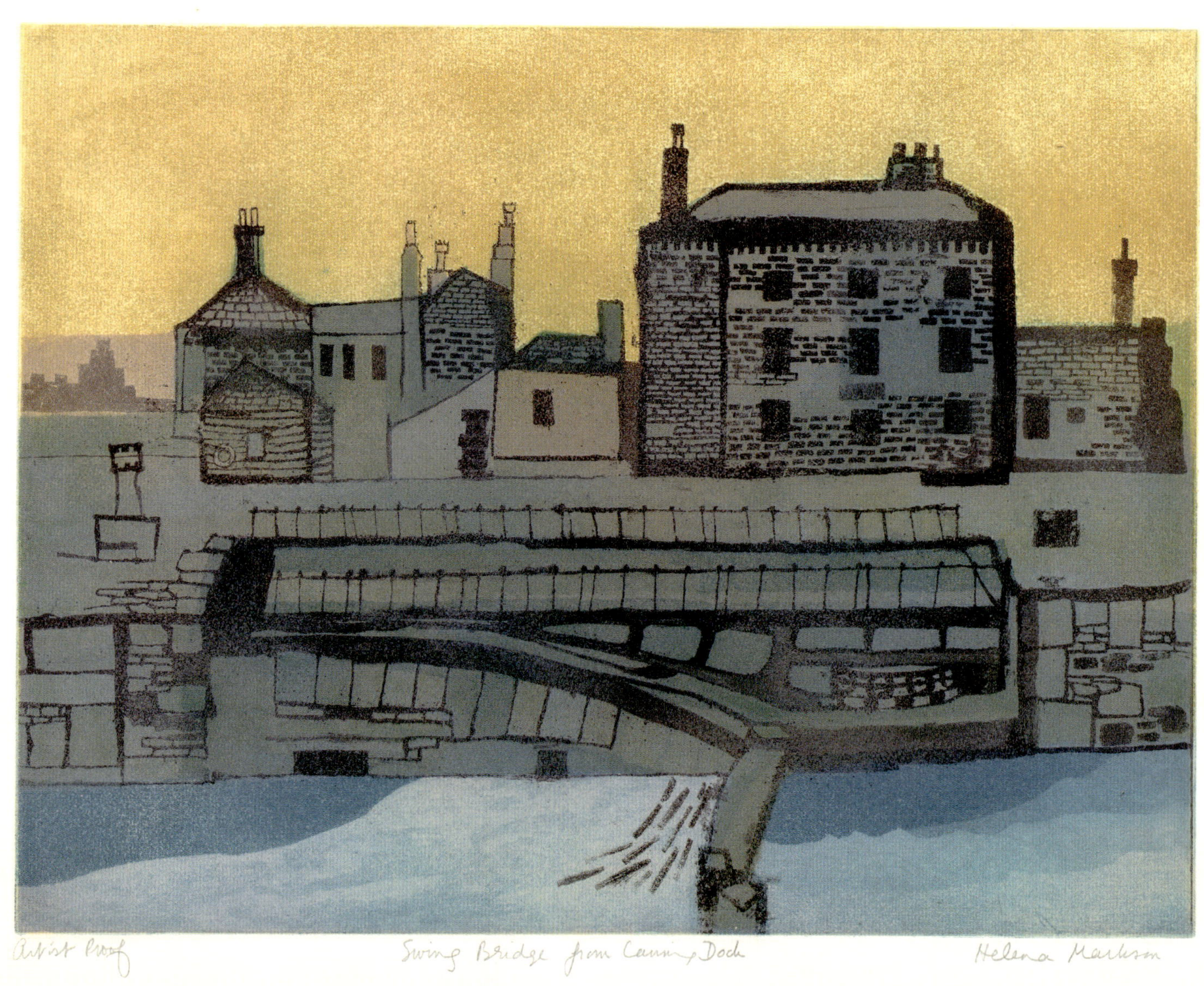


*Swing Bridge from Canning Dock*    1966–67 etching and aquatint 42.5cm x 55cm

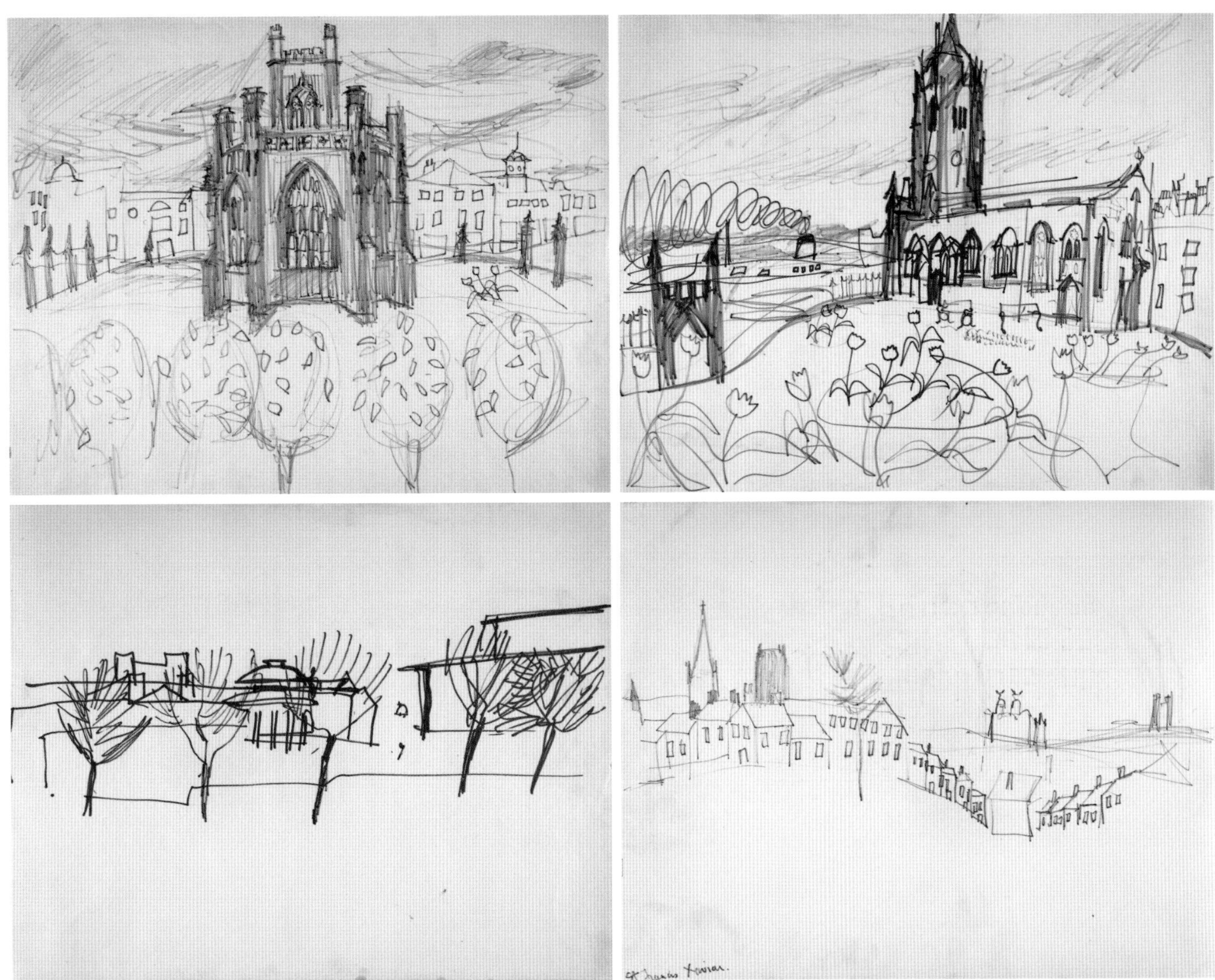

Pages from Helena's Liverpool sketchbook    1963–64 pencil 40cm x 50cm

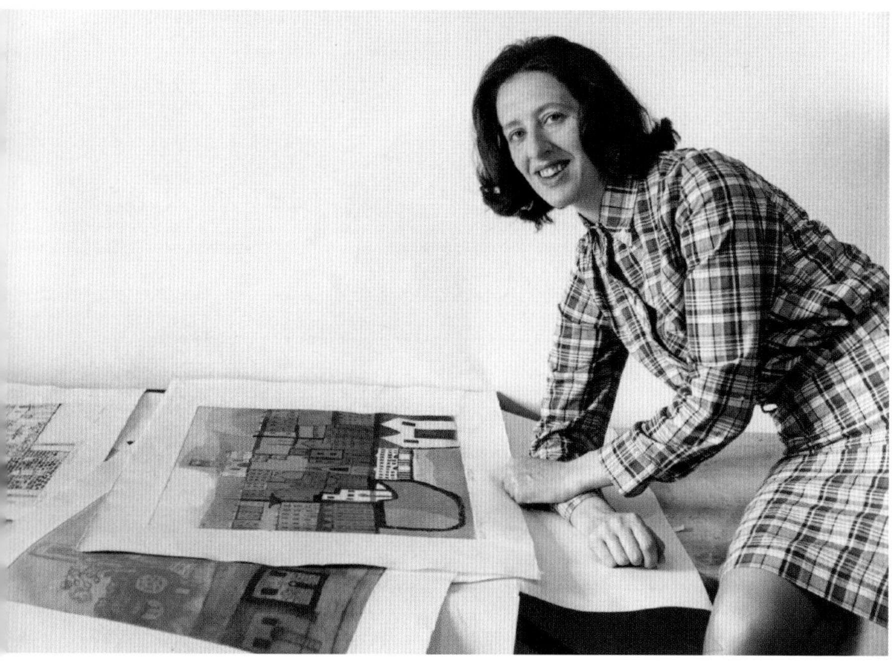

Helena and Liverpool prints

Helena worked on her Liverpool Series over a five-year period. The prints were well received from the outset and the first prints she made in 1963 were noticed by Paul Cornwell-Jones of Editions Alecto, who himself had studied architecture.

Editions Alecto, pioneering print publishers, opened in London in 1962 with the aim of producing limited edition prints for artists, which could be sold through the company. To some extent it took on the role started by the St George's Gallery in 1954 and in fact Editions Alecto acquired the remaining stock of prints from Robert Erskine of St George's Gallery.

Editions Alecto was keen to work with artists and printmakers who were already attracting public and media attention and were often buying in existing work by established printmakers.

Paul Cornwall-Jones approached Helena to discuss publishing and selling a small number of her Liverpool prints as *The Liverpool Suite*. Helena agreed and began working with Editions Alecto with *The Liverpool Suite* published in 1964–5. Helena went on to produce more prints of Liverpool which are the later prints from 1966-68, some of which Editions Alecto also chose to publish as part of a further collection of Helena's work called, *New Suite* 1968.

EDITIONS ALECTO
LIVERPOOL SUITE 1964–65

*Six colour etchings each in an edition*
*of 100 with 10 artist proofs*

*'There is a powerful position of the cathedral but also a balance between the community (of houses), the dock and the church'.[12]*

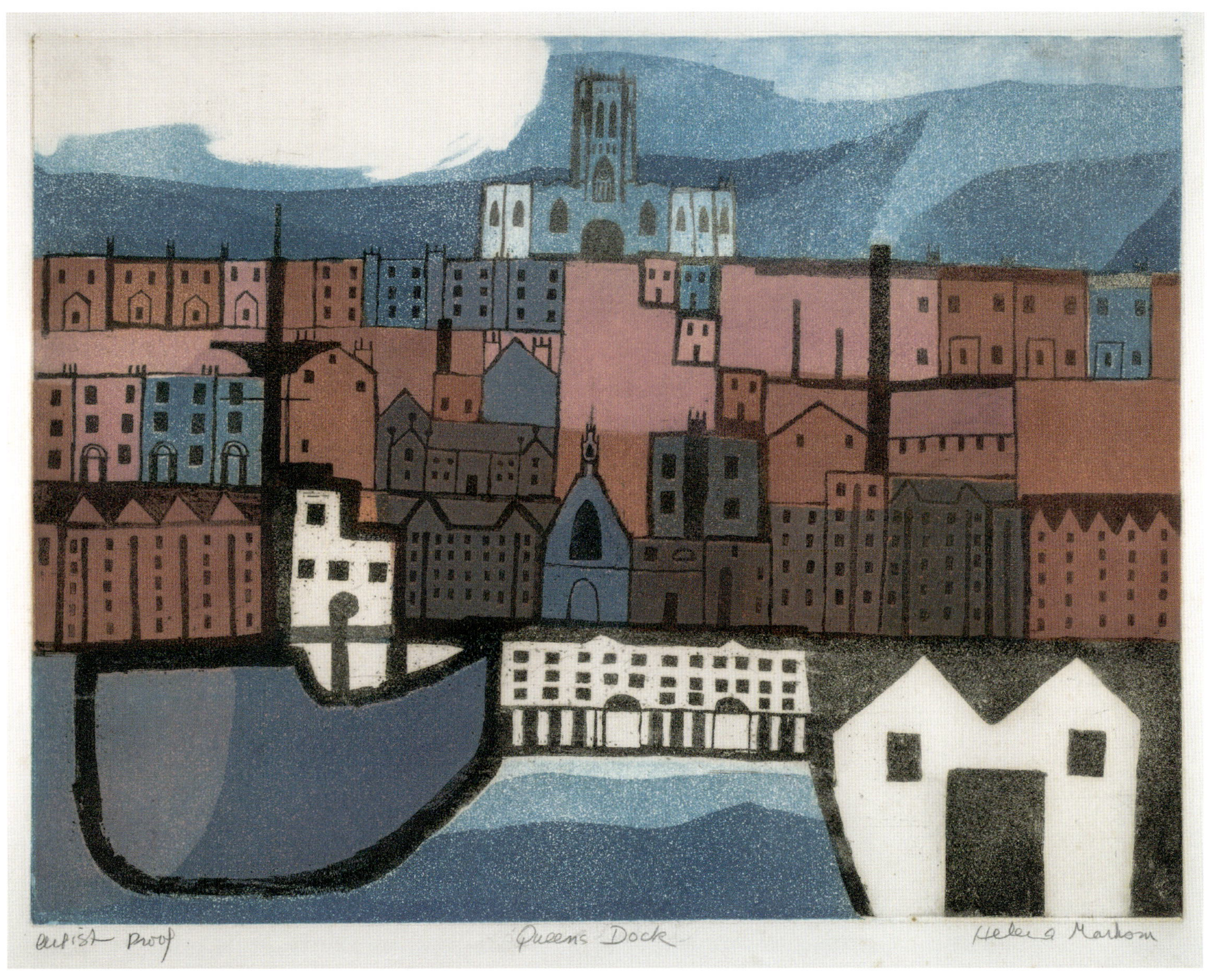



*Queens Dock*    1964–5 etching and aquatint 42cm x 55cm

*'This is how it looked in Everton, line upon line of houses on steep hills. … There were some sparkling houses, and then not far away some very neglected areas … Also some extraordinary sunsets, mixed with pollution of course'.*[13]

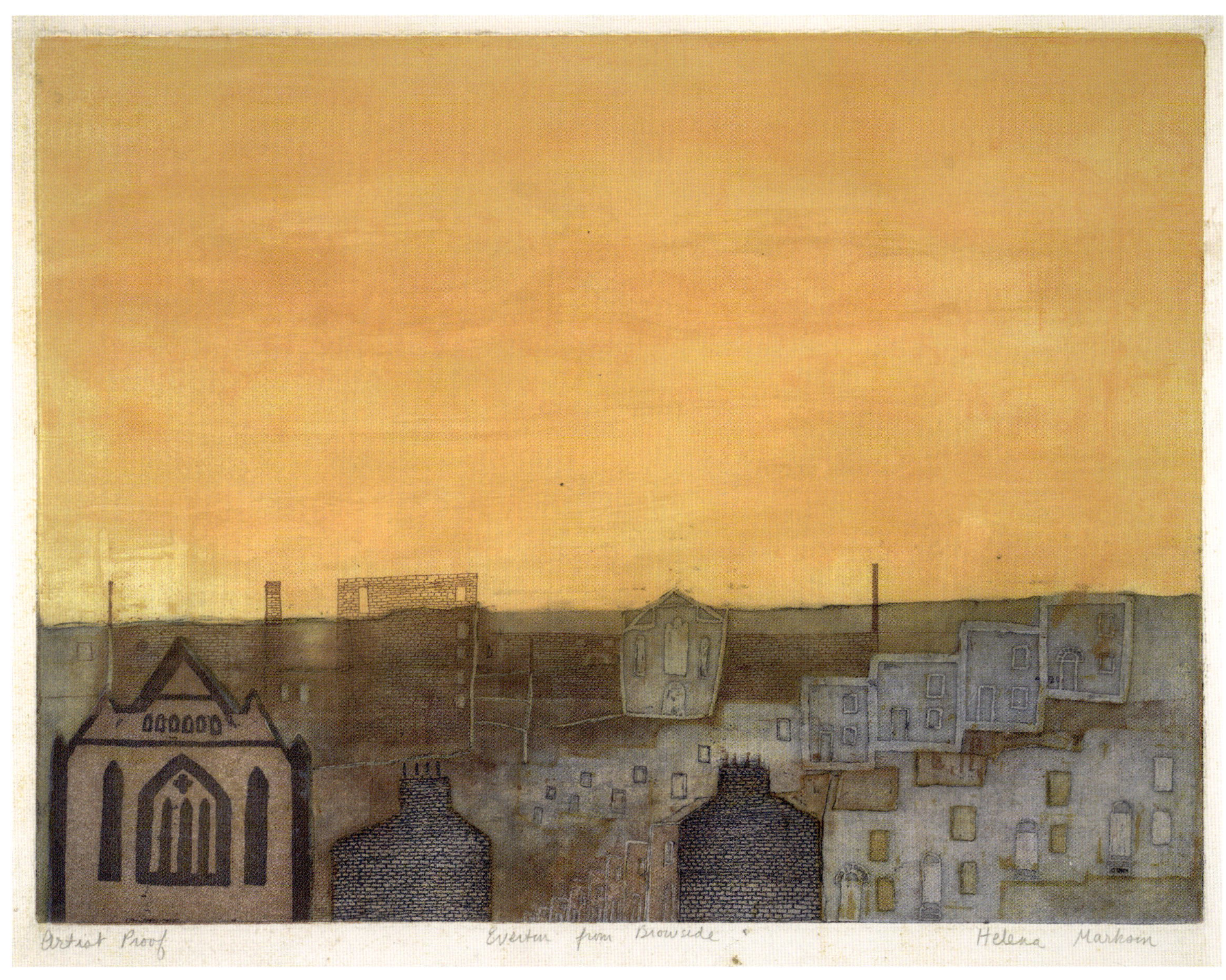



*Everton from Browside*   1964–5 etching and aquatint 41cm x 55cm

*'Walking round I got to know individual buildings,*

*their form and particular place in the wider scheme of things.*

*At the time I was becoming quite minimal, this project pulled*

*me in a different direction …'[14]*

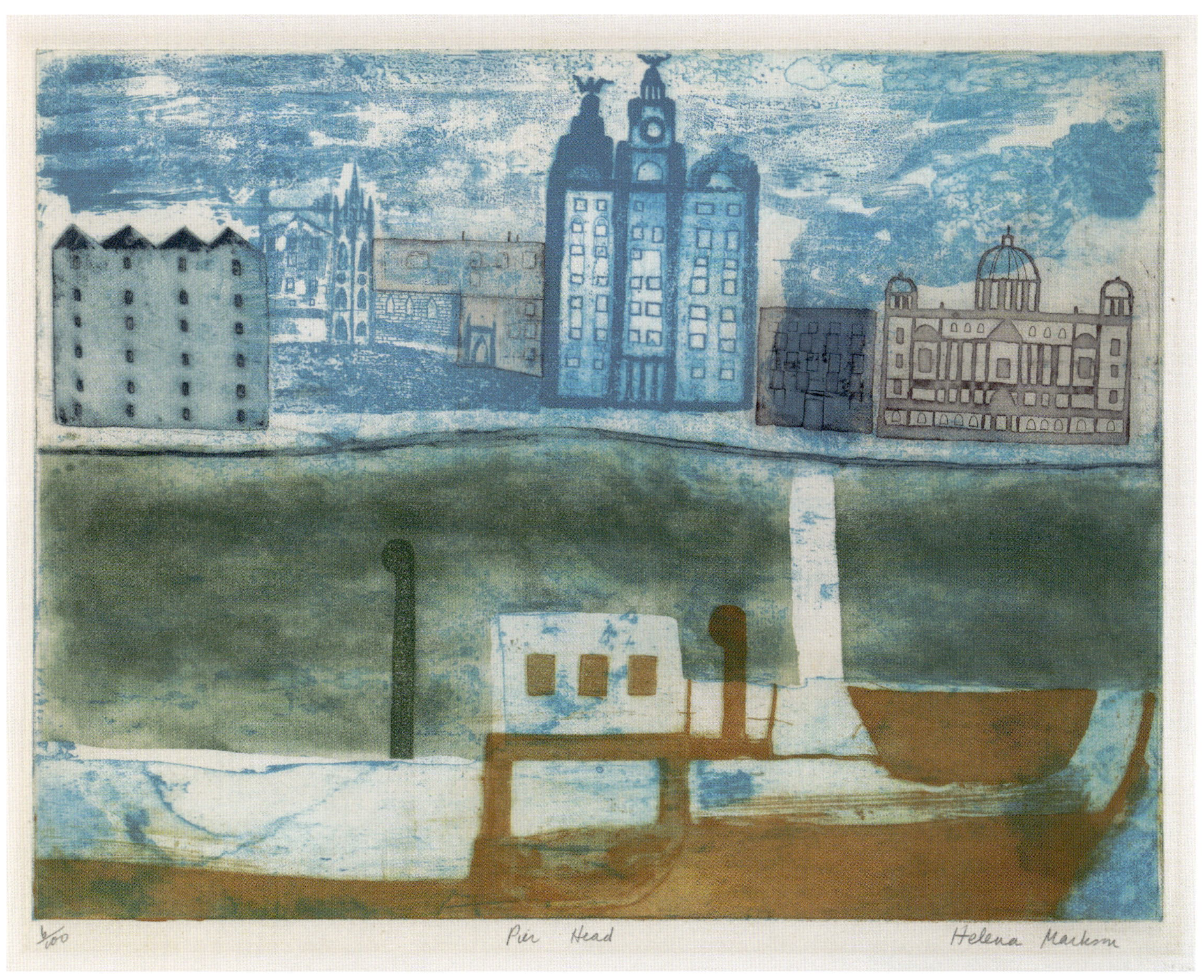

*Pier Head*   1964–5 etching and aquatint 42cm x 55cm

'I like to isolate a certain structure and present a sense of place …

At the time they were threatening to pull all of this (Albert Dock) down.

I remember John Betjeman getting involved …'[15]

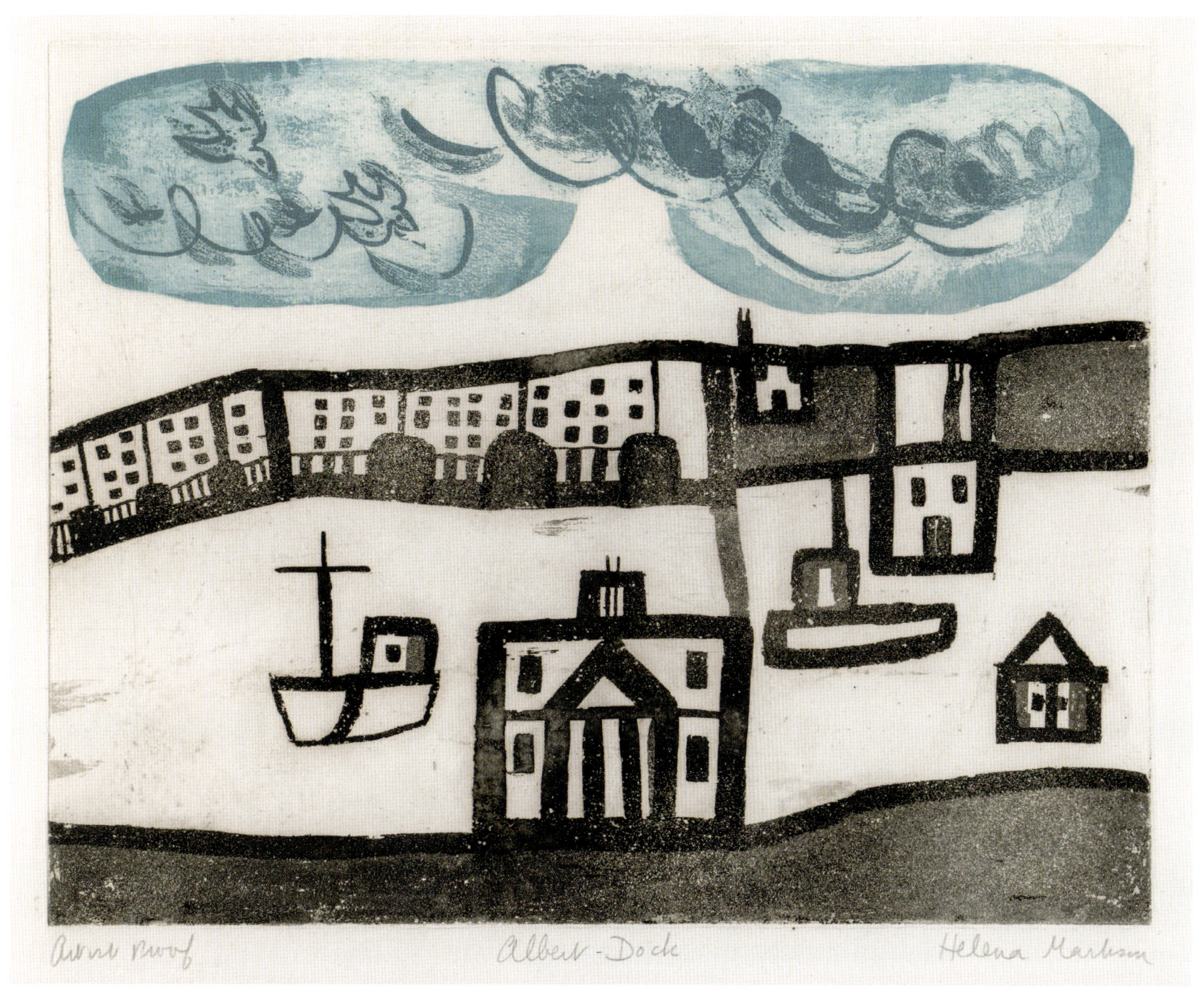


*Albert Dock*   1964–5 etching and aquatint 40cm x 50cm

*'I would walk around getting to know different buildings,
civic and residential, and their particular features …'[16]*

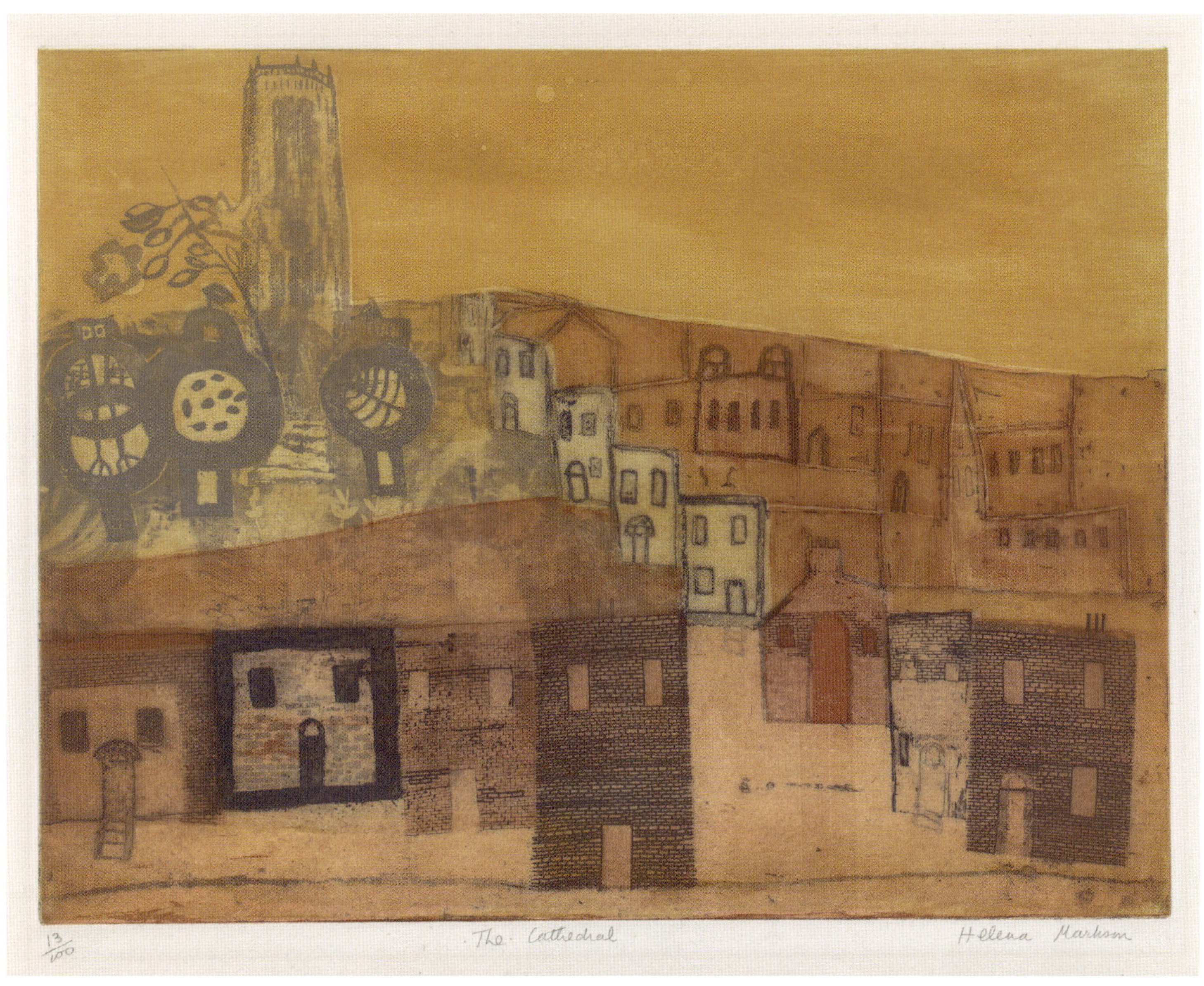



*The Cathedral*    1964–5 etching and aquatint 42cm x 54cm

An exhibition showing *The Liverpool Suite* was held by Editions Alecto at their gallery, The Print Centre in Holland Street, London in October 1964. The gallery was located in an area of West London, which was becoming recognised for the interesting artists living and working there:

*'The choice of 8 Holland Street in 1962 as an initial London base therefore appears significant. With the unambiguous name of The Print Centre, this ground floor gallery, with stock room in the basement and offices on the first, second and third floors, was located close to the future BIBA shops in Kensington as well as the Royal College of Art. It can be seen as the most tangible indication of Editions Alecto's aspiration to be part of a new generation of art and consumerism.'*[17]

Helena also worked with Editions Alecto to produce three prints for the Public Schools Series 1961–4, which had begun in 1961 with John Piper's lithographs of Westminster School. Helena made prints of *Beaumont School*, *Haileybury College* and *Dover College*.

A few years later in 1968 she also published *New Suite* with Editions Alecto, who chose six colour etchings of London and Liverpool scenes.

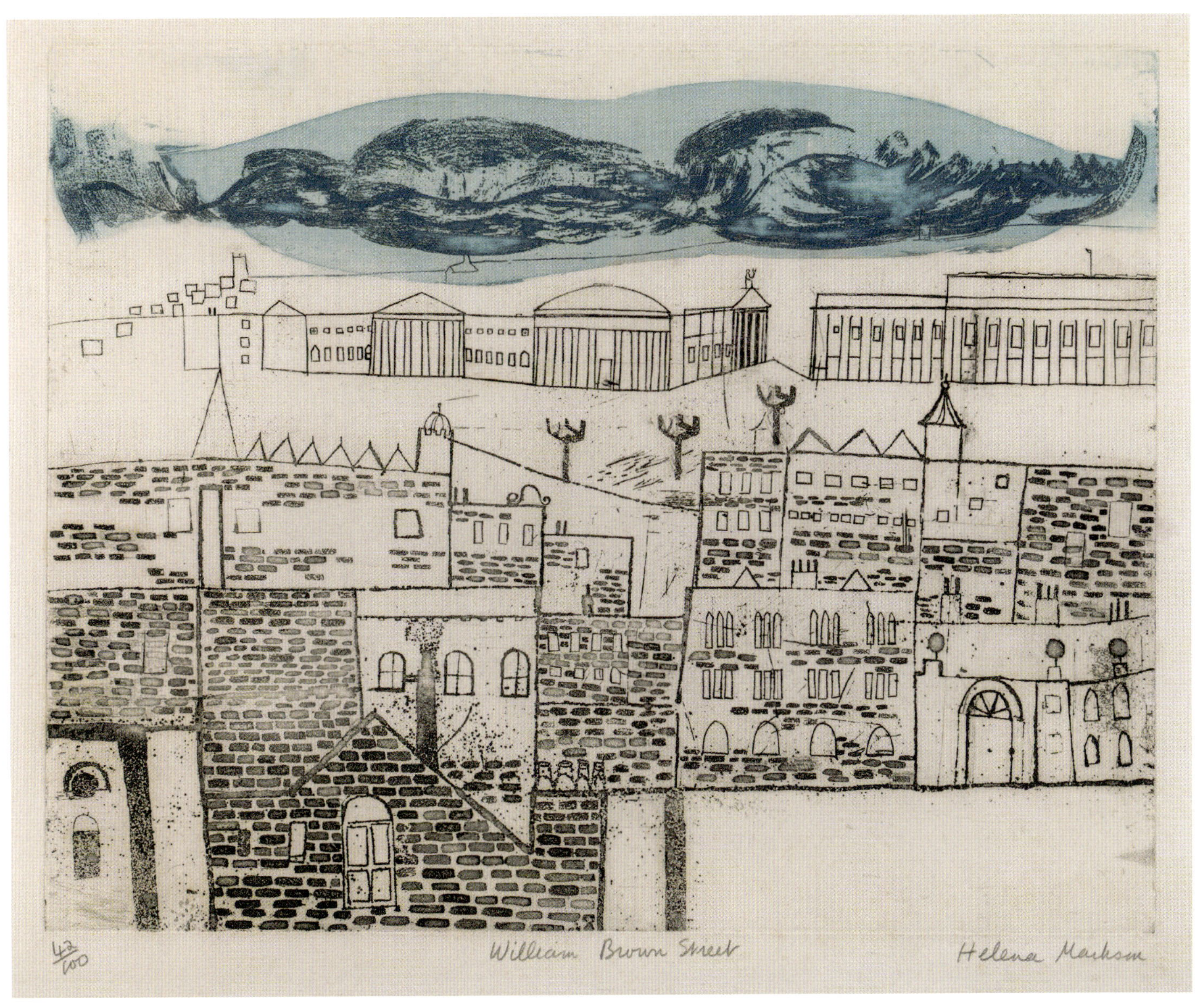

*William Brown Street*    1964–5 etching and aquatint 39cm x 50cm

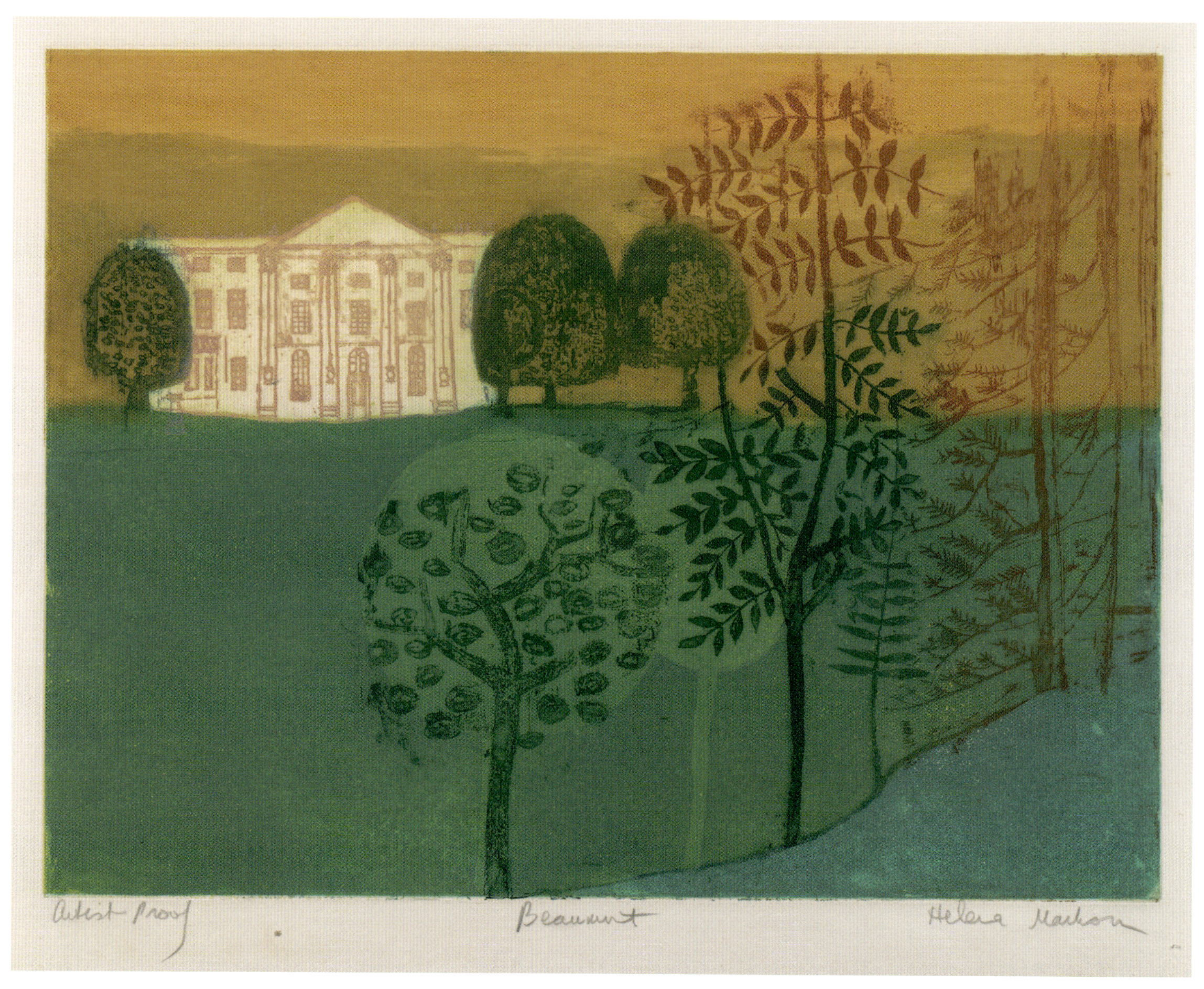


*Beaumont*   1964 etching and aquatint 42cm x 55cm

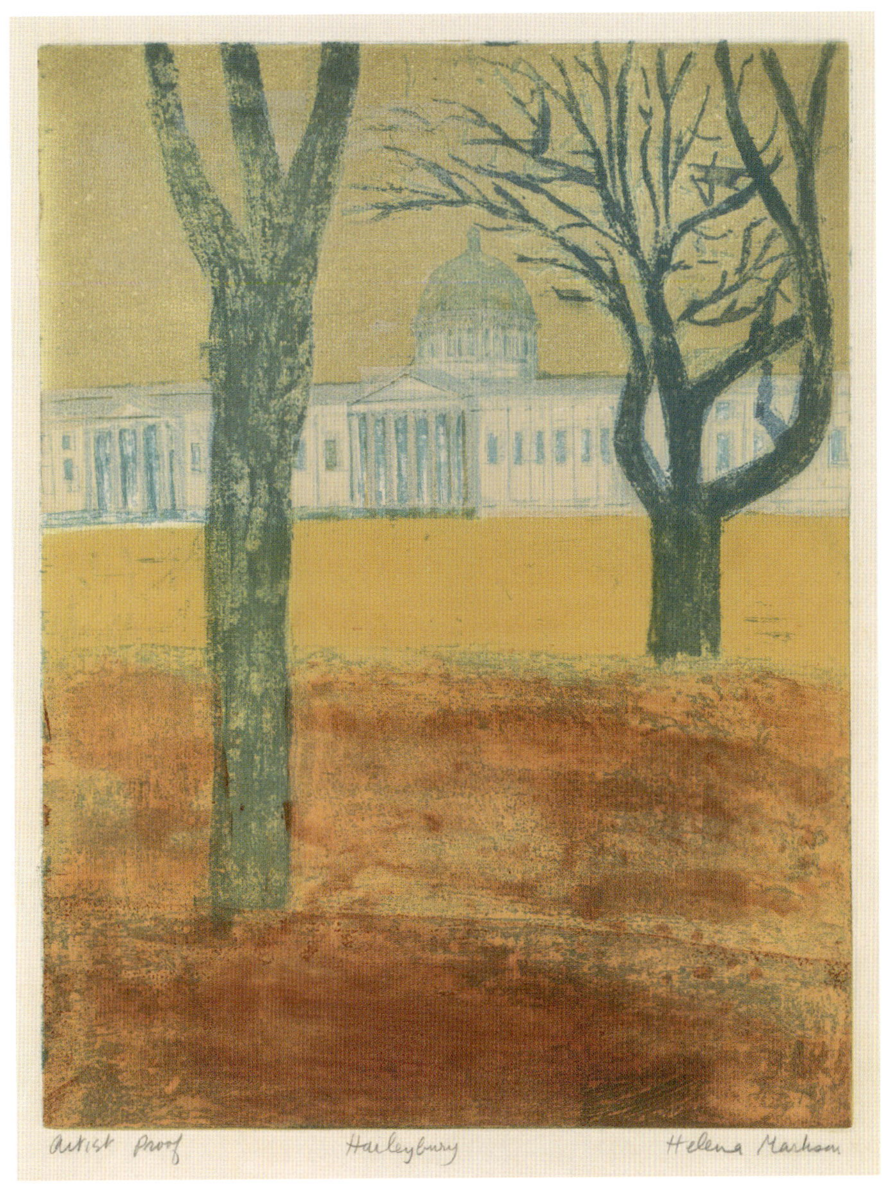



*Haileybury*    1964 etching and aquatint 75cm x 56cm

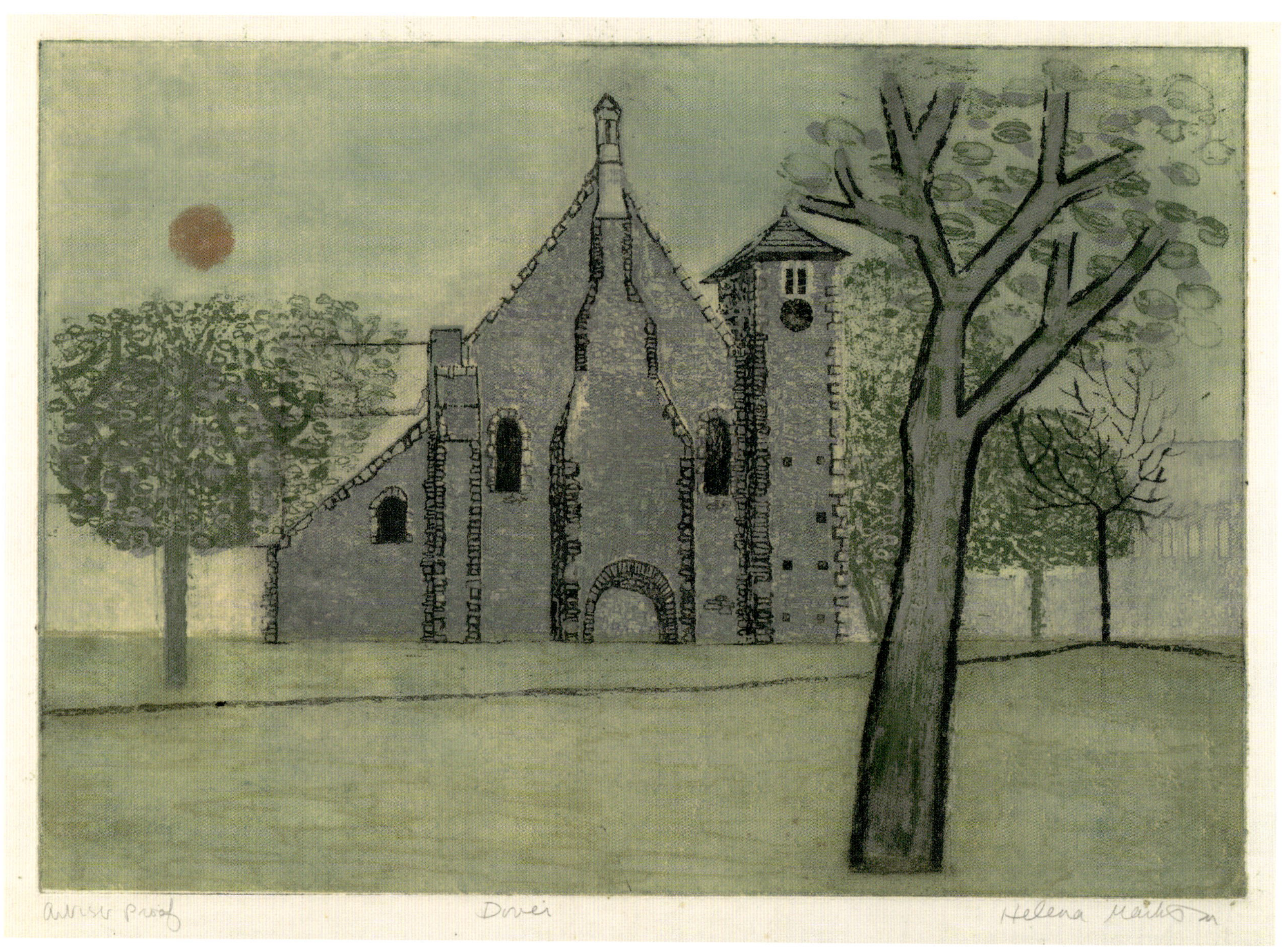



*Dover*   1964 etching and aquatint 42cm x 50cm

EDITIONS ALECTO
NEW SUITE 1968

*Six colour etchings each in an edition
of 100 with 10 artist proofs*

'This is the church in Pentonville [London] where Richard Bonnington is buried. This is now owned by a corporate firm with the grave stones moved to one side. … The house on the right is symbolic of houses/dwellings there.'[18]

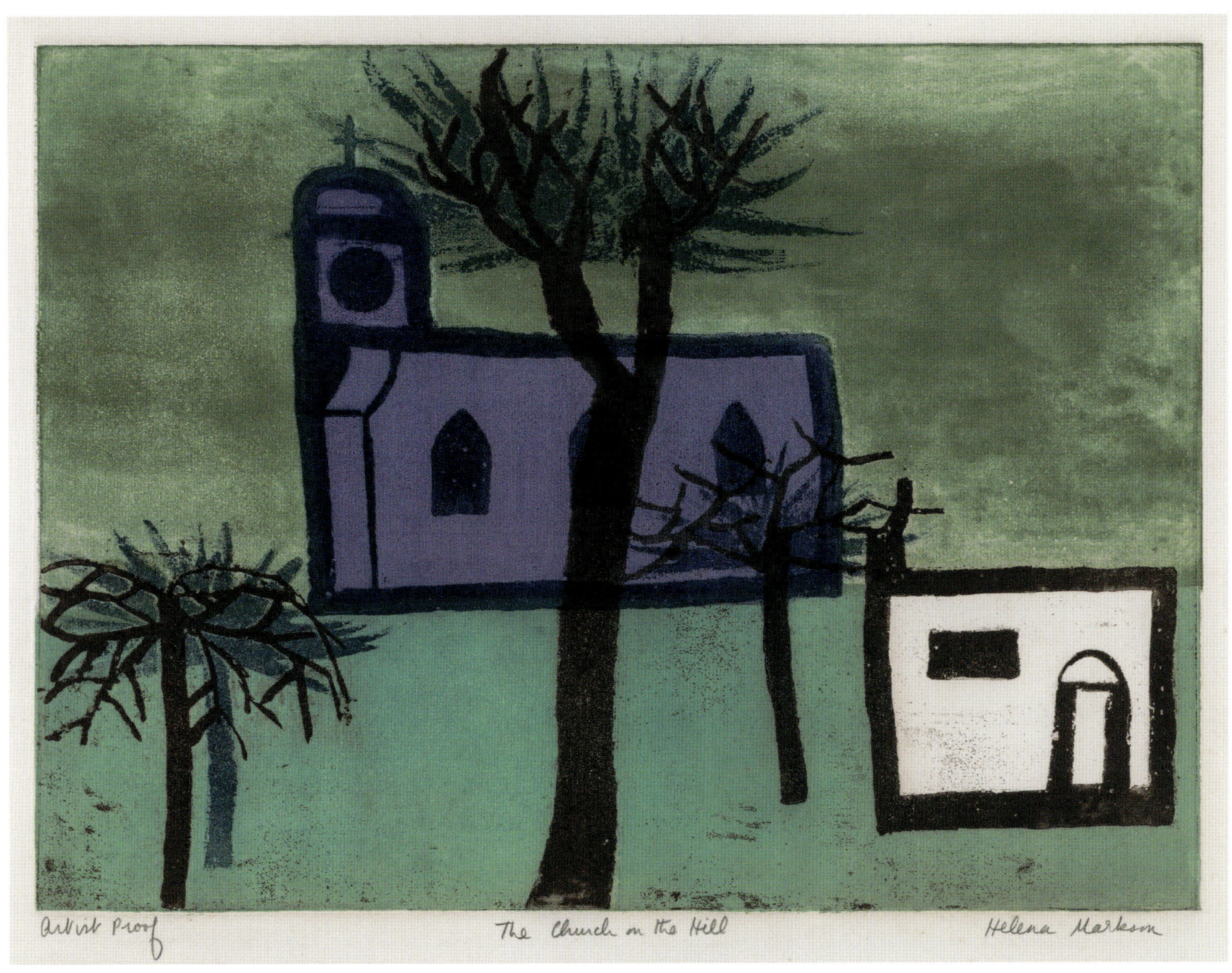



*The Church on the Hill*    1968 etching and aquatint 43cm x 58cm

'I used pigment and oil not tins of paint so I could control the colour better … I remember Michael Rothenstein said I worked on the plates "like a painting". Falconer Square was a residential area in Liverpool where I stayed.'[19]

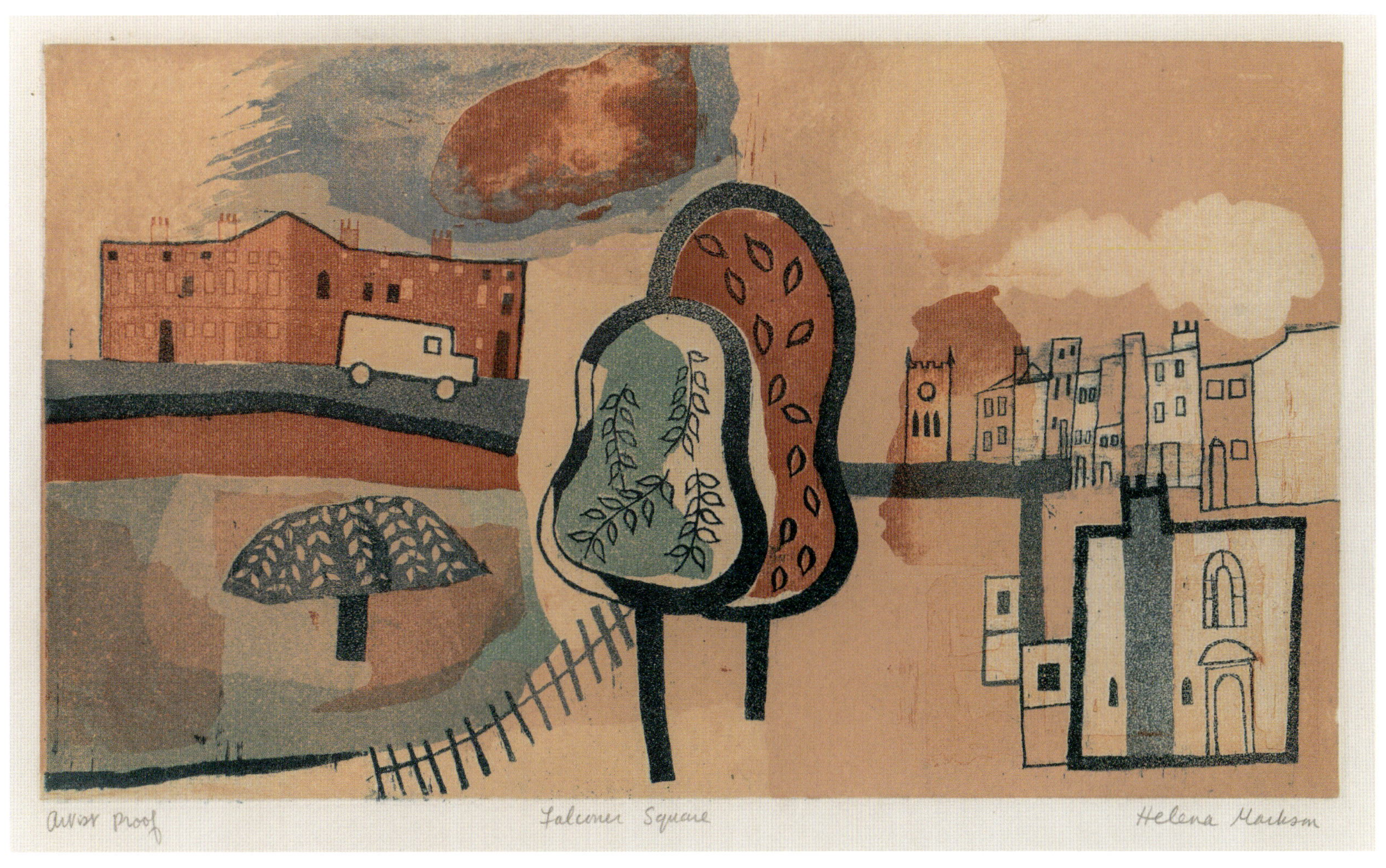



*Falconer Square*   1968 etching and aquatint 35cm x 60cm

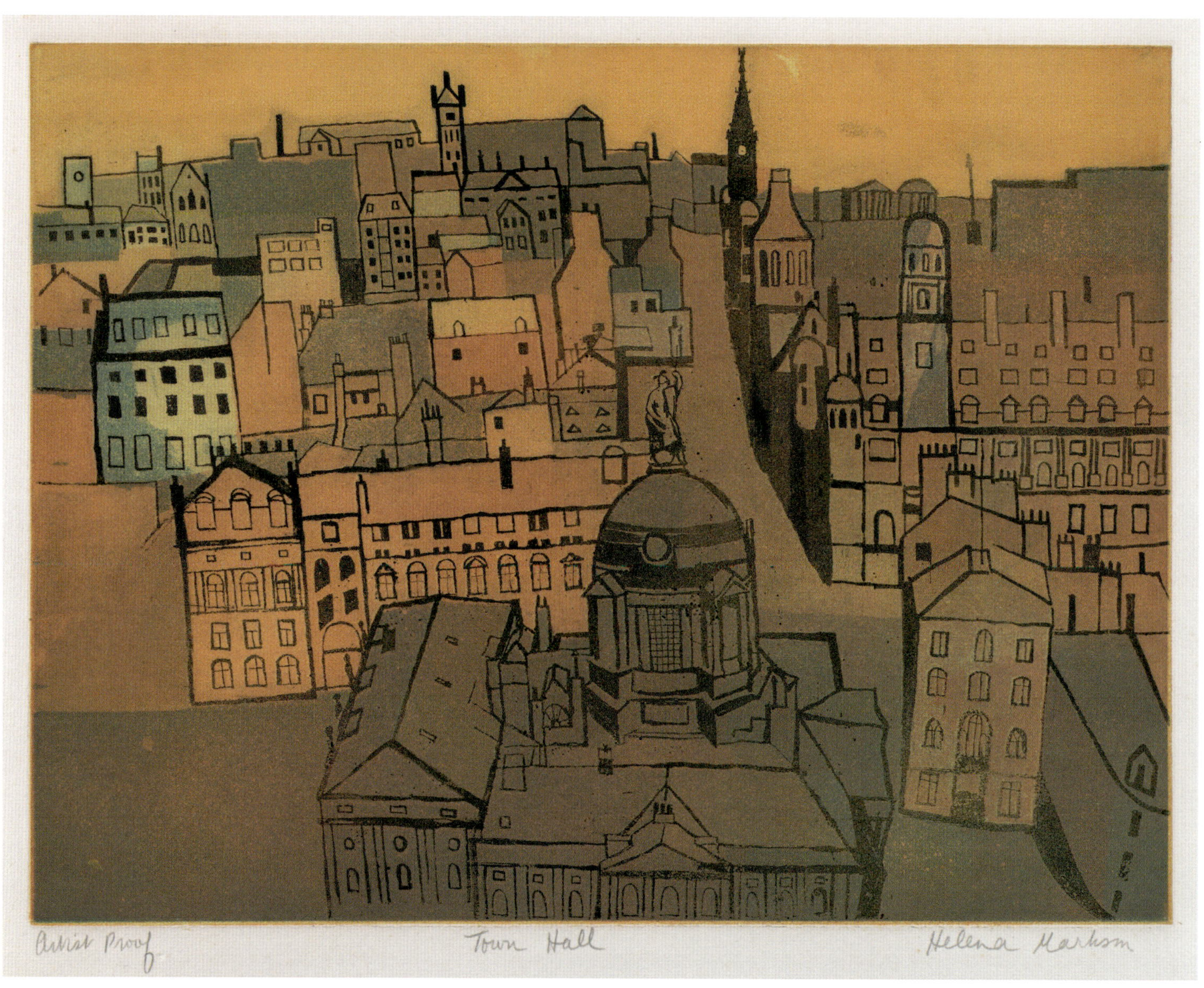



*Town Hall*    1968 etching and aquatint 43cm x 55cm

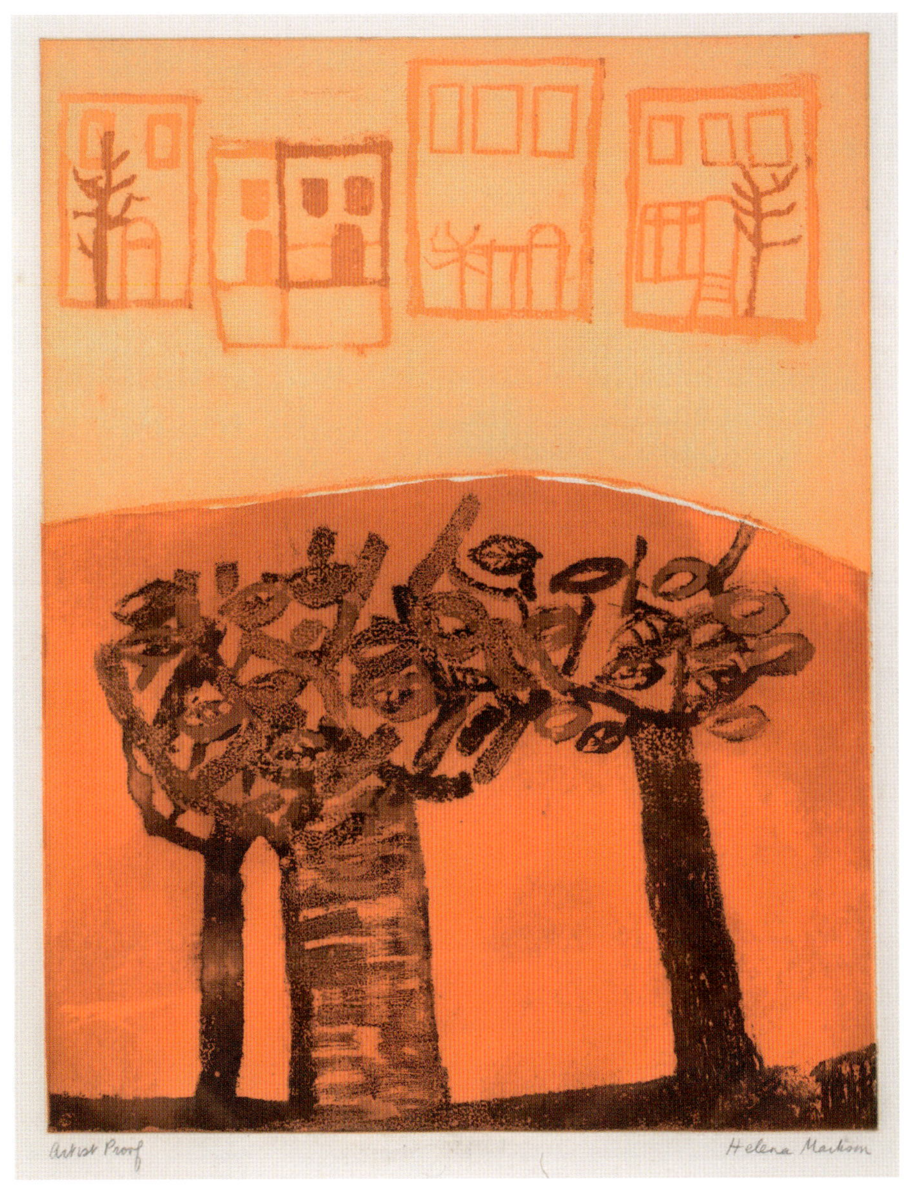



*Hampstead Pond*    1968 etching and aquatint 59cm x 44cm

'The large warehouse on the right was designed by Jesse Hartley and torn down soon after I completed this print. All the docks in Liverpool connect …'[20]

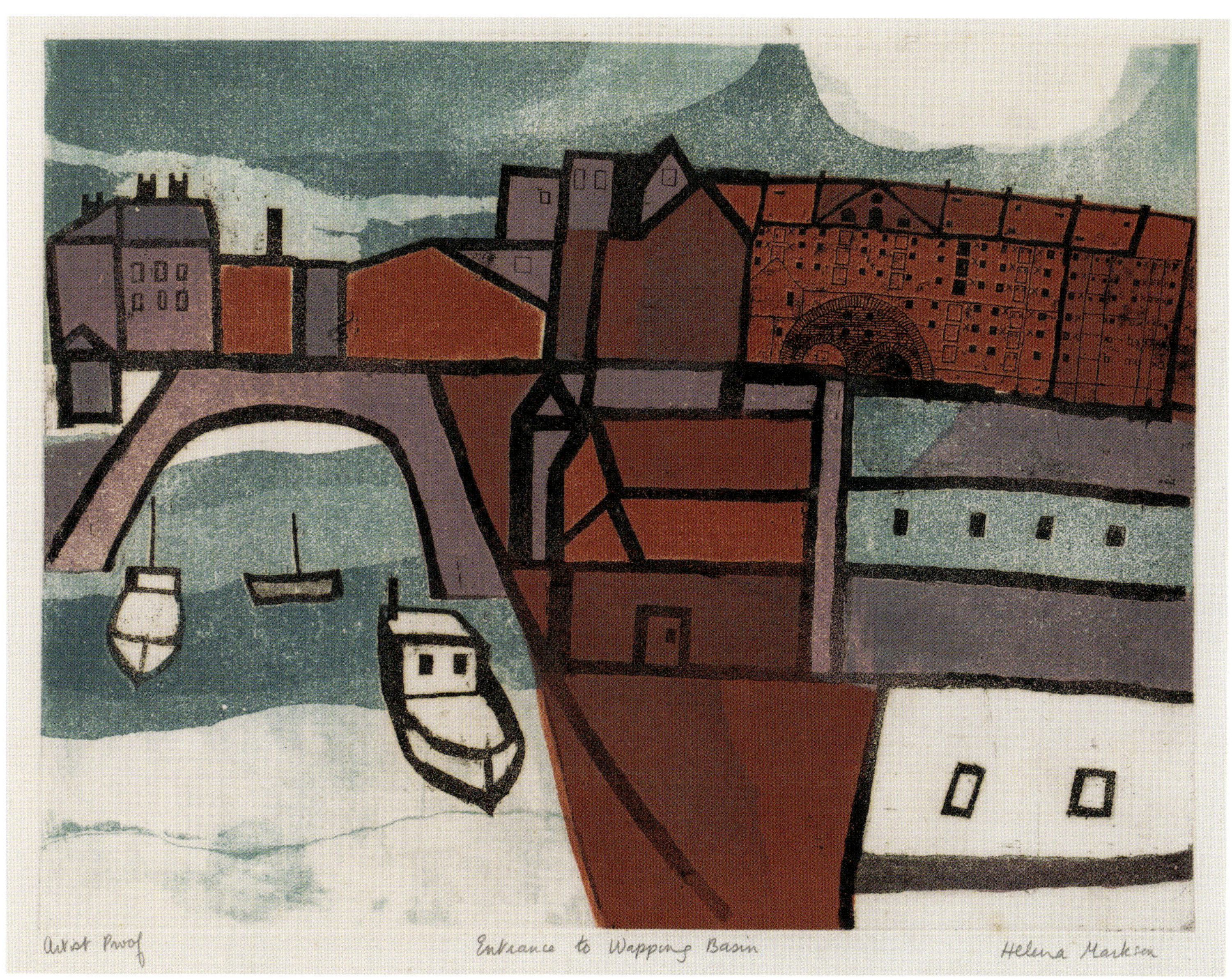

*Entrance to Wapping Basin*    1968 etching and aquatint 42cm x 54cm

'A student plate which Paul Cornwell-Jones later picked out …
a general idea of an area I knew well … people waiting for buses,
going about a dreary day.'[21]

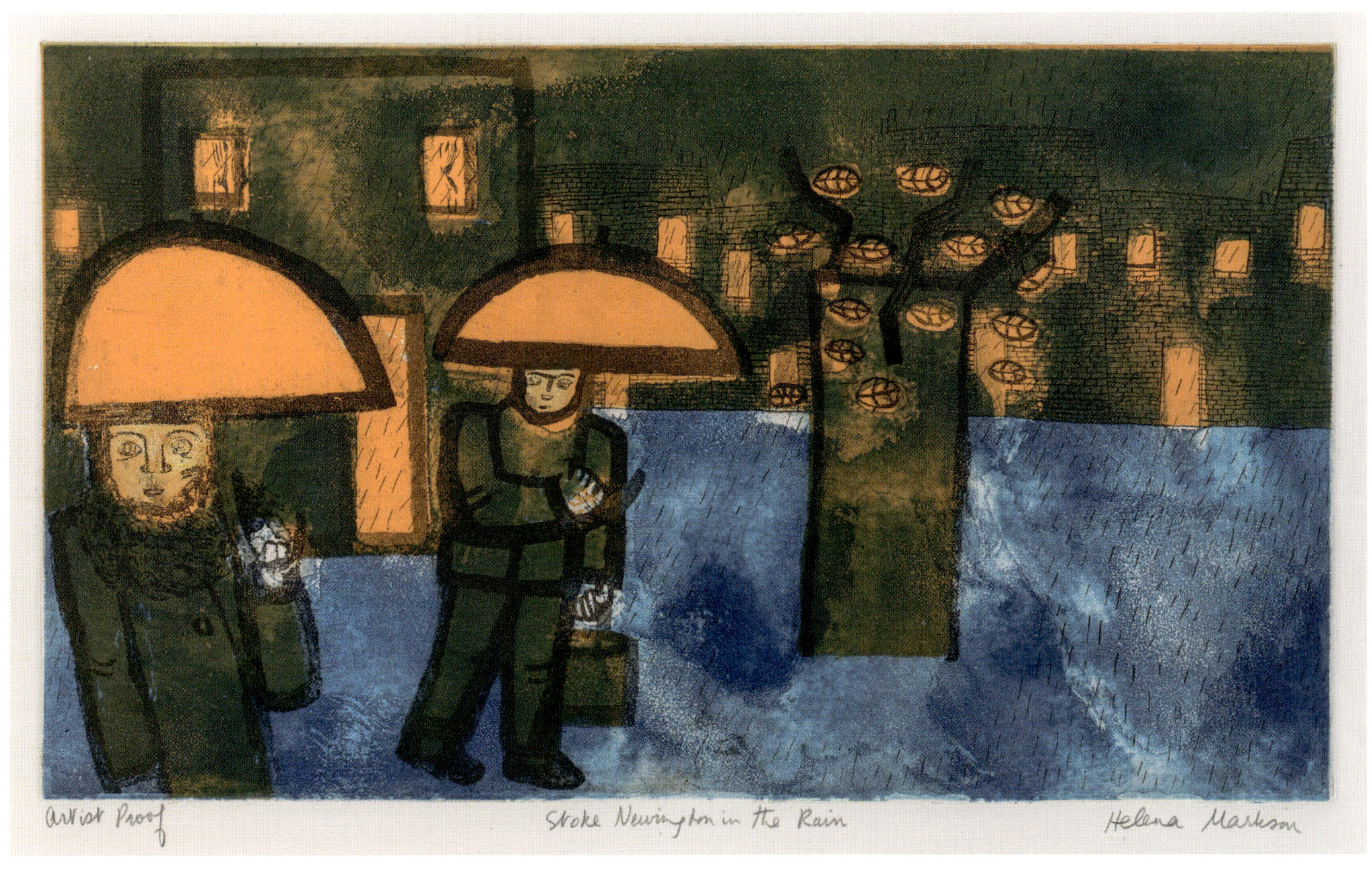


*Stoke Newington in the Rain*    1968 etching and aquatint 30cm x 52cm

Working with Editions Alecto brought Helena's work to a wider audience and raised her profile as a printmaker. She was elected to join The Printmakers Council, a newly formed group set up in London in 1965 by Anthony Gross, Michael Rothenstein and Julian Trevelyan and other leading artists and printmakers of the day. The vision was to create a forum for artist printmakers, to protect the integrity and standards of prints and to enable members to exhibit and sell their work. Members were elected and could then exhibit their original prints in the Printmakers Council exhibitions. Helena exhibited an etching *Queens Dock* in their travelling exhibition of 1967–8.

Helena's prints were also included in the 'Pictures for Schools Exhibition' in 1966, an annual exhibition founded by Nan Youngman, that had been running since 1947. Organised by the Society for Education through Art with the support of the Arts Council the works in the exhibition were available to educational bodies to buy and included original prints, paintings, sculpture and collages and embroideries. The Pictures for Schools exhibitions had been very successful for many years and had led to many local education authorities, schools and colleges owning excellent collections of art, which could be enjoyed by the children and students. Carel Weight wrote in his foreword to the 1966 exhibition:

*'I have always thought that these exhibitions are among the best mixed shows to be seen in London nowadays. Artists as a rule like exhibiting pictures or sculpture for children; and they are generally quite happy to sell their works at prices that can meet the modest budget of schools.'*[22]

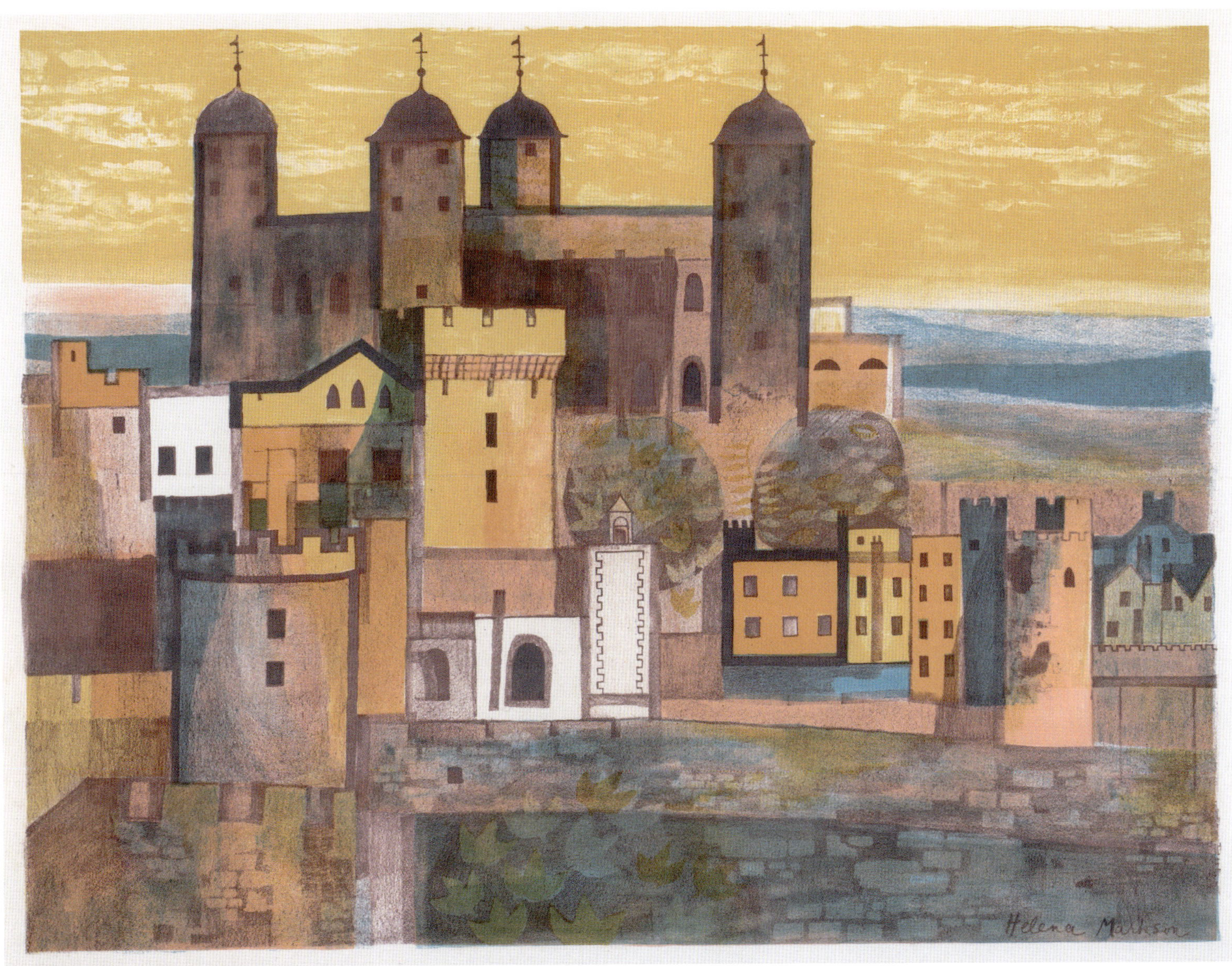

*Tower of London*    1968 lithograph 43cm x 56cm

# ISRAEL, USA,
# UK AND TRAVELS

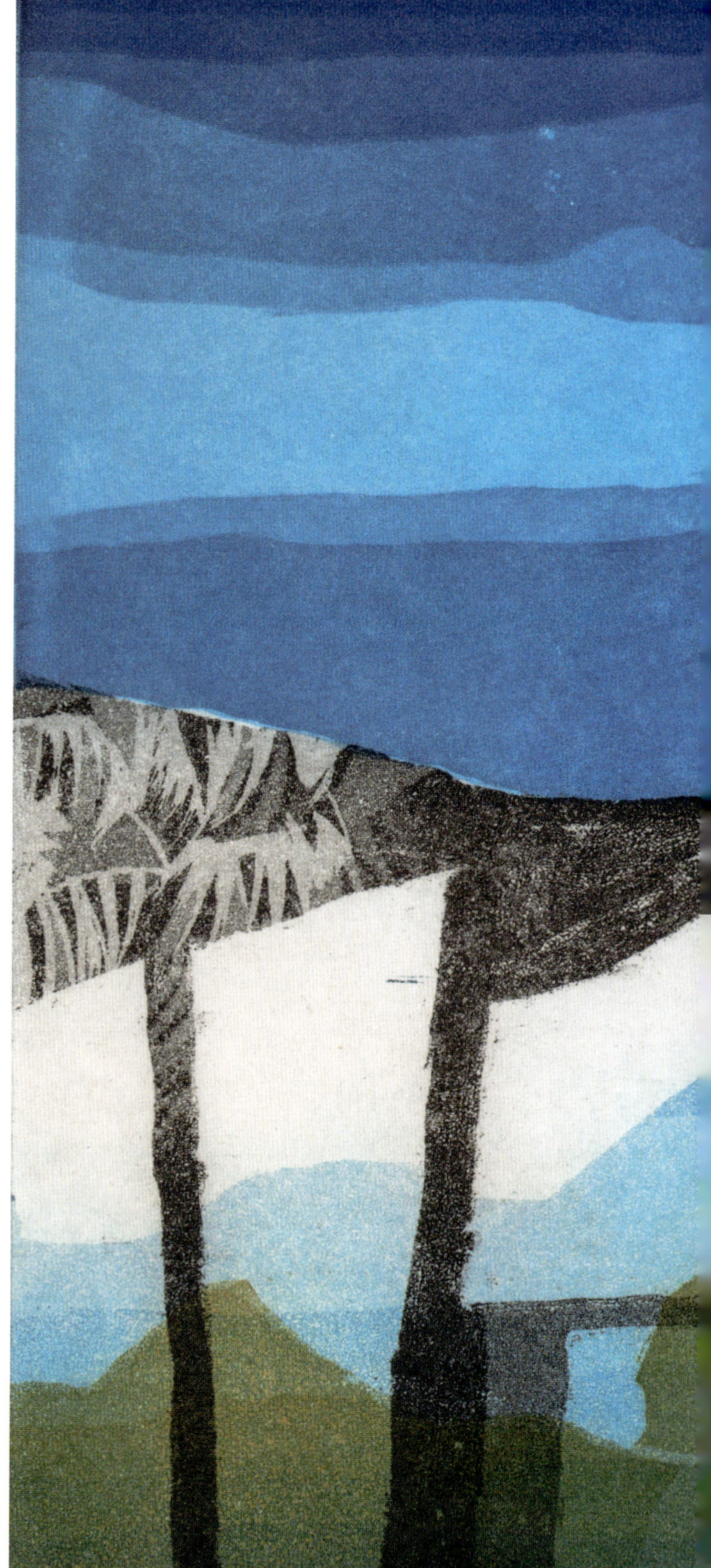

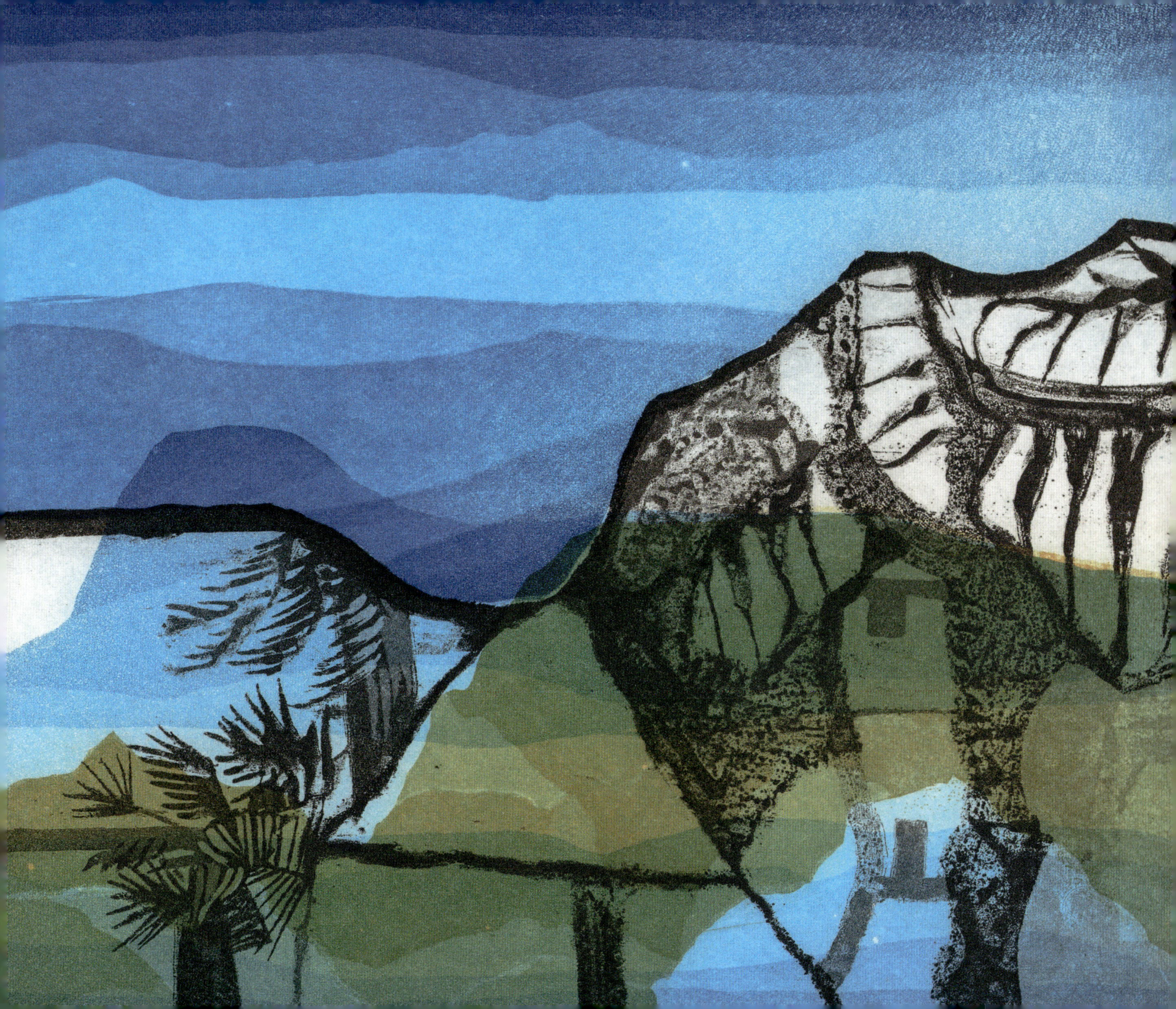

In 1967 Helena visited Israel. This was to be a turning point in her life and by 1970 she was living and working in Israel almost full time.

Prior to travelling to Israel Helena seems to have been interested in its changing history and the tremendous change for the lives of Jews in Israel. In 1960 she had designed a book cover for Eyre and Spottiswoode. The book, *Rebel Against the Light* by Alexander Ramati, tells the story of three characters set against the backdrop of the Arab-Israeli war as it follows their lives in a changing world.

In the autumn of 1967 a fuller version of the design was used for the cover of the *Association Journal of the Professional and Technical Workers Aliyah*, the Israeli organisation whose purpose was to encourage and assist the settlement of professional and technical workers in Israel. It was published just a few months after the events of June 1967, the Six Day War (1967 Arab-Israeli War). The editorial in this edition of the journal calls upon Jewish people to go to live in Israel and use their skills to help build a Jewish state. The events and changing history of Israel must surely have been in Helena's mind when in November 1967 the Israel Association of Painters and Sculptors organised an exhibition, 'Helena Markson Etchings' at their gallery, The Jerusalem Artists' House in Jerusalem, Israel.

Helena travelled to Israel to see the exhibition and here she met artists and teachers from the newly founded University of Haifa. A short while after she returned to England the university invited Helena to return to Israel to help set up the new art department. Helena decided to make the move and set off for a new life in Israel. Once living there, just as in the UK in the previous decades, she threw her energies into her work.

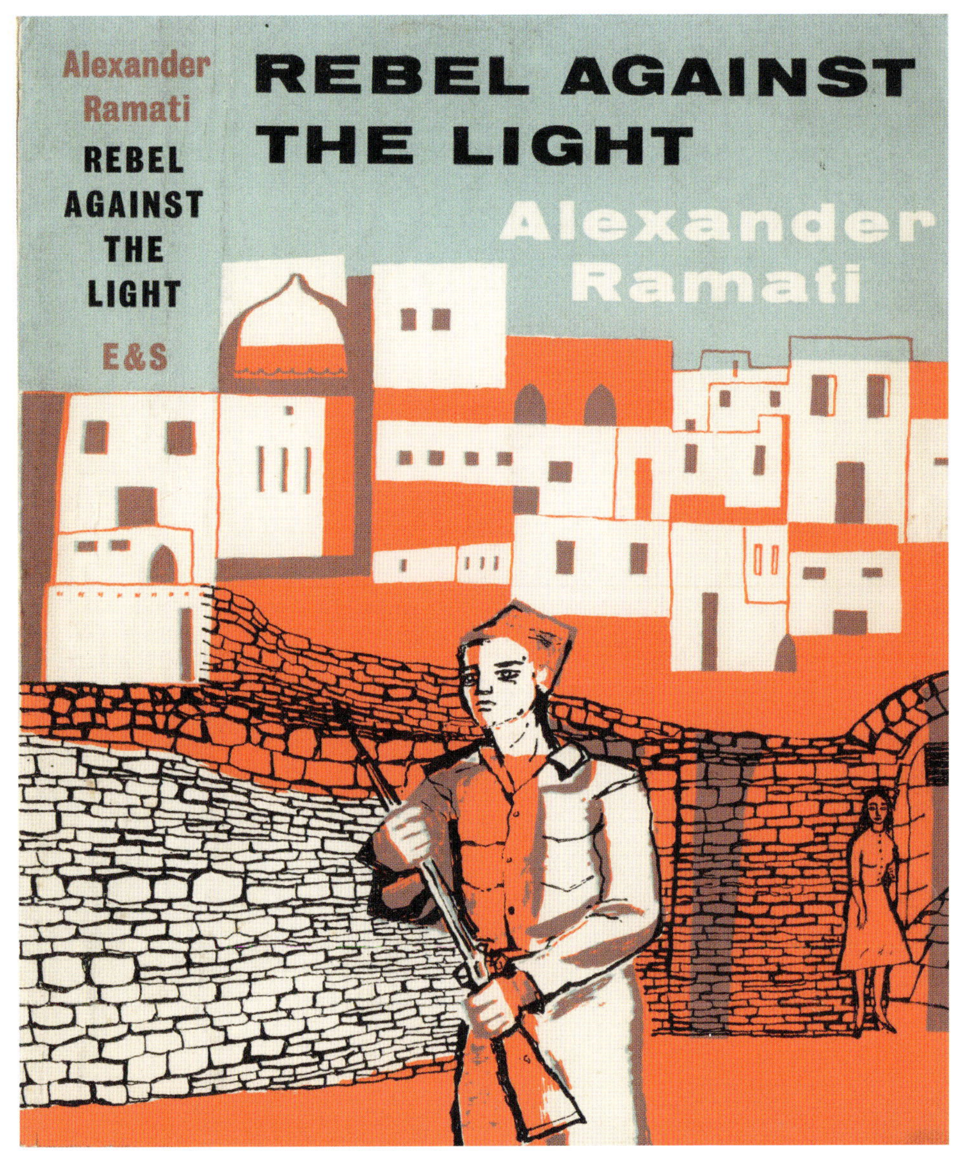


Book cover illustration *Rebel Against the Light*

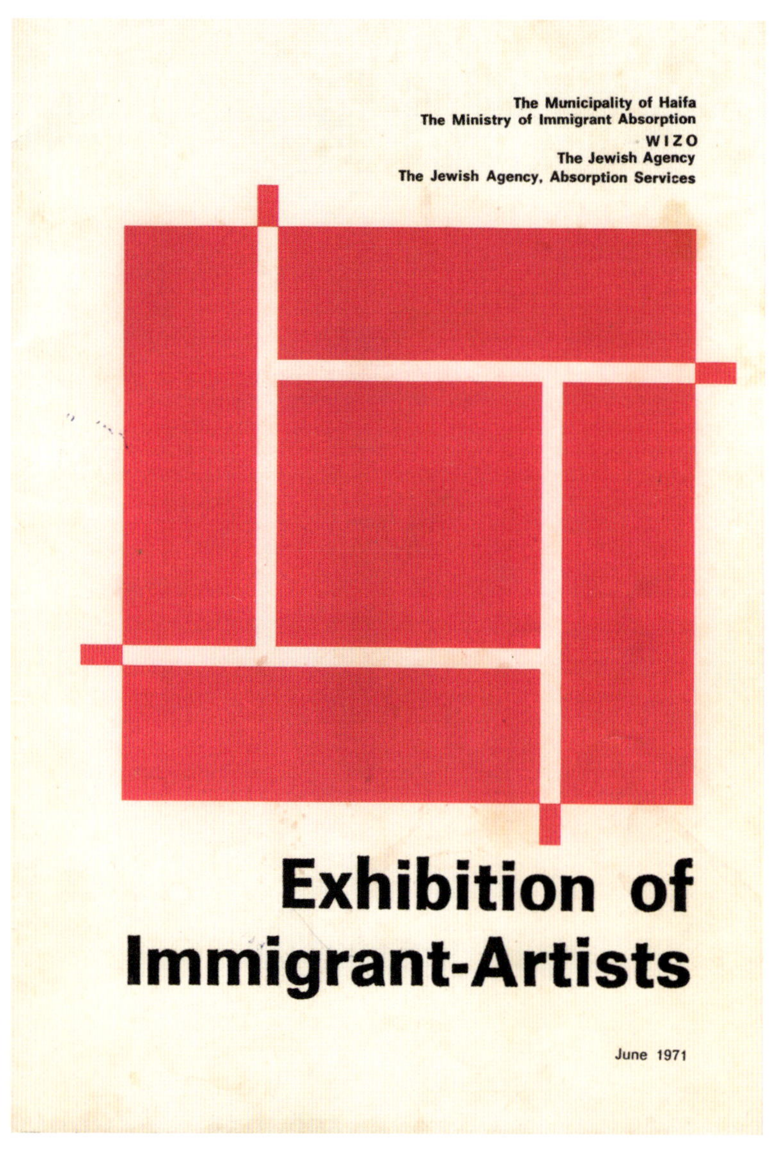


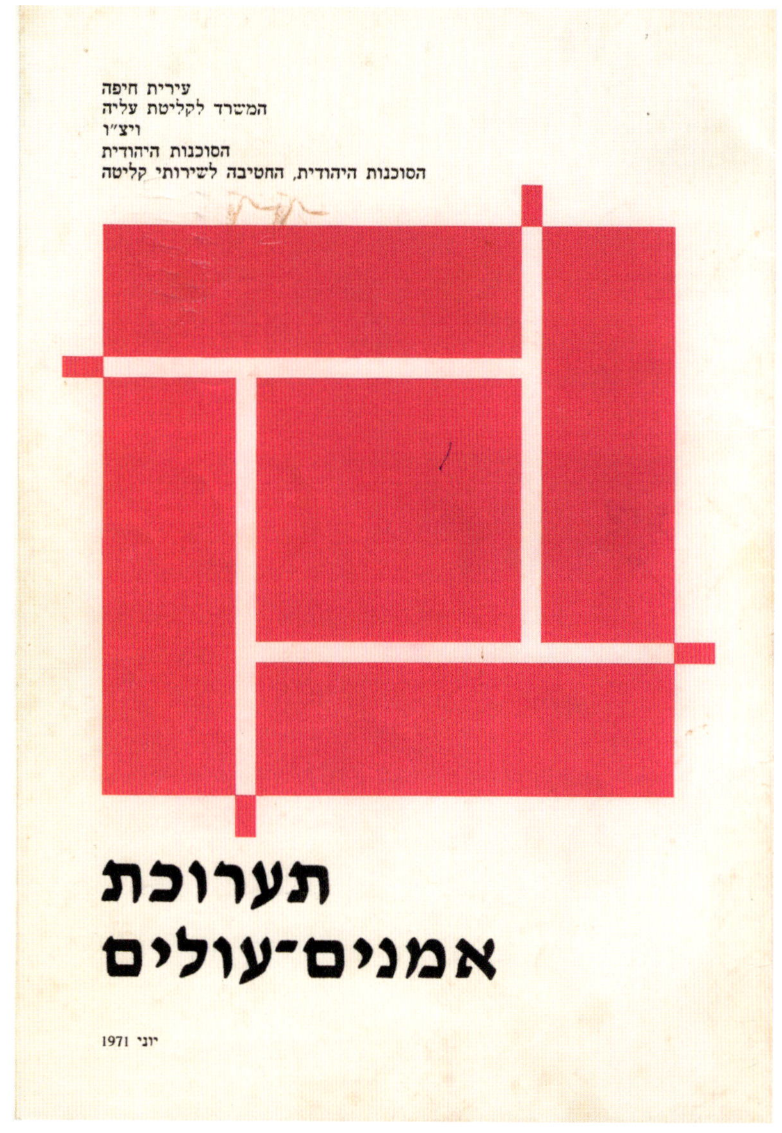


Catalogue Immigrant-Artists Exhibition

Helena first taught at Bezalel Academy of Arts and Design and the Avni Institute of Art and Design before starting work at the University of Haifa where she became co-founder faculty member of the art department and founded the Fine Art Printmaking Studios. This was no easy task but she was very resourceful and worked hard to get everything needed for a print studio. She found a large litho press at the Israel Museum in Jerusalem, stones from a commercial print workshop in Tel Aviv and the other materials she brought over from England. She knew all the suppliers and ordered an etching press from Hunter Penrose and rollers and tools from Lawrence's. With the new studio set up Helena gave her time and commitment to teaching printmaking. She was dedicated to her students who all benefitted from her knowledge and experience, much of it gained from her time running The Print Workshop in London. She recalled that as she became more and more involved with her new life and teaching her own work was put on hold:

*'I absorbed the culture and environment and the light and life were different and I put my energies into teaching and felt awkward with my own work'.*[23]

However, in the initial years after arriving in Israel she did show her prints in a small number of exhibitions. On the whole this involved exhibiting prints previously made in England. In December 1969 there was an exhibition of her lithographs of Liverpool such as *Falconer Square* and *Dock Traffic Office* which was opened by the British Ambassador to Israel at the Nahmani's Art Gallery in Haifa.

As a newcomer to the country she also exhibited in an 'Exhibition of Immigrant-Artists' in 1971 organised by the Ministry of Immigrant Absorption in Haifa. This exhibition showed work by artists from the Jewish community who were new to Israel as the organisers explain in the catalogue:

*'The advantages of such an exhibition are two-fold: firstly to the Israeli residents, who thus have an opportunity of making a closer acquaintance with the work of new immigrants; and secondly to the immigrants themselves, who can thus become part of the artistic life and spirit of the country.'*[24]

Helena's early years in Israel were filled with setting up the art department and university print studio. It was an exciting time and she met many new colleagues and friends with whom she was able to share her enthusiasm for the work. She was also fortunate to meet several Israeli artists who had practised printmaking in Europe and could help with her vision for a print studio. One such artist was Yehuda Bacon who was teaching at the art school in Jerusalem but had previously studied alongside Helena in London at the Central School of Arts and Crafts. He was particularly helpful not only in supporting Helena with her work but also in helping her get orientated with her new life in Israel. He recalls how Helena stood out, being tall and open-eyed and enthusiastic at being in this new country, which seemed like a new world to her.

It took about five years for Helena to establish the print studio but gradually life and work settled and she had more time for herself. She began to travel around and see Israel, fascinated by the fact that this was not a large country but the spaces and geographical forms of the Negev and Sinai desert gave an impression of vast space. Moved by the open spaces, the light and the spirituality of the desert she made a series of colour etchings of the Negev and Sinai. Other travels and sights gave her visual ideas for prints and a sense of place returned to her work and inspired her to start again on her own practice.

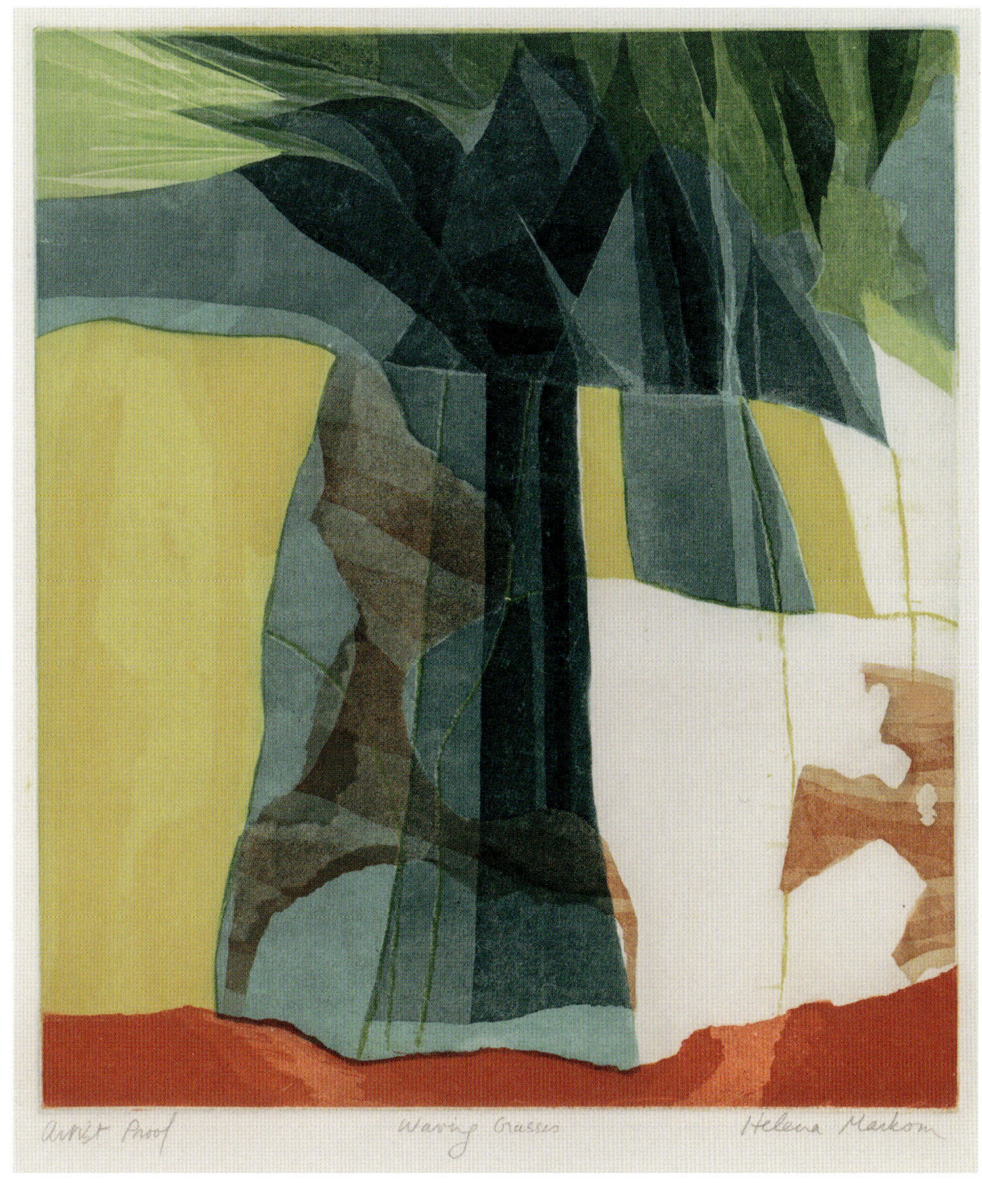


*Waving Grasses*    1987 etching and aquatint 49cm x 41.5cm

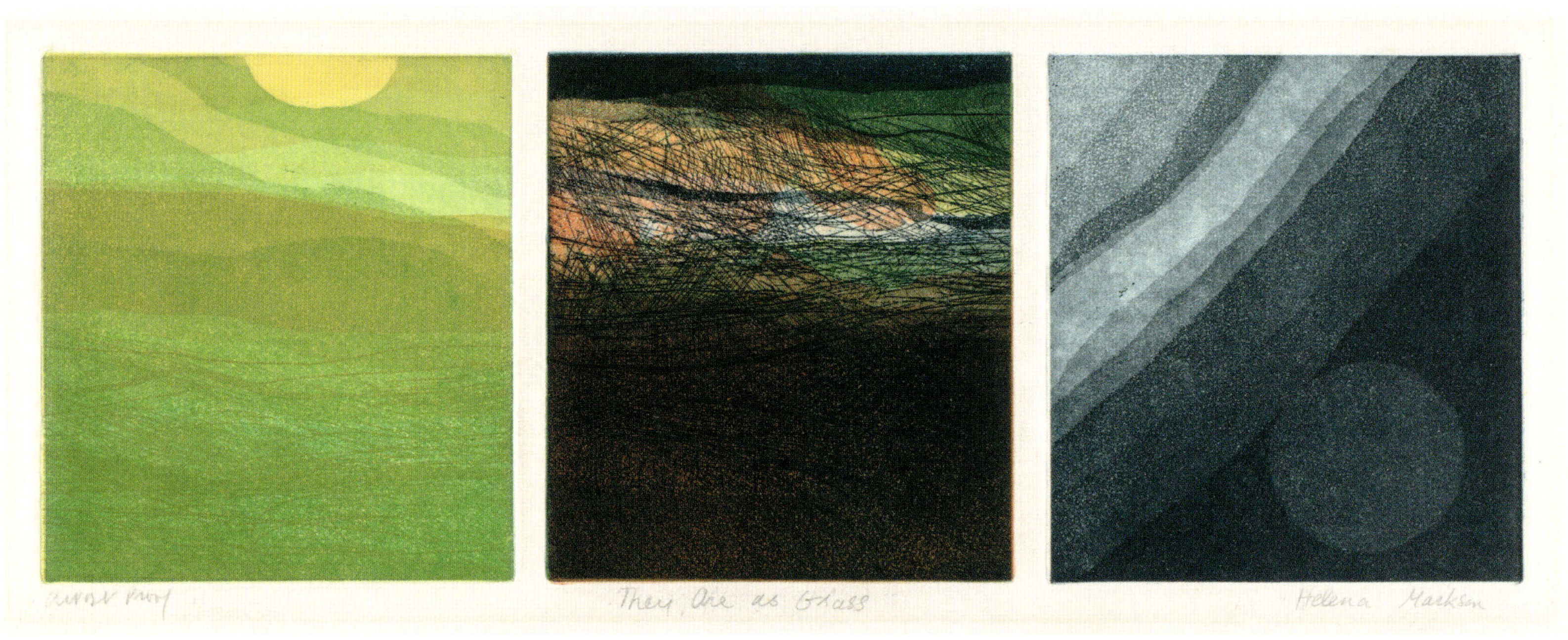

*They are as Grass*   c.1980 etching and aquatint 22cm x 58cm

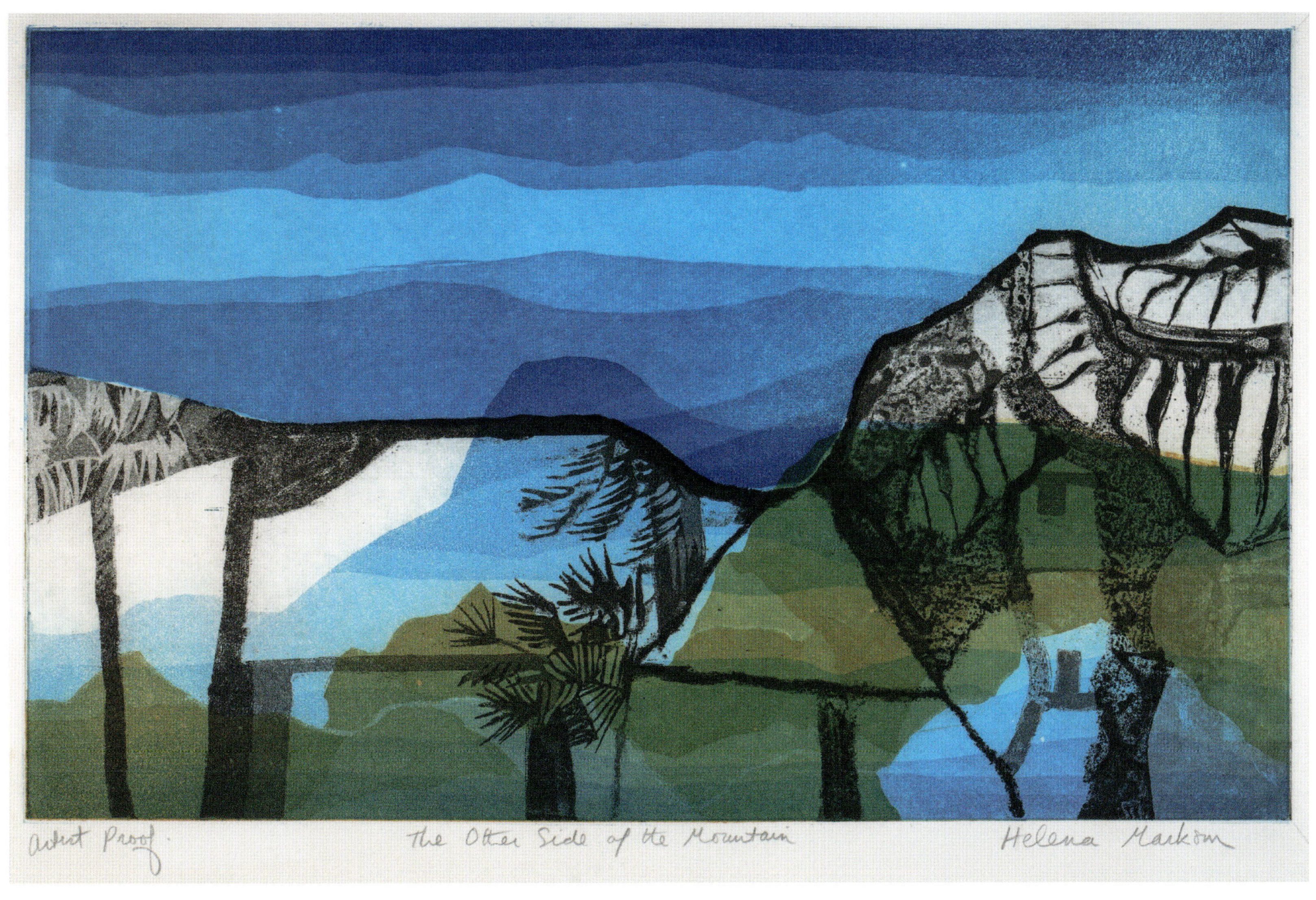



*The Other Side of The Mountain*    c.1980 etching and aquatint 35cm x 55cm

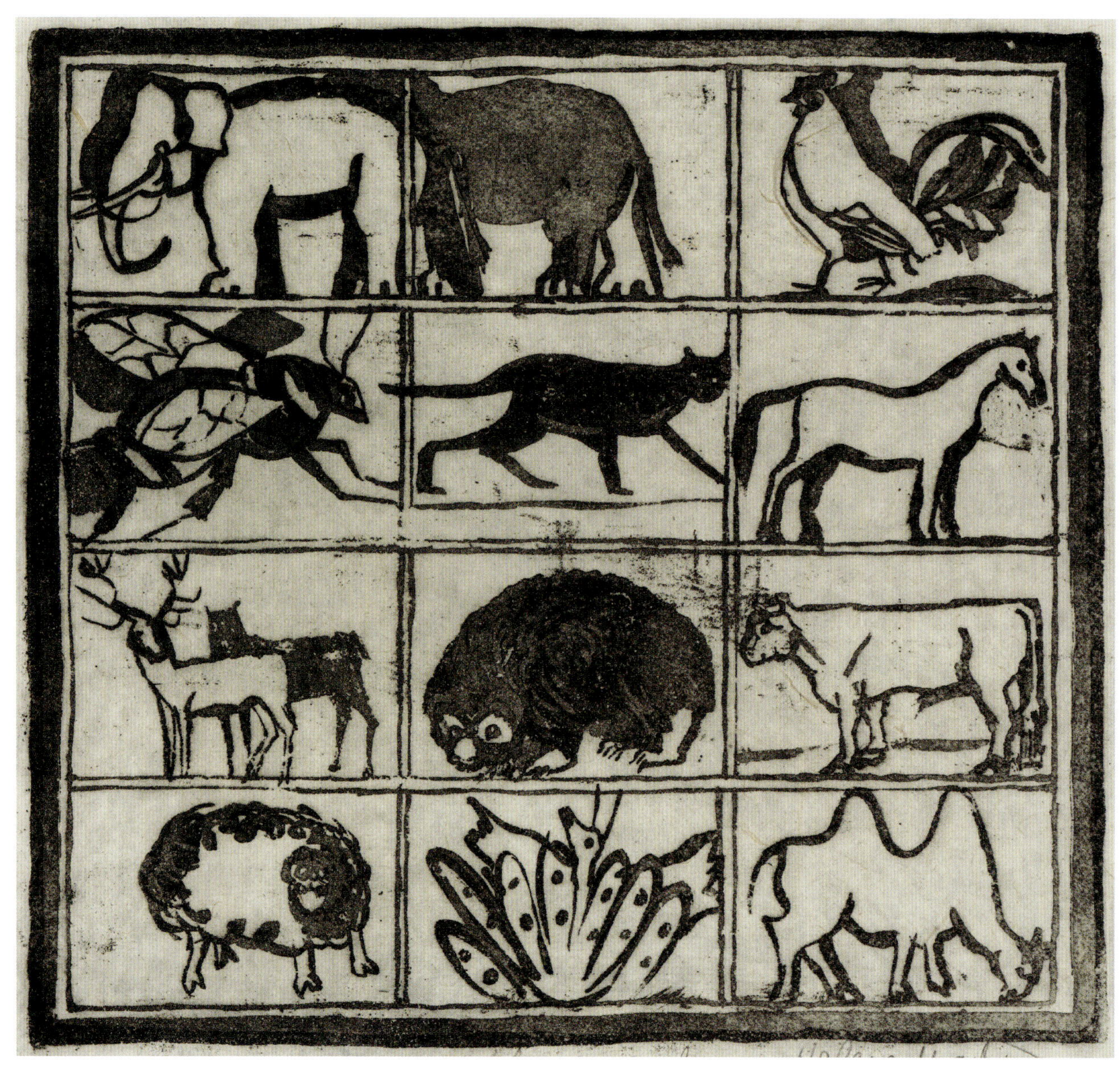

*Animals (Noah)*   1999 etching 28cm x 30cm

## USA, UK AND TRAVELS

Through fellowships and sabbaticals Helena was able
to travel and work in other countries. She visited Italy,
Switzerland, France, the USA (including New York,
Connecticut, Arizona and Los Angeles) and the UK.
The influences from these visits pushed Helena's work in
different directions, as she responded to and interpreted
the world around her.

In the 1980s and 1990s Helena made several visits to
the USA. She spent a sabbatical year at the University of
California at Los Angeles (UCLA). Helena's print of *America*
shows her apartment in Westwood, near UCLA. It is a very
personal image, which shows Helena in the mirror, her feet
on the bed, and typifies how she made images inspired by
her sense of place.

Whilst in California she exhibited her work including
showing a small number of prints on the subject of *Grasses*
and *Swan Lake*. The subjects reflected different aspects of
her life, places and memories:

*'When my interest in an idea or image is aroused,
I research the facts around it. In visual and literary
terms, the subject gathers its own momentum and extends
it in many directions. My objectives are enquiry and study
to express a personal view through drawing, paintings
or print. The recent work in this exhibition* Grasses
*and* Swan Lake *represents part of the process I describe
above. With regard to the later my early training in
classical ballet and continued interest in the performing
arts as well as my study of migratory habits of certain
birds, have influenced the choice of subject. Israel evokes
a great source of ideas to me and I have begun to express
them in landscape.'*[25]

In 1992 she took a residency at the Tamarind Institute in
New Mexico, USA (established in the 1960s as a centre
for research, education, and artistic projects in fine art
lithography) and here Helena made the lithographs *Muse*,
*Myth* and *Taco*.

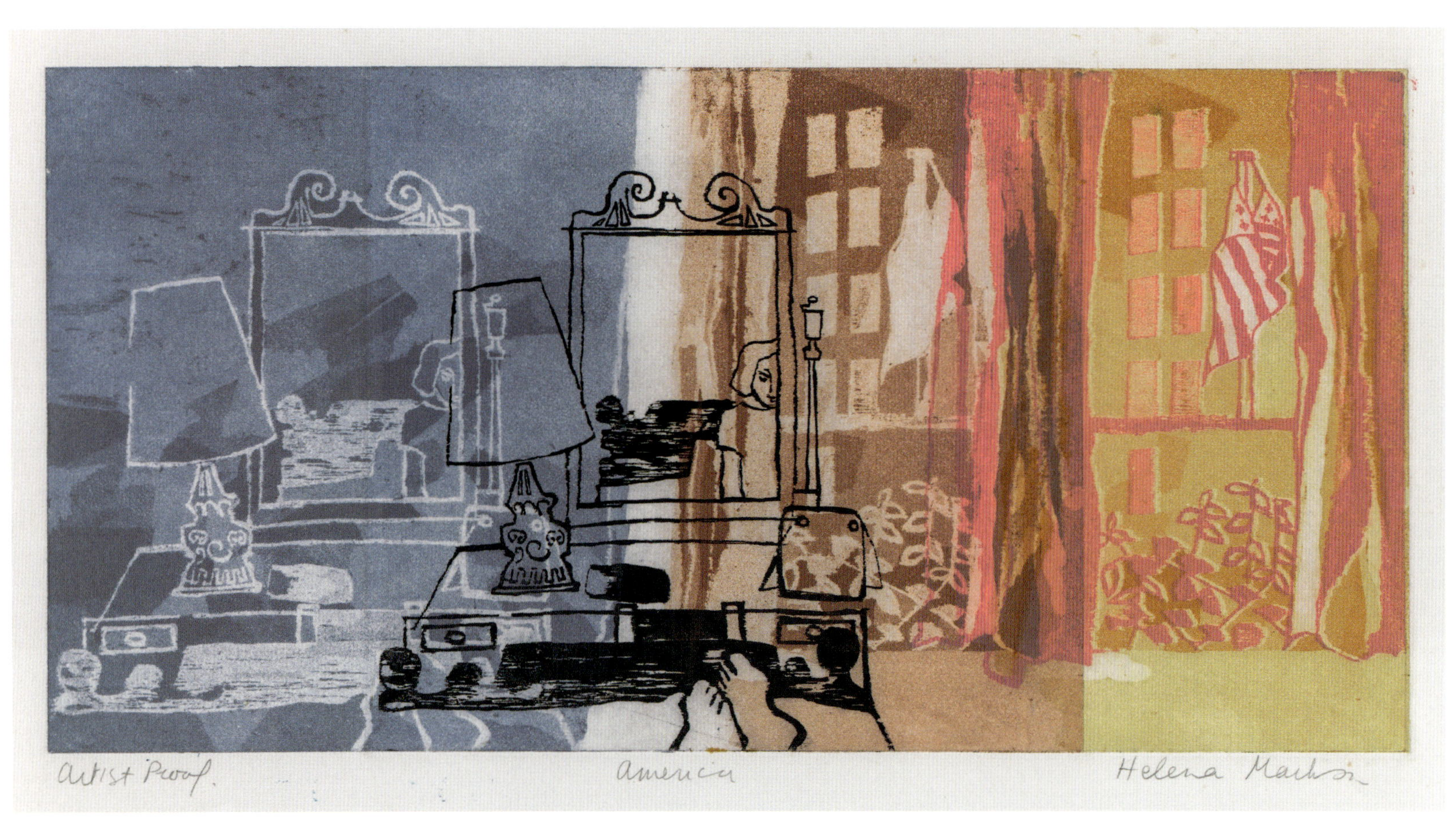



*America*   c.1990 etching and aquatint 29.5cm x 59cm

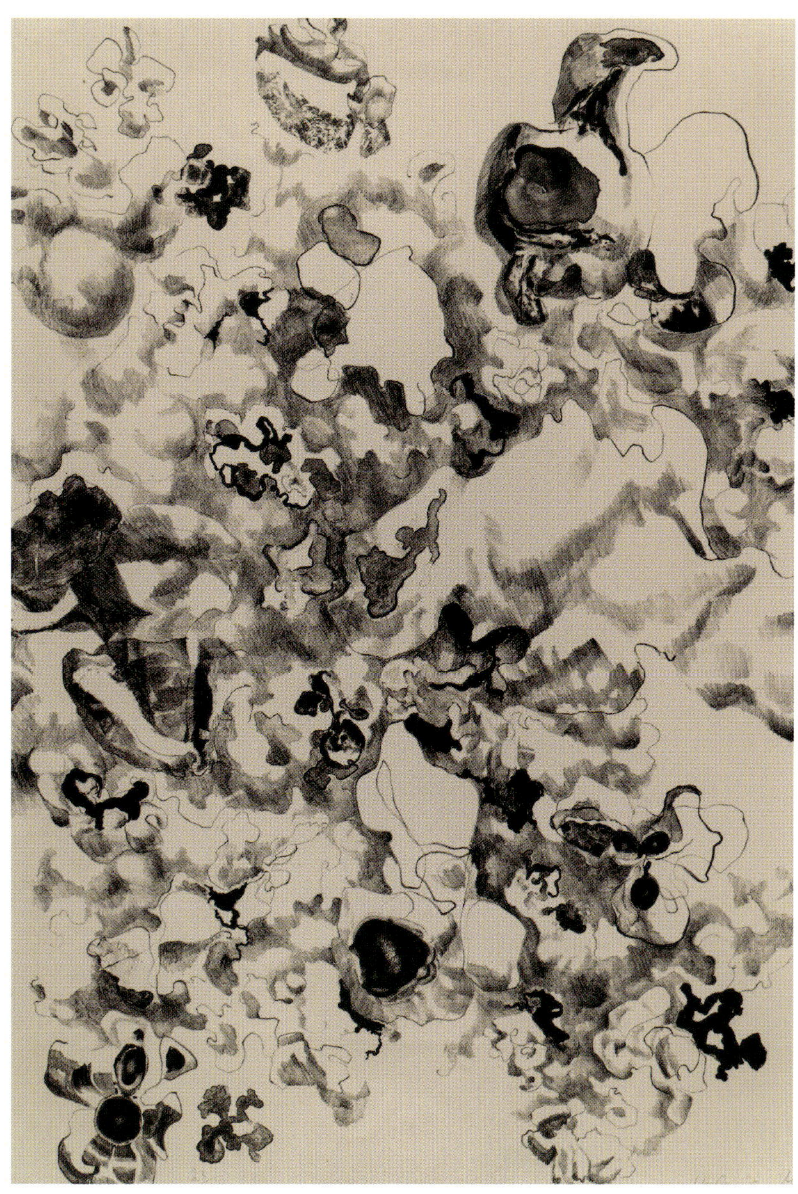

*Popcorn*　lithograph 76cm x 56cm

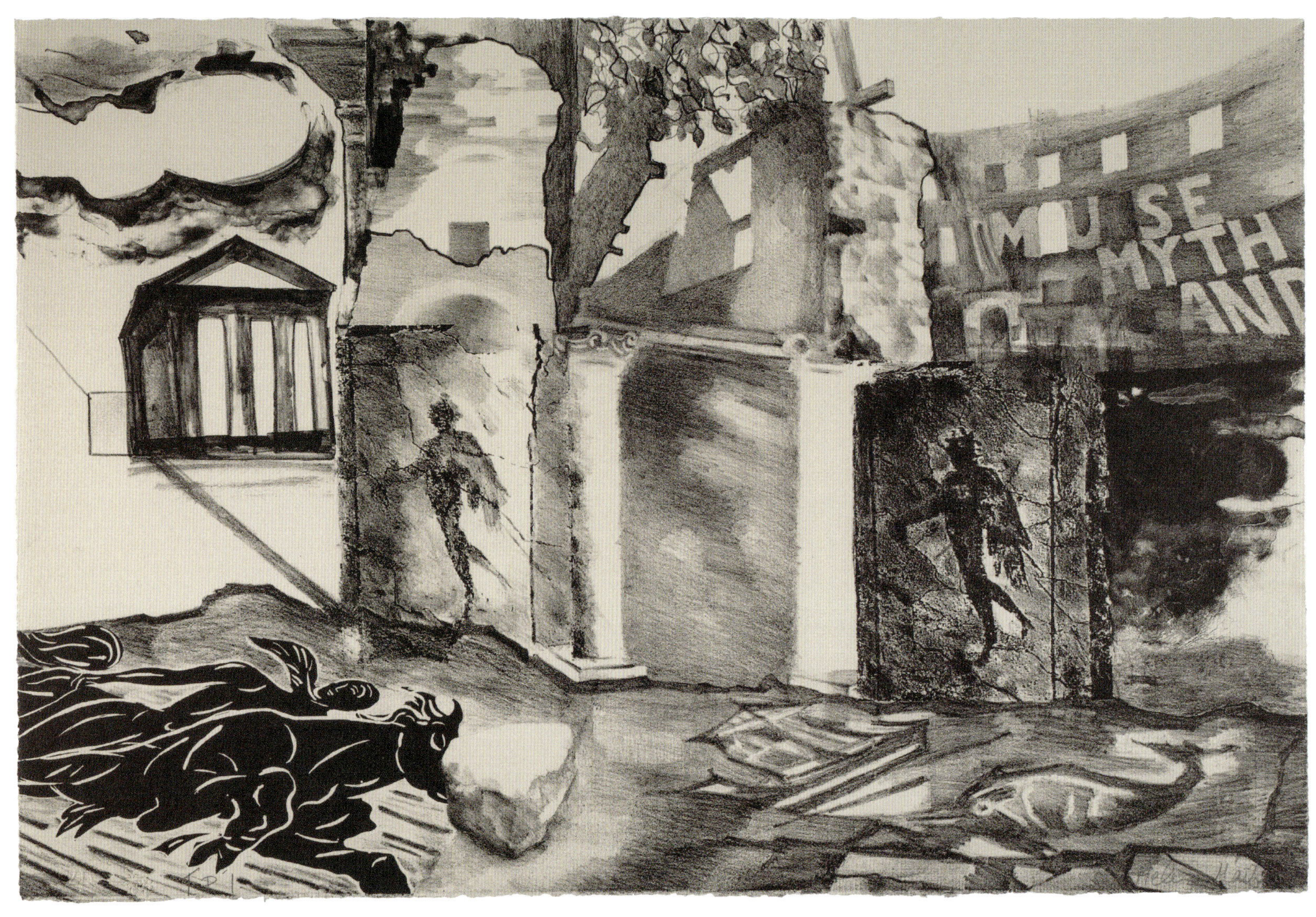



*Muse, Myth*    1992 lithograph 38cm x 56cm

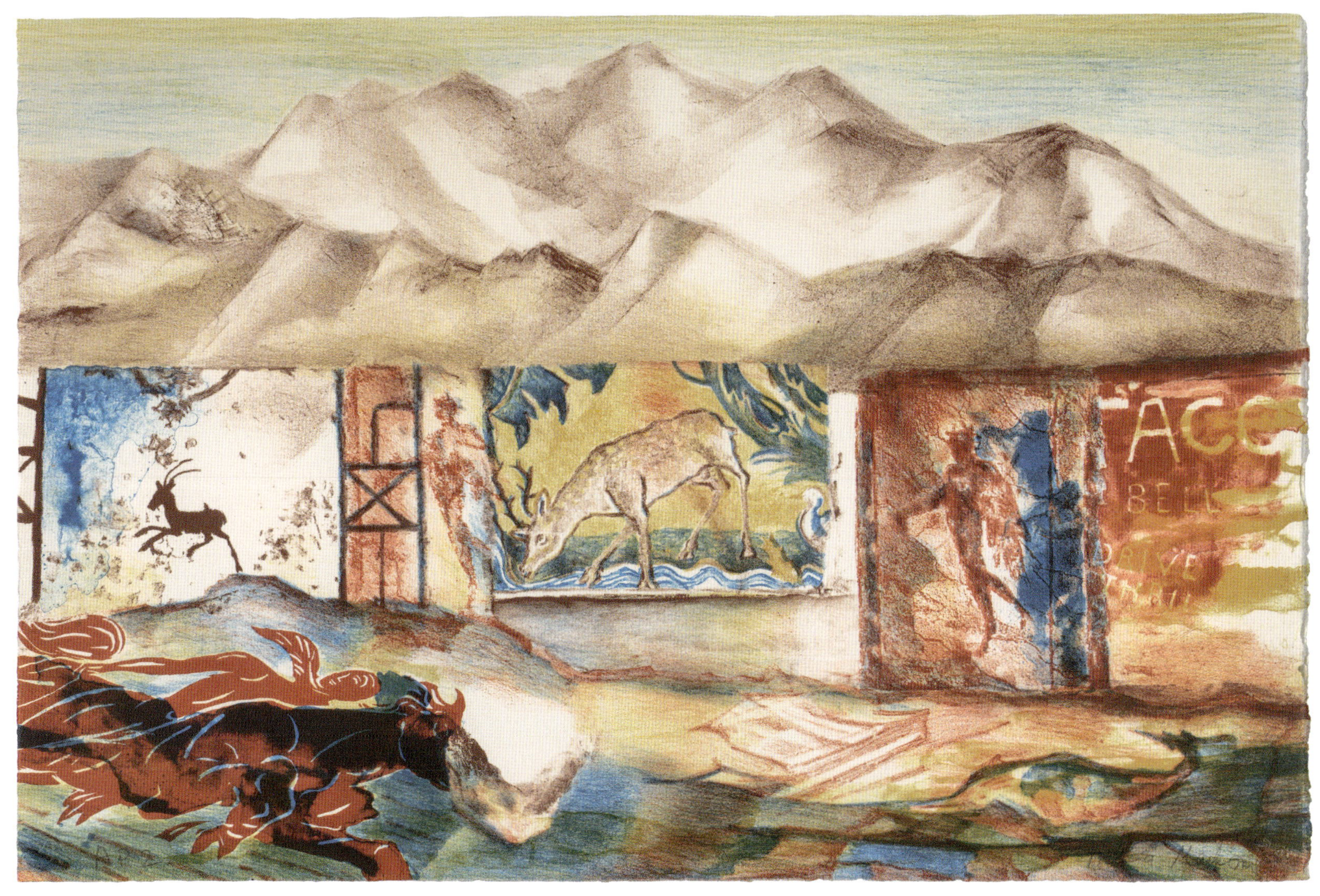

*Taco*   1992 lithograph 38cm x 56cm

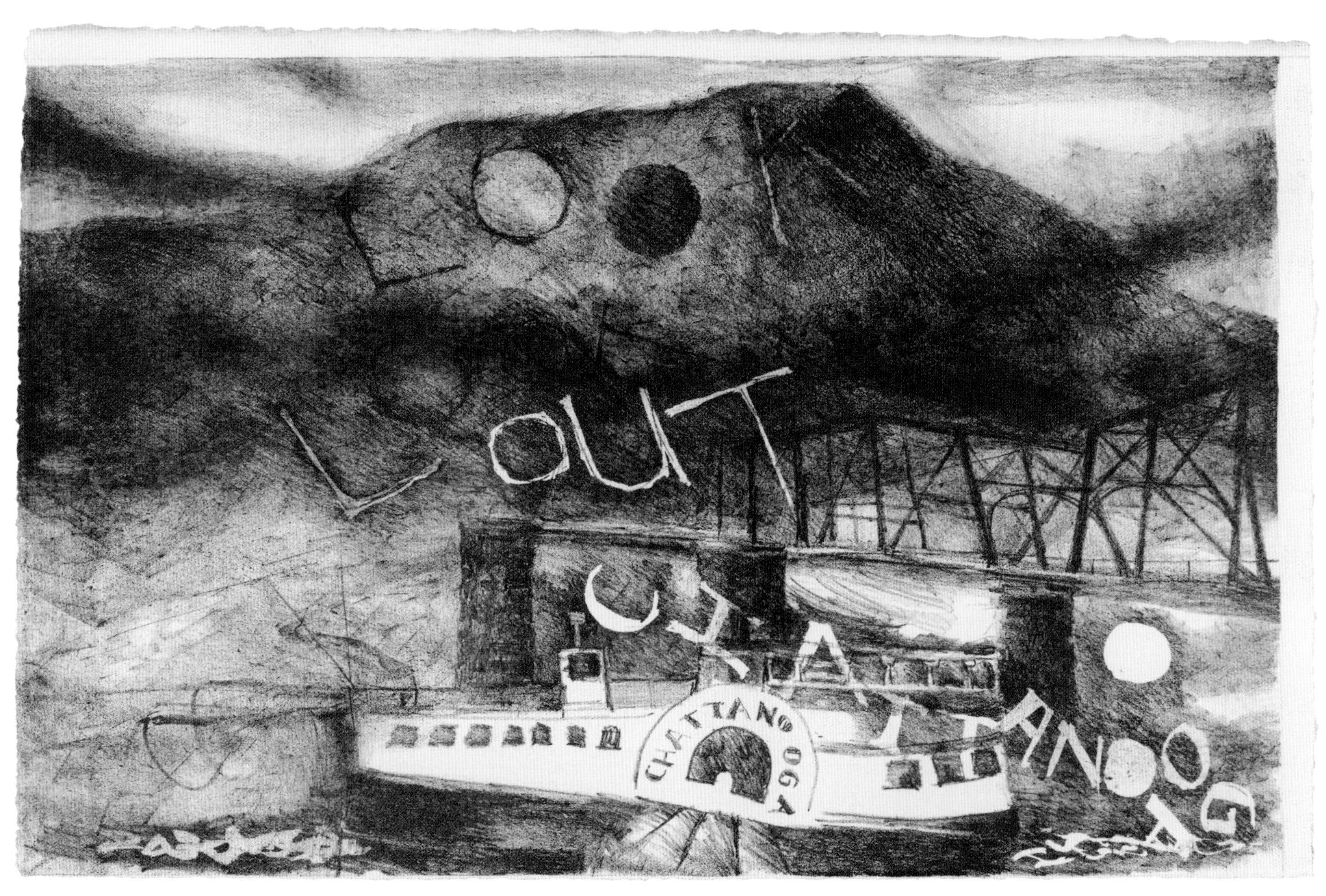


*Chattanooga*   c.1990 lithograph 26.5cm x 41.5cm

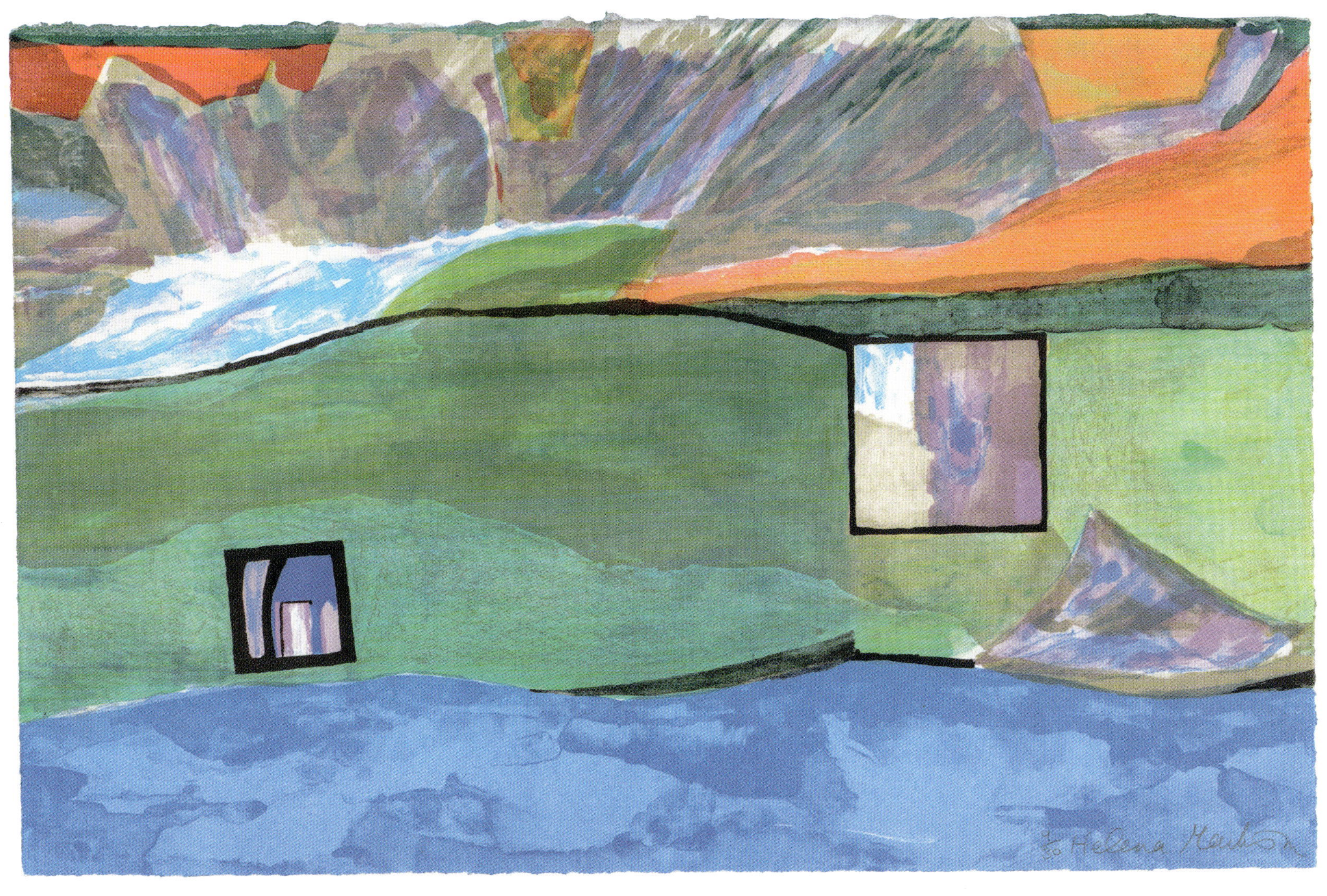

*The Water House*   lithograph 29cm x 44.5cm

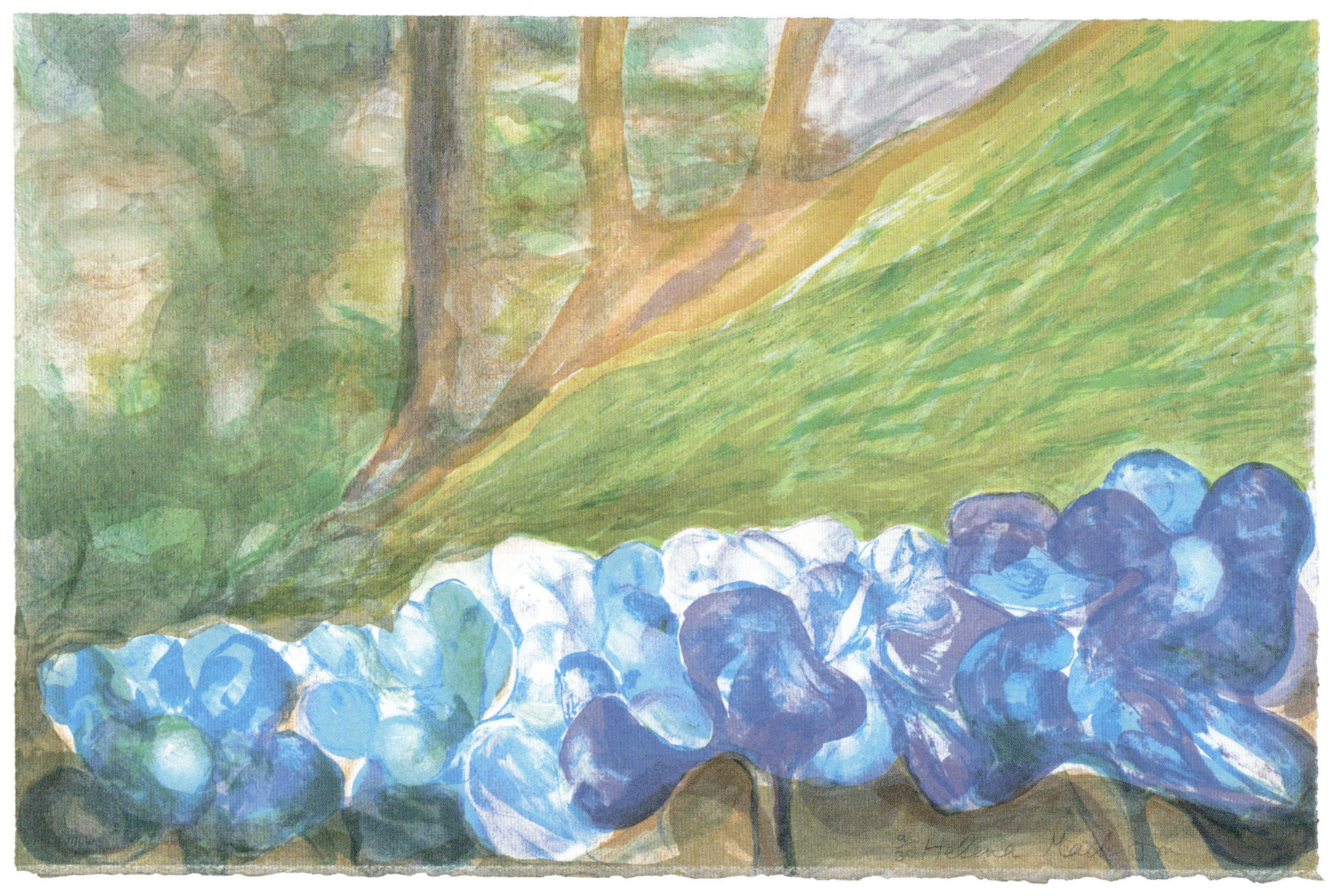

*The Cabbage Field*   lithograph 29cm x 44.5cm

In 1993 Helena also set up a new home in Israel moving to Ein Hod, an artist's village near Haifa, a village which sits in an enviable position on a hill, at the foot of Mount Carmel overlooking the Mediterranean coast. Ein Hod was founded 1953 by a group of artists led by the acclaimed Dada artist Marcel Janco. With perseverance and vision they established Ein Hod as a place where artists could live and create across a wide range of media to include visual arts, music, theatre and literature. Here Helena made her home and in 1994 she set up her own studio press, The HM Press under which Helena described herself as 'Artist/Publisher' and listed the press as having available, 'Etchings, Lithographs, Folios and Artist Books'.

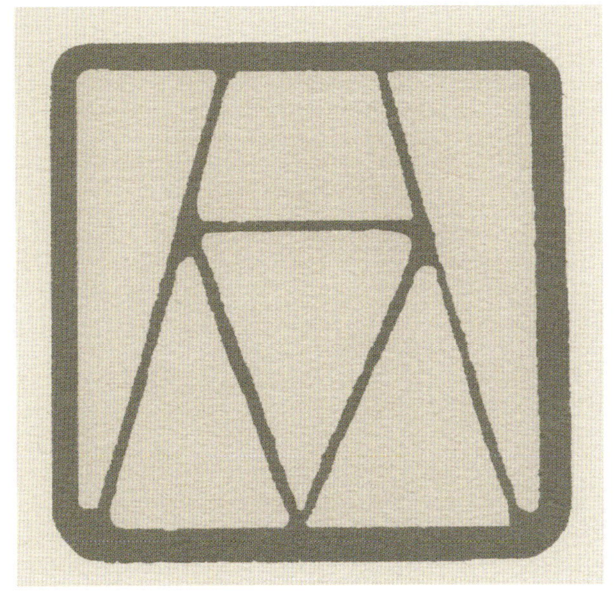

The HM Press logo

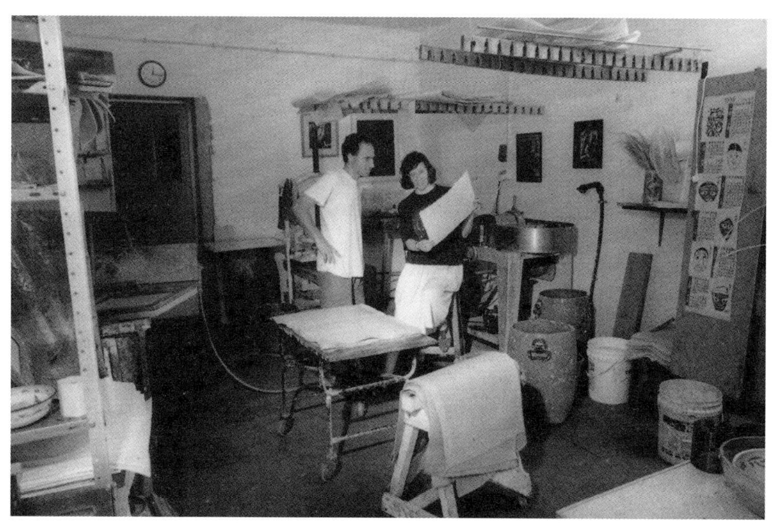

From the mid-1990s onwards Helena also made many visits back to England where she also had a home in Essex. From here she was able to visit places from her childhood and enjoy being in England, visiting her family and friends. She often wrote about how she felt she was a part of two worlds, with a life in Israel and a life in England. The visits between the two countries became increasingly important to Helena and this can be particularly seen in her work on a large print series she made in the mid-1990s, based on the work of poet Dylan Thomas.

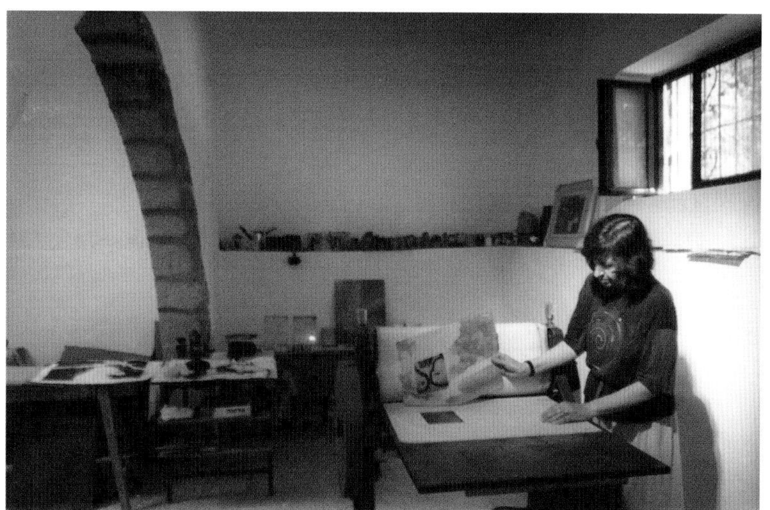

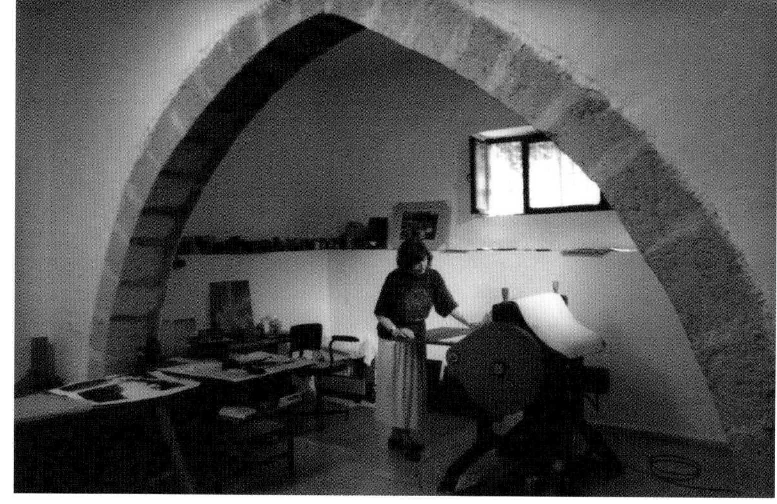

Helena in her studio in Ein Hod

*'Deaths and Entrances' and other poems by Dylan Thomas* is a
series of aquatints hand printed by Helena between 1993–4
on hand made paper. Helena learnt that Israel had a great
interest in papermaking and she took to using it in her work,
experimenting with how it could be used and adapted to her
printmaking. She chose to use handmade paper, which came
from the nearby mill of paper-maker Izhar Neumann. In the
Dylan Thomas series of prints Helena used layers of aquatint
to create the sky and cloud of the background over which
she printed discreet typography with lines from the poems.
Helena printed the series at the Jerusalem Print workshop,
a centre dedicated to the promotion and fostering of the
art of printmaking, founded in 1974 by Arik Kilemnik.
He was very supportive of Helena and it was the perfect
environment for Helena to make her prints. A full edition of
Helena's Dylan Thomas print series is held in the archive
of the Jerusalem Print Workshop.

Helena had been inspired by the writings of Dylan Thomas
since being a student and she was surprised at how this
interest had stayed with her. Between 1990 and 1993 Helena
visited various places from her childhood in England, which
encouraged her to look back and made her think of Dylan
Thomas and his poems. Initially Helena made a series of five
etchings, soon adding a further five, all based on Thomas'
poems. Helena continued with the series over the following
months, to make a final group of twenty-two etchings. The
last etchings in the series were made in 1994 after Helena's
visit to her childhood hometown of Salisbury. The series
brings together elements from Helena's life in England and
from her life in Israel as she describes:


*'In the series on Dylan Thomas' Deaths and Entrances,
the images I make of nature, language, memory and
war trauma are immediate responses to the words from
my own experience and impressions. The text is chosen
as a descriptive core idea of the poem. The techniques
I use allow me to express the "sound" of the words and
their spiritual and sensual content, as a visual whole.
The colour plate is developed from sketches made of
cloud formations during my many fights from Israel to
England …'*[26]

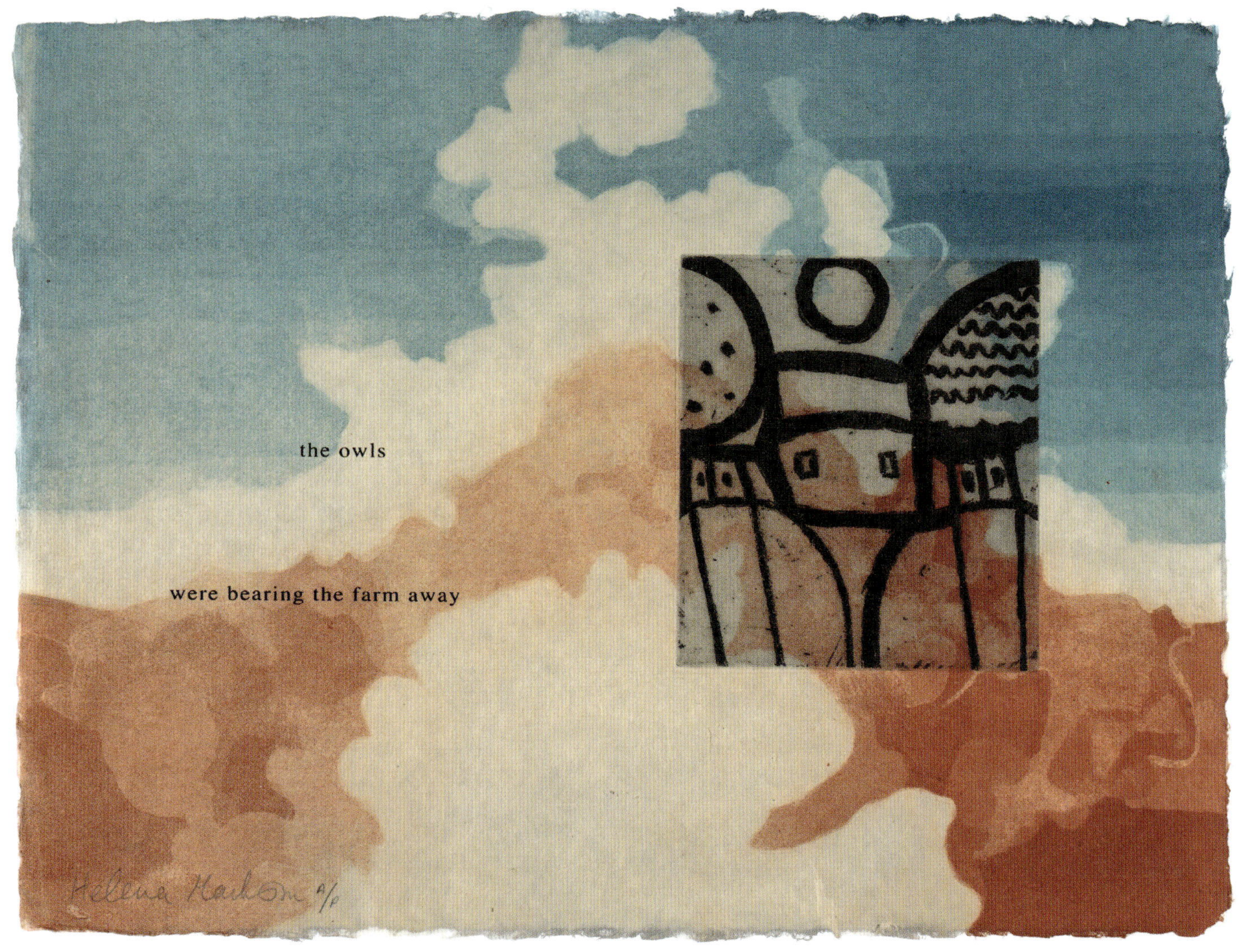



Dylan Thomas Series Aquatints on '"Deaths and Entrances" and other Poems' by Dylan Thomas    1993–4 aquatint 32cm x 42cm

## The owls were bearing the farm away

*Fern Hill*

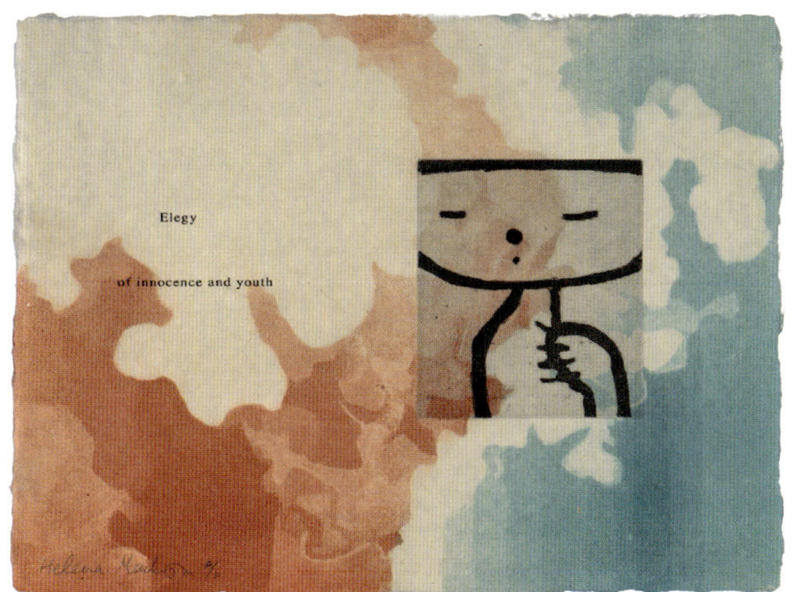


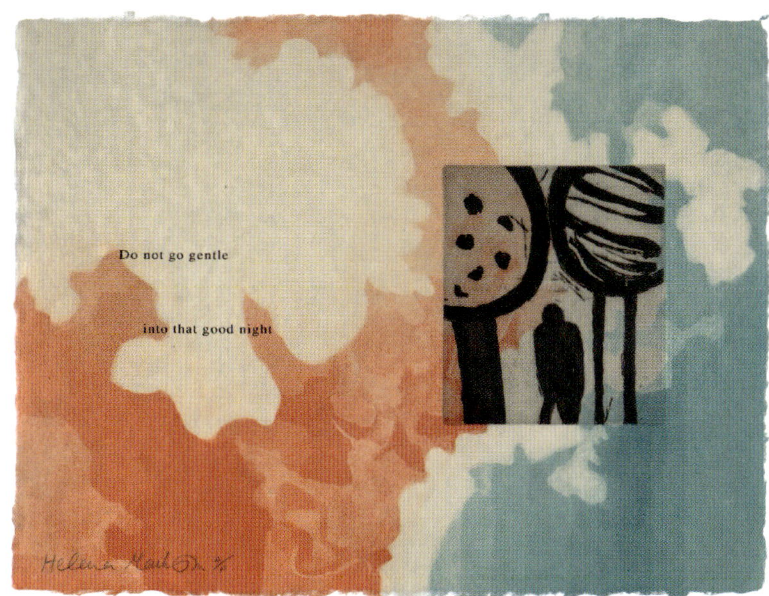


Elegy of innocence and youth

*A Refusal to Mourn the Death, by Fire, of a Child in London*

Do not go gentle into that good night

*Do Not Go Gentle into that Good Night*

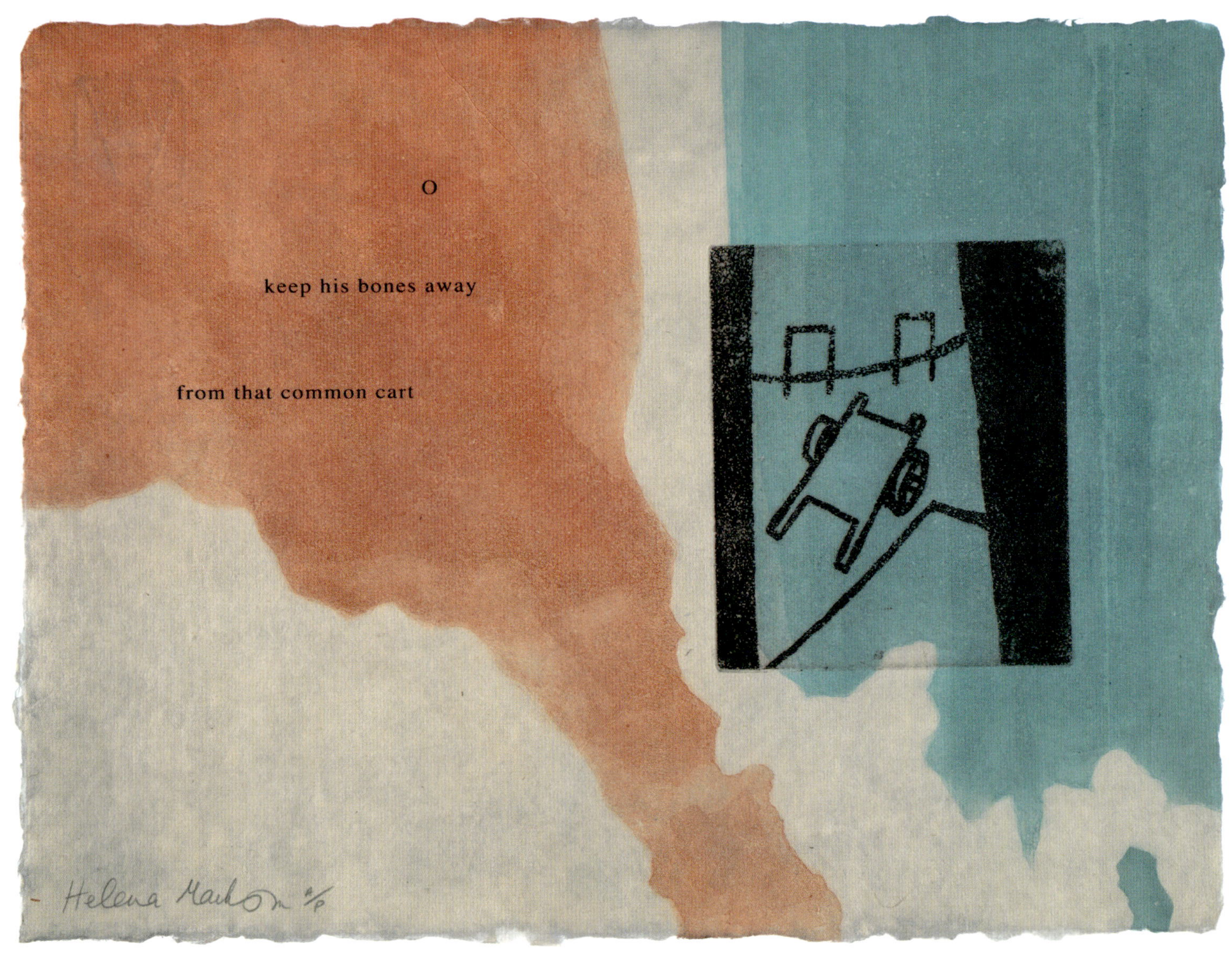



O keep his bones away from that common cart

*Among Those Killed in the Dawn Raid was a Man Aged a Hundred*

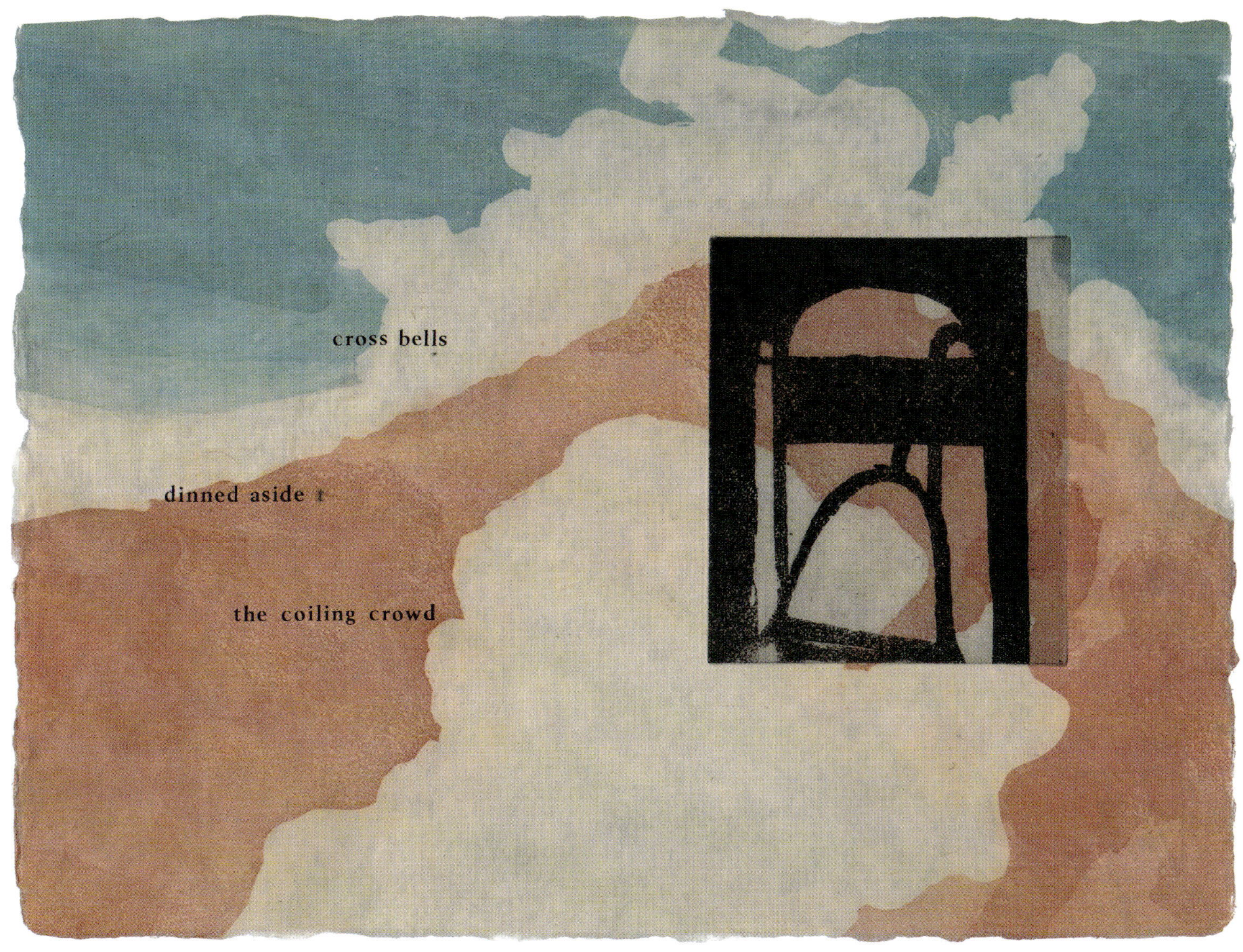


Cross bells dinned aside the coiling crowd

*When I Woke*

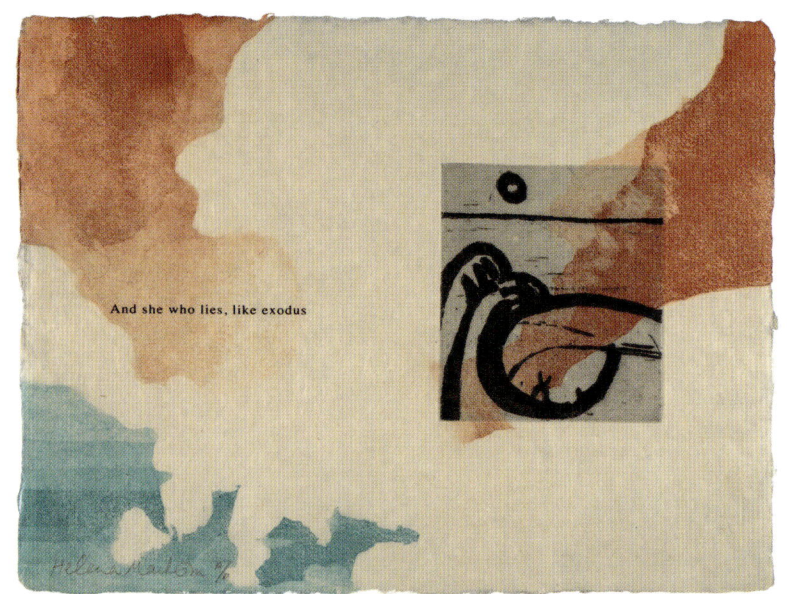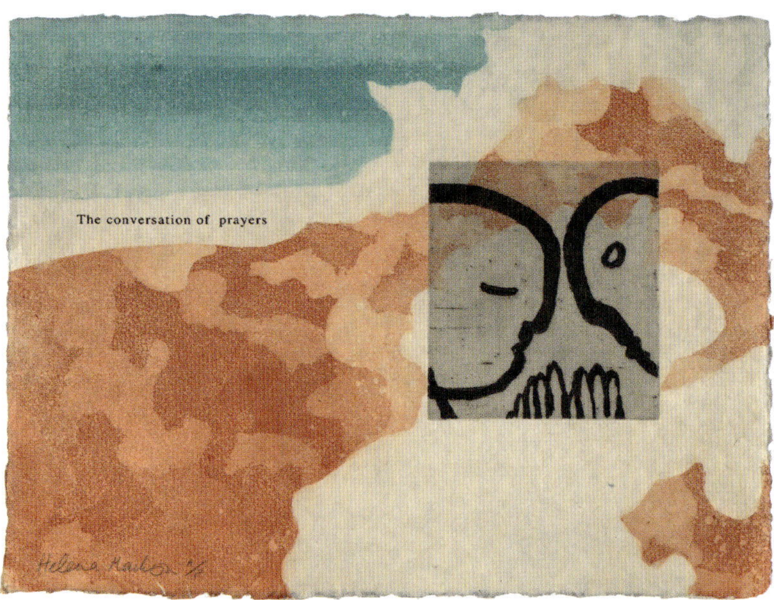

And she who lies, like exodus

*A Grief Ago*

The conversation of prayers

*The Conversation of Prayers*

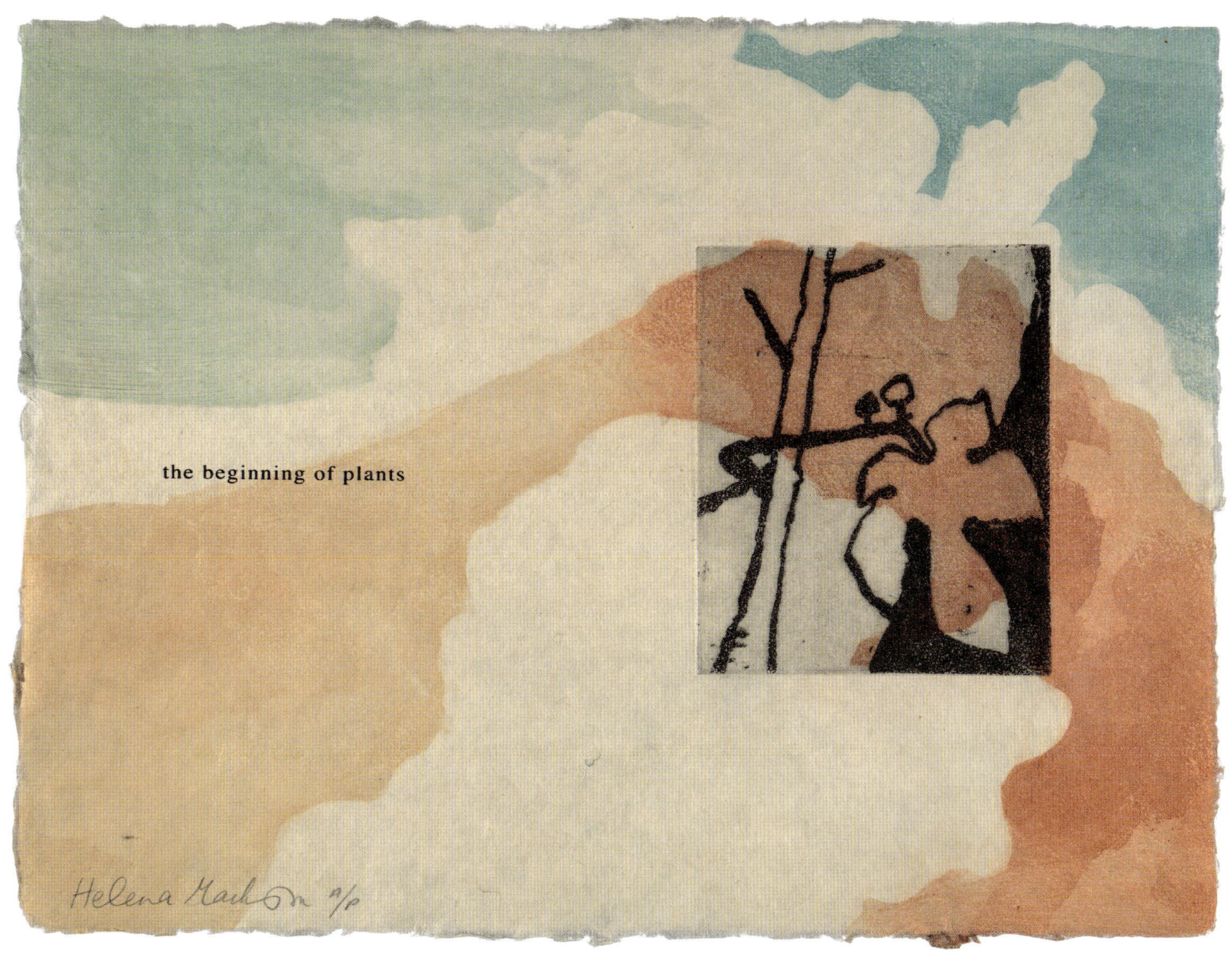


The beginning of plants

*This Side of the Truth*

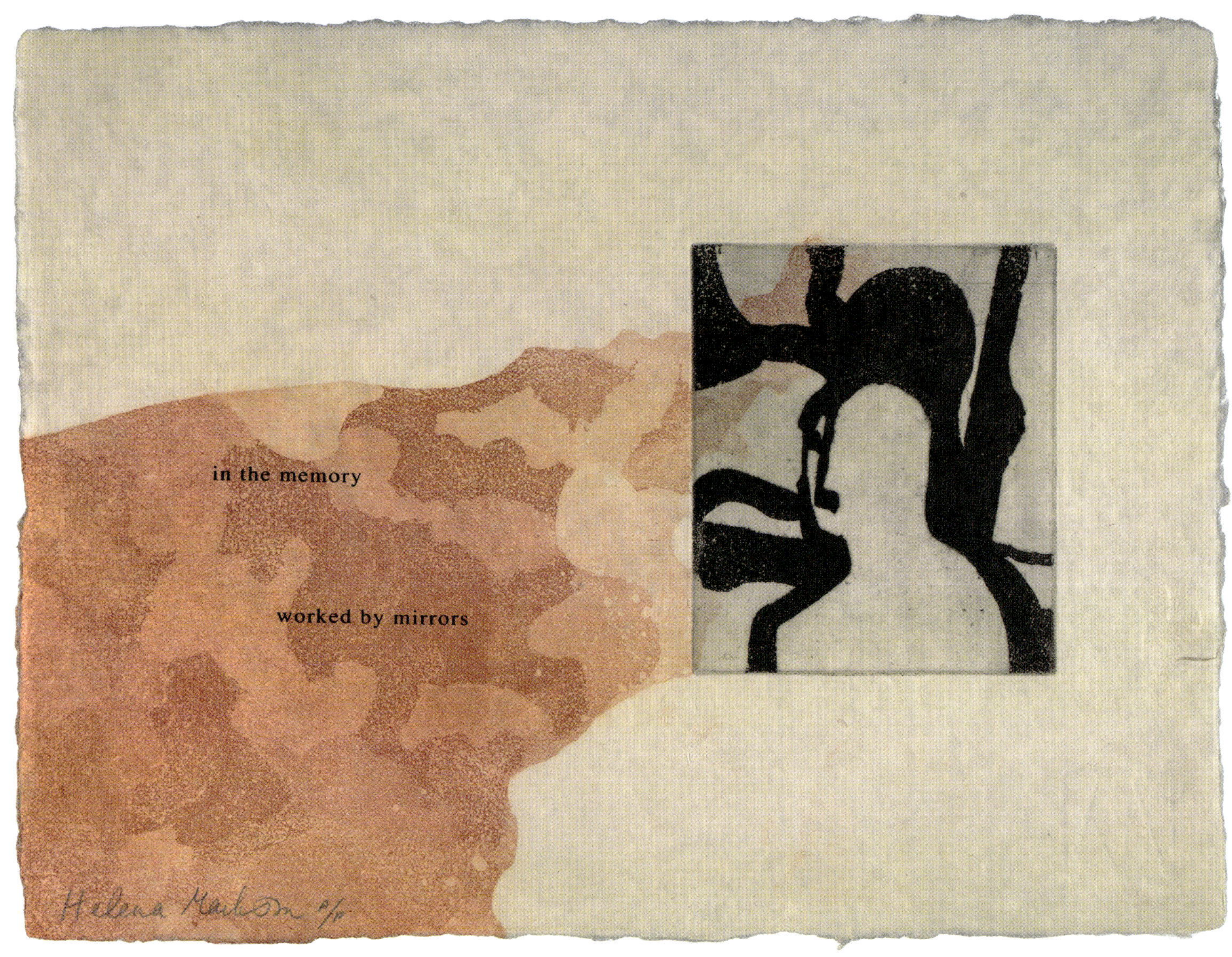



In the memory worked by mirrors

*To Others than You*

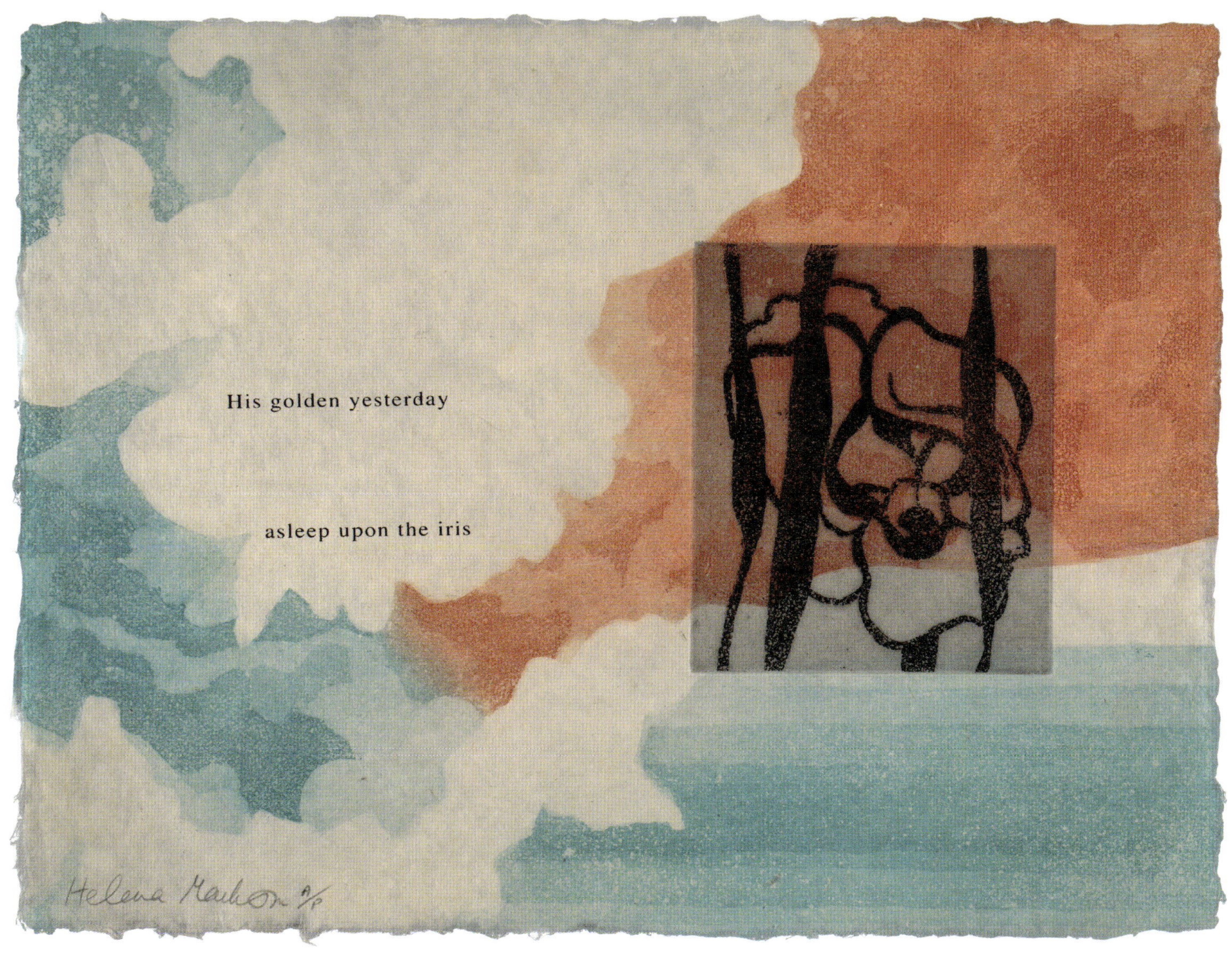



His golden yesterday asleep upon the iris

*On the Marriage of a Virgin*

In 1996 Helena held an exhibition of her Dylan Thomas Series in the Gallery of Art at the University of Haifa. This displayed all the prints and was accompanied by a catalogue. The following year in 1997 Helena exhibited *Deaths and Entrances* in the 22nd Ljubljana Print Biennale when she was selected to represent Israel alongside three other artists working in graphics in Israel at the time; Yehiel Shemi, Moshe Kupferman and Yigal Ozeri.

That same year Helena organised an exhibition of lithographs all made by teacher-artists at the University of Haifa. She was an important part of the team working at the university and enjoyed bringing people together. This project suited her very well. For the project Helena made a lithograph linked to her working life as a printmaking teacher. *Lithography Studio* a lithograph in black and white from 1997 illustrates the day-to-day life of the print studio.

In her later years Helena spent more time in England, in part for family reasons, as her brother Edward was unwell. However she was also drawn back to the familiarity of England. In 2000 she spent two months in England working at Spike Island Print Workshop in Bristol. It gave her great pleasure to be working in Bristol, which she liked as it was not too far from Salisbury where she grew up. In Bristol she made a series of prints called *Dwelling Places,* ten etchings with aquatint. These images are again influenced by a sense of place looking at memories of her childhood and life in England, the titles reflecting personal memories of place.

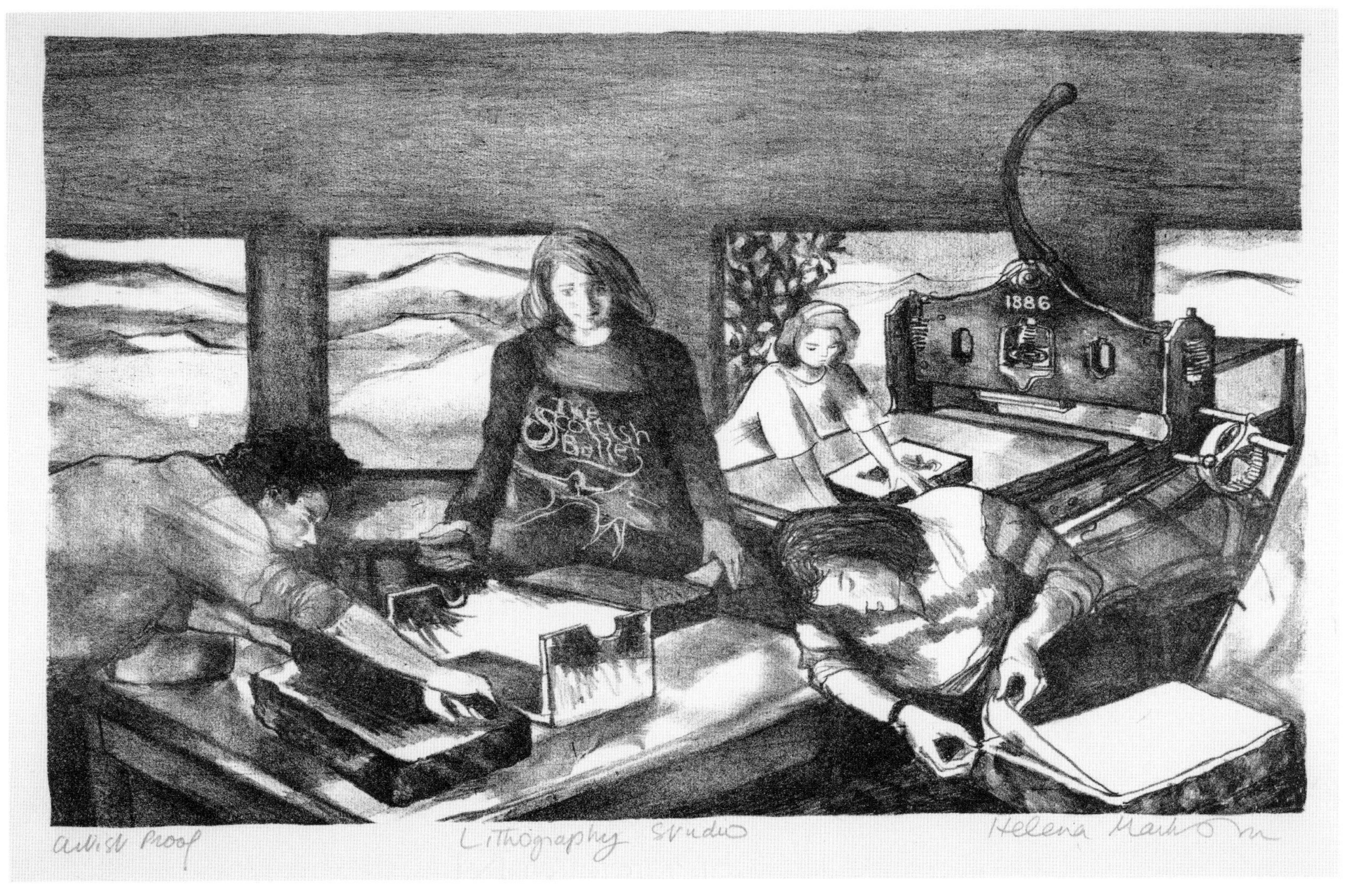



*Lithography Studio*   1997 lithograph 29cm x 40cm

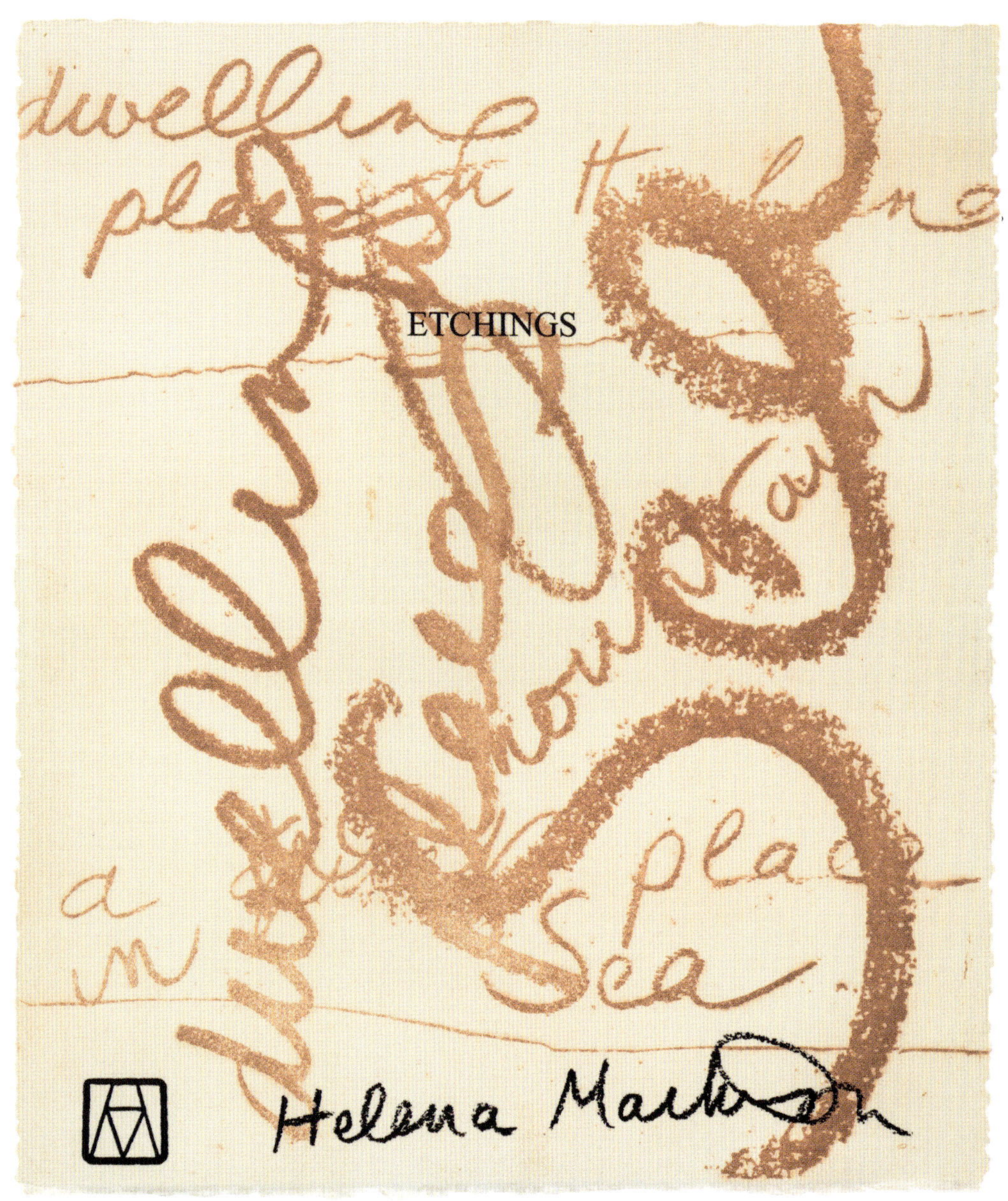


*Dwelling Places* Series   (10 images plus title page) 2000 etching 28cm x 24cm

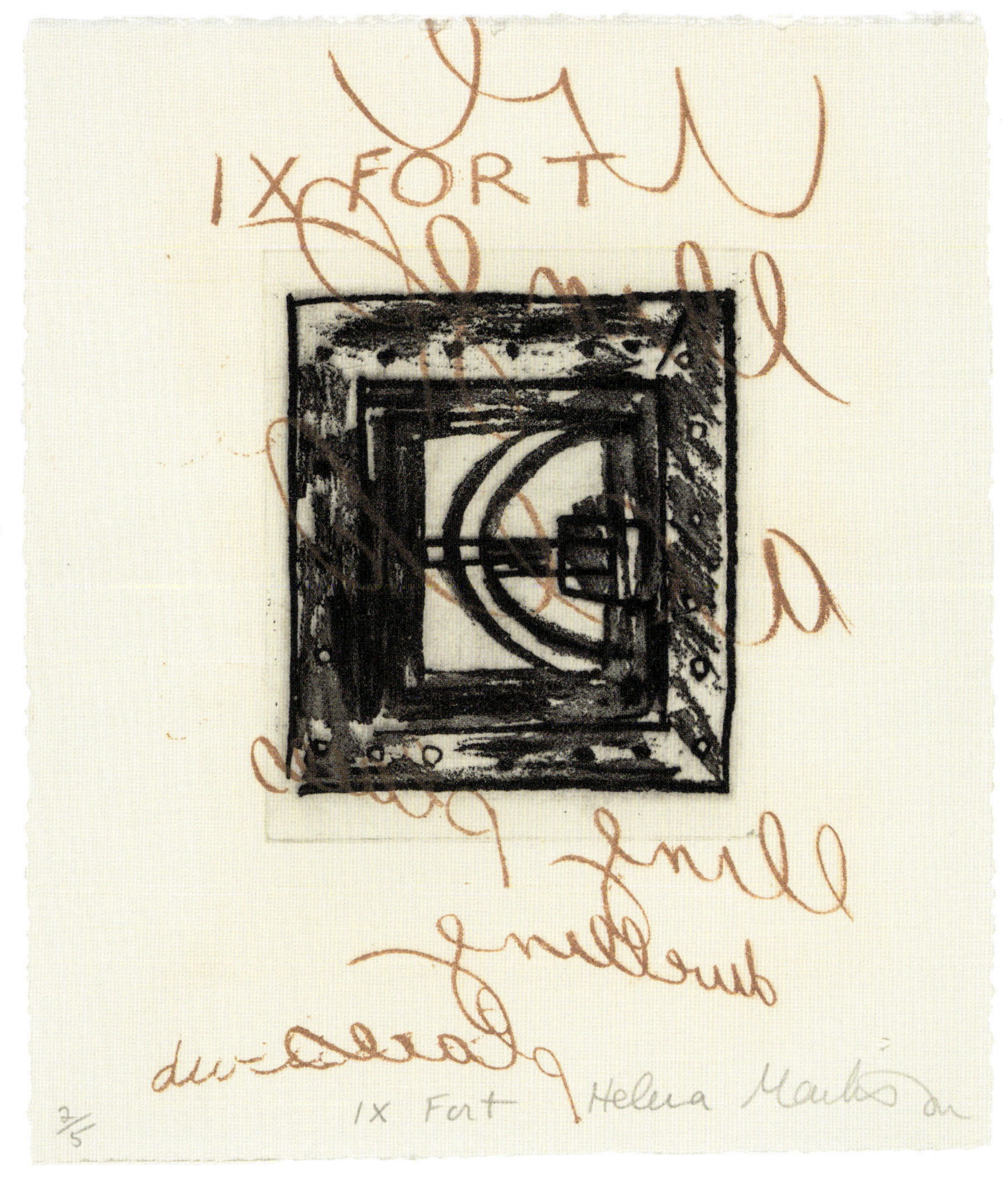

*Fort*

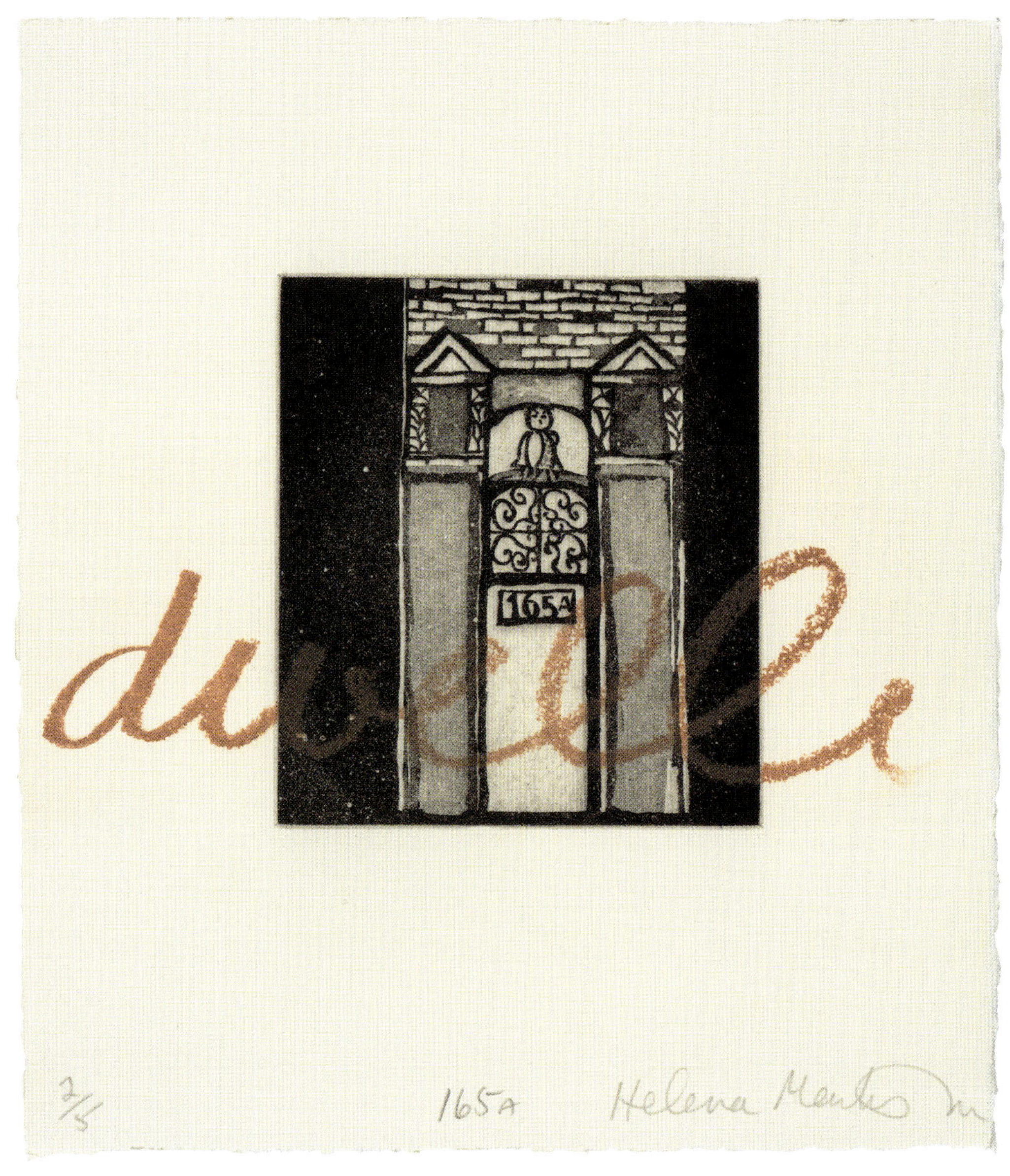

*165A*

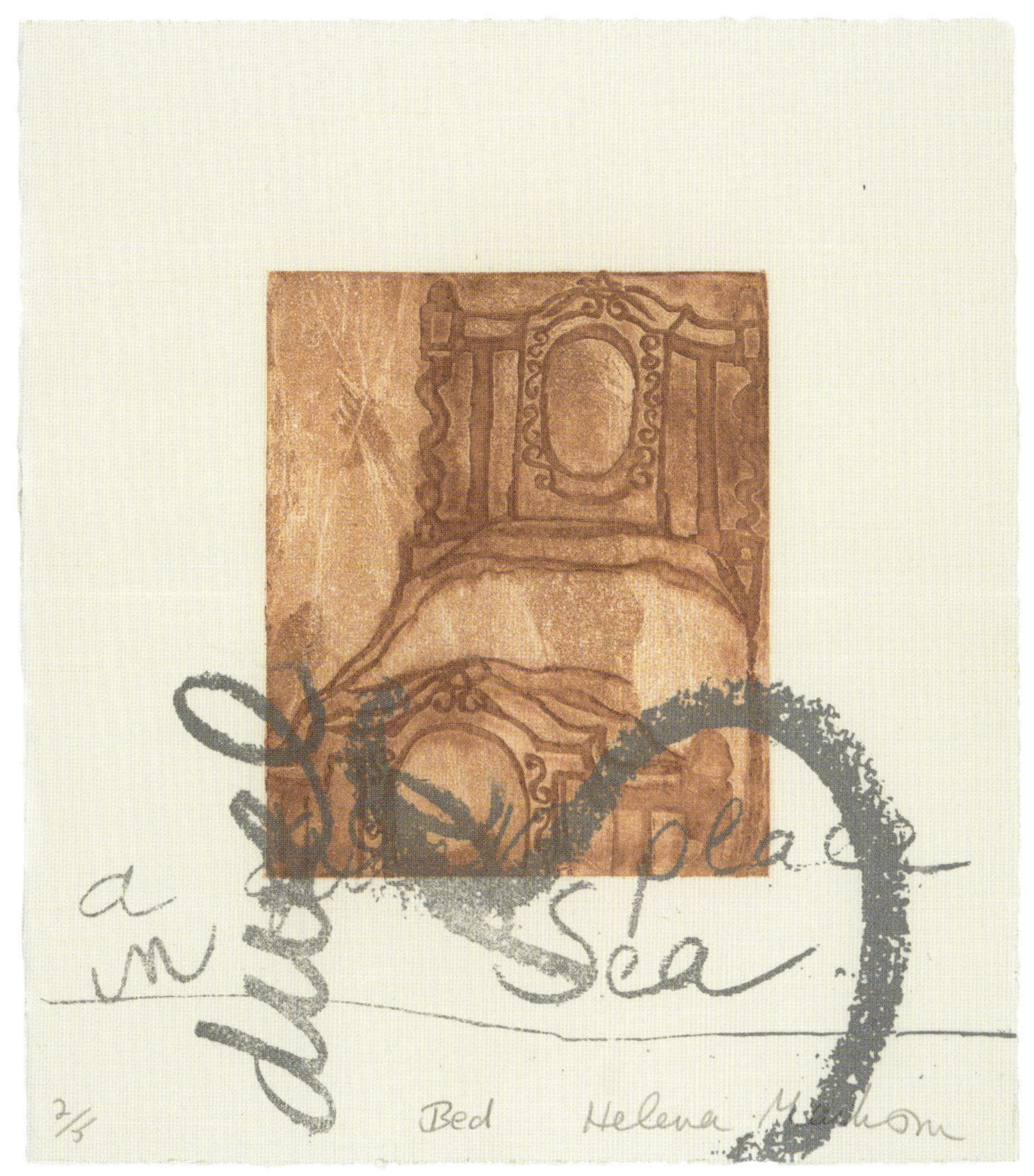

*Bed*

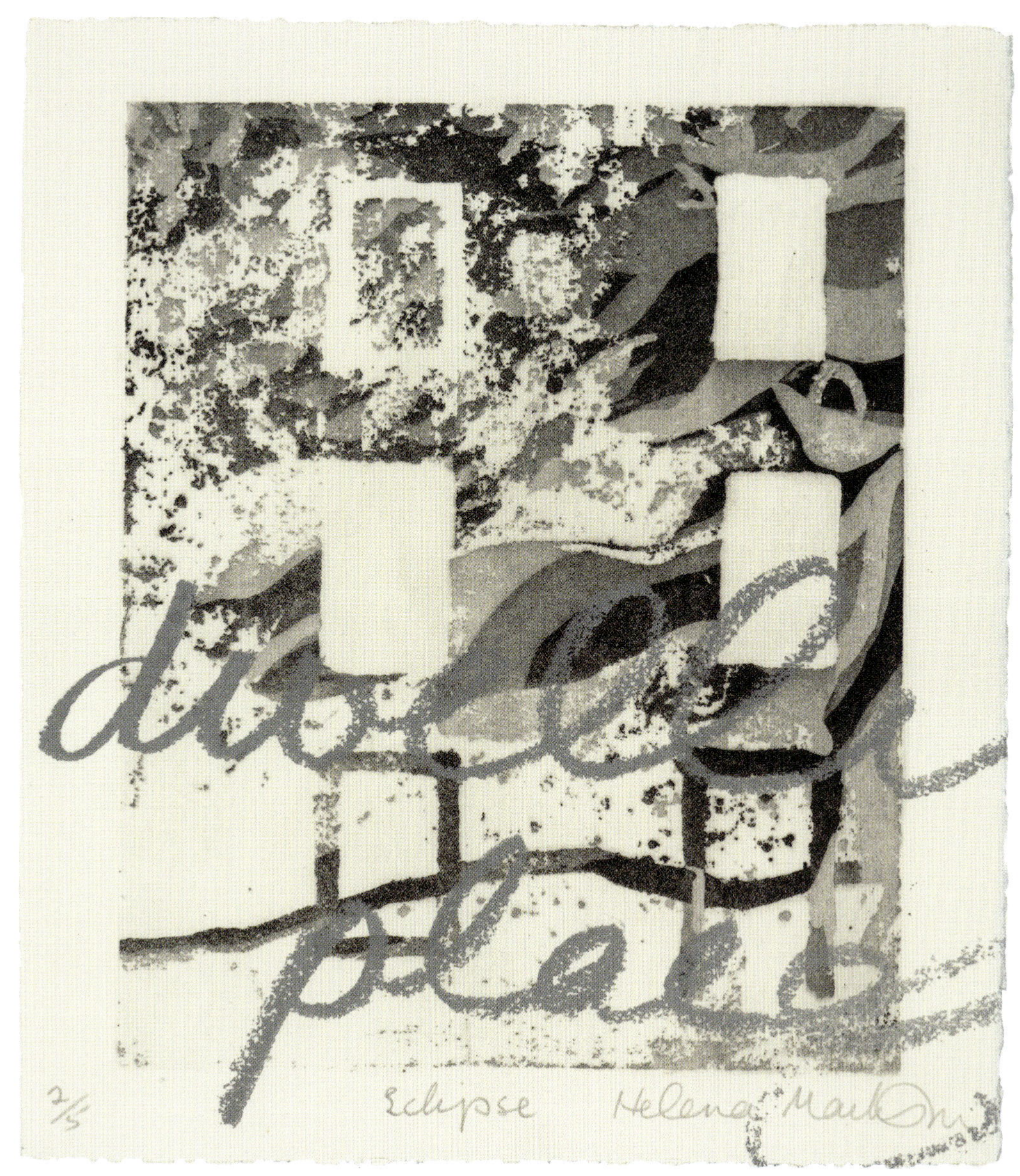



*Eclipse*

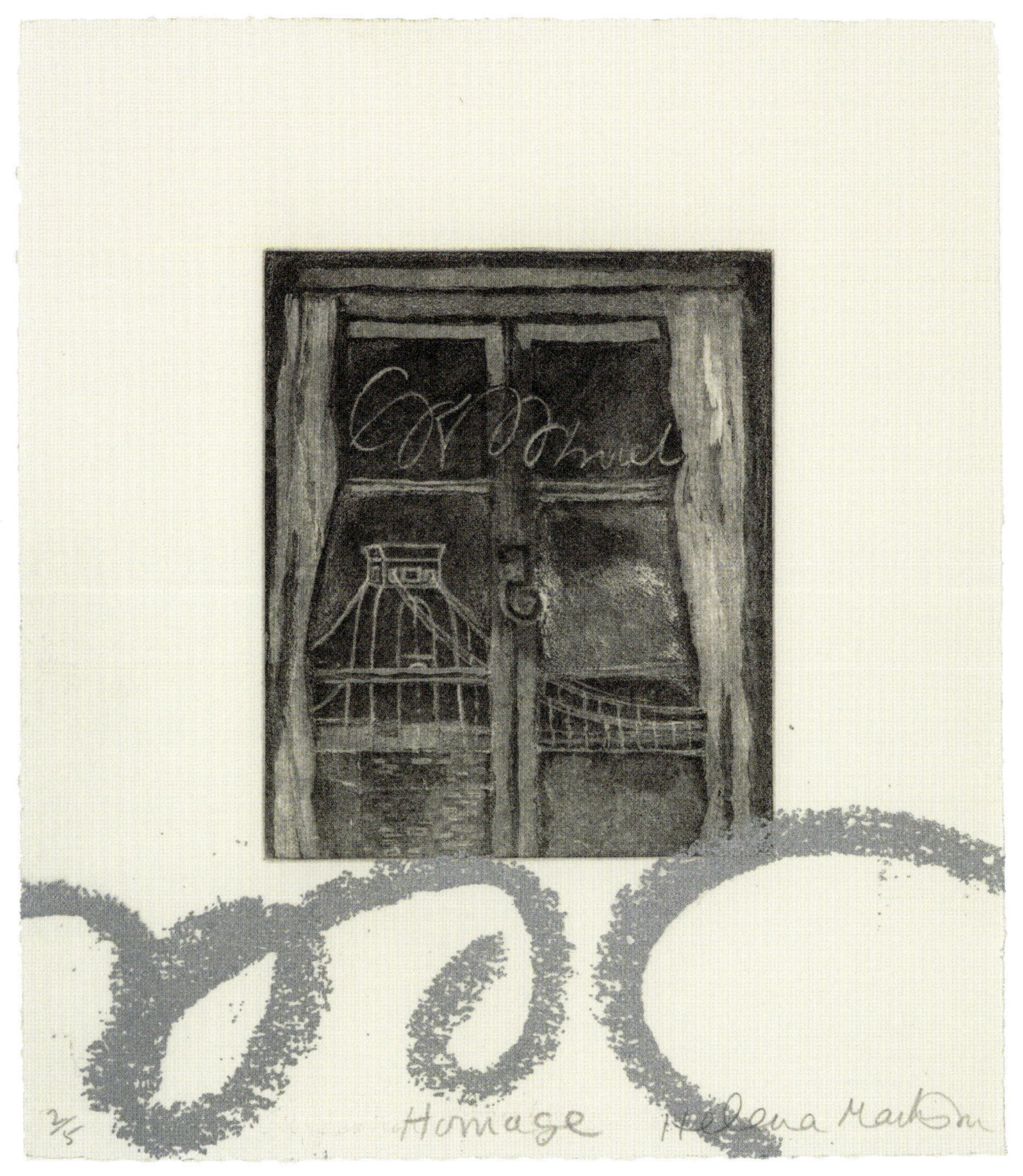

*Homage*

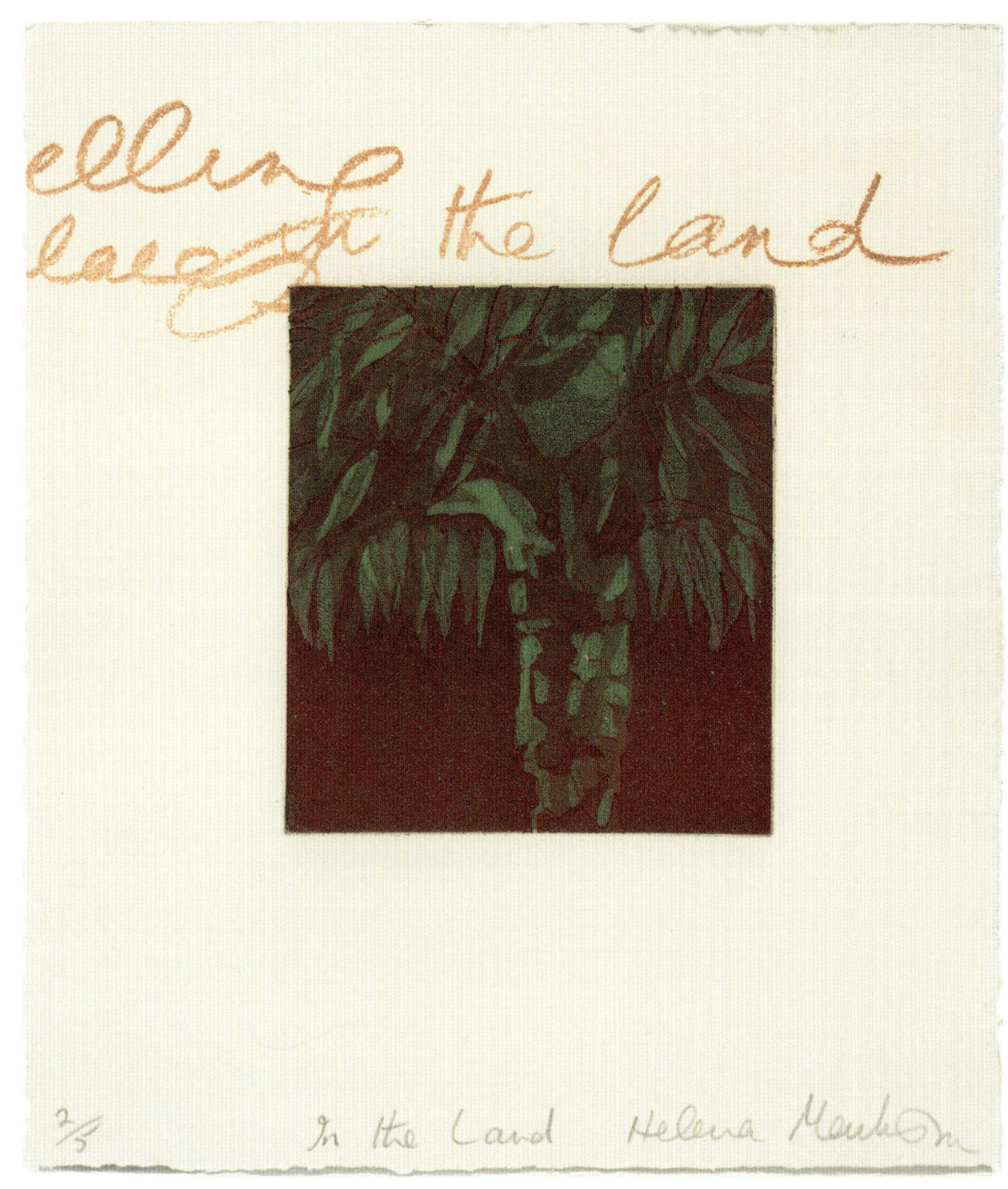

*In the Land*

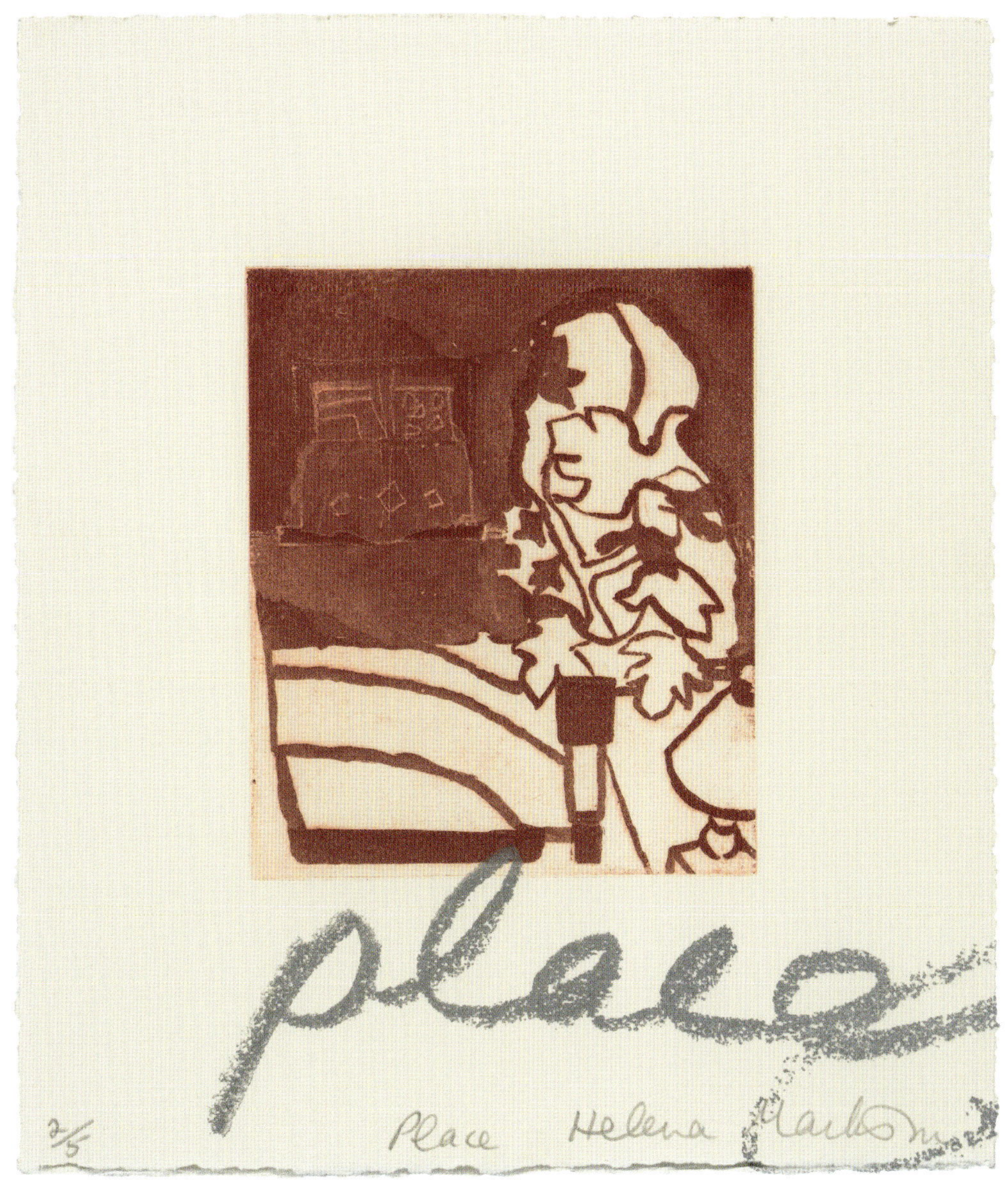


*Place*

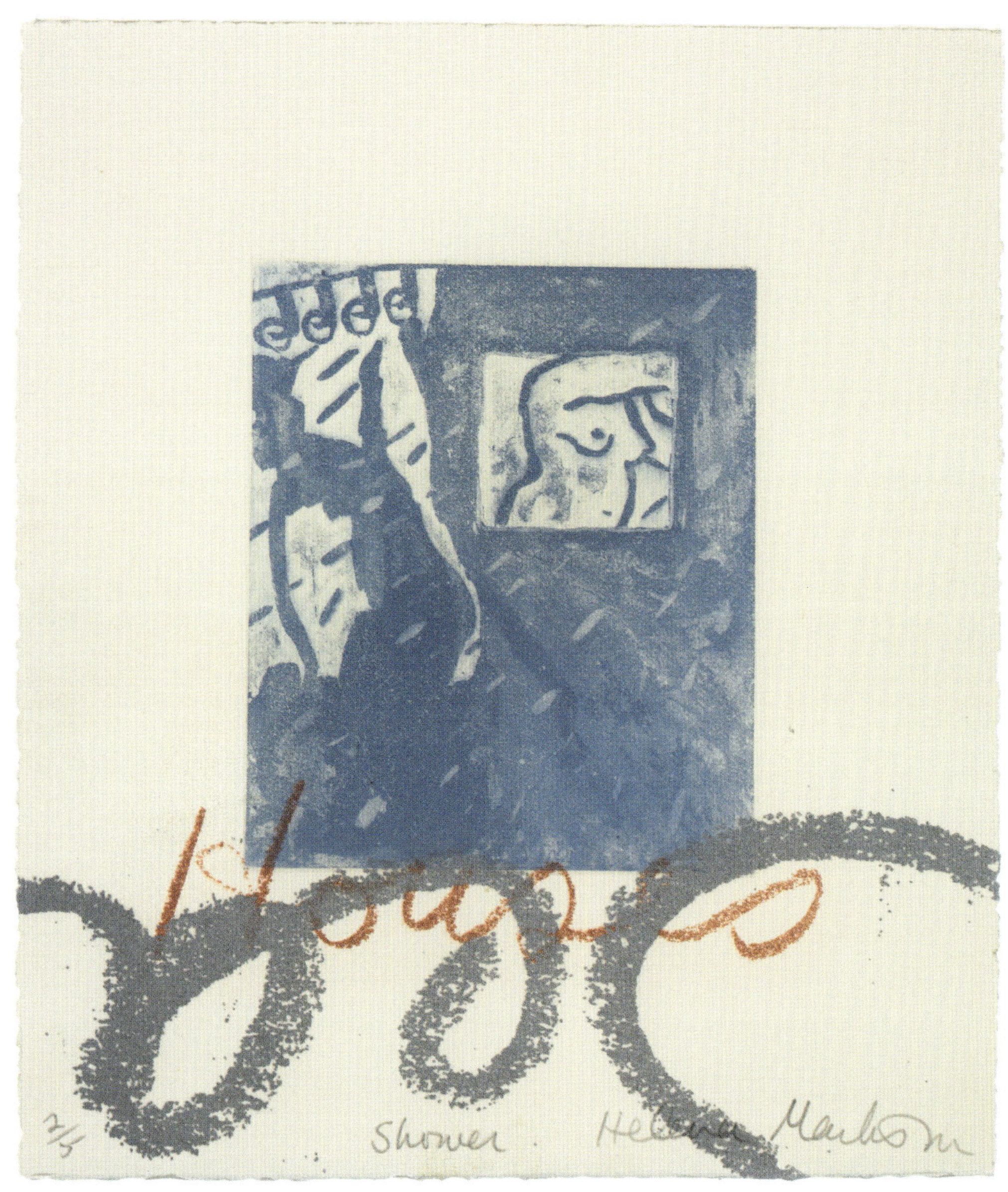

*Shower*

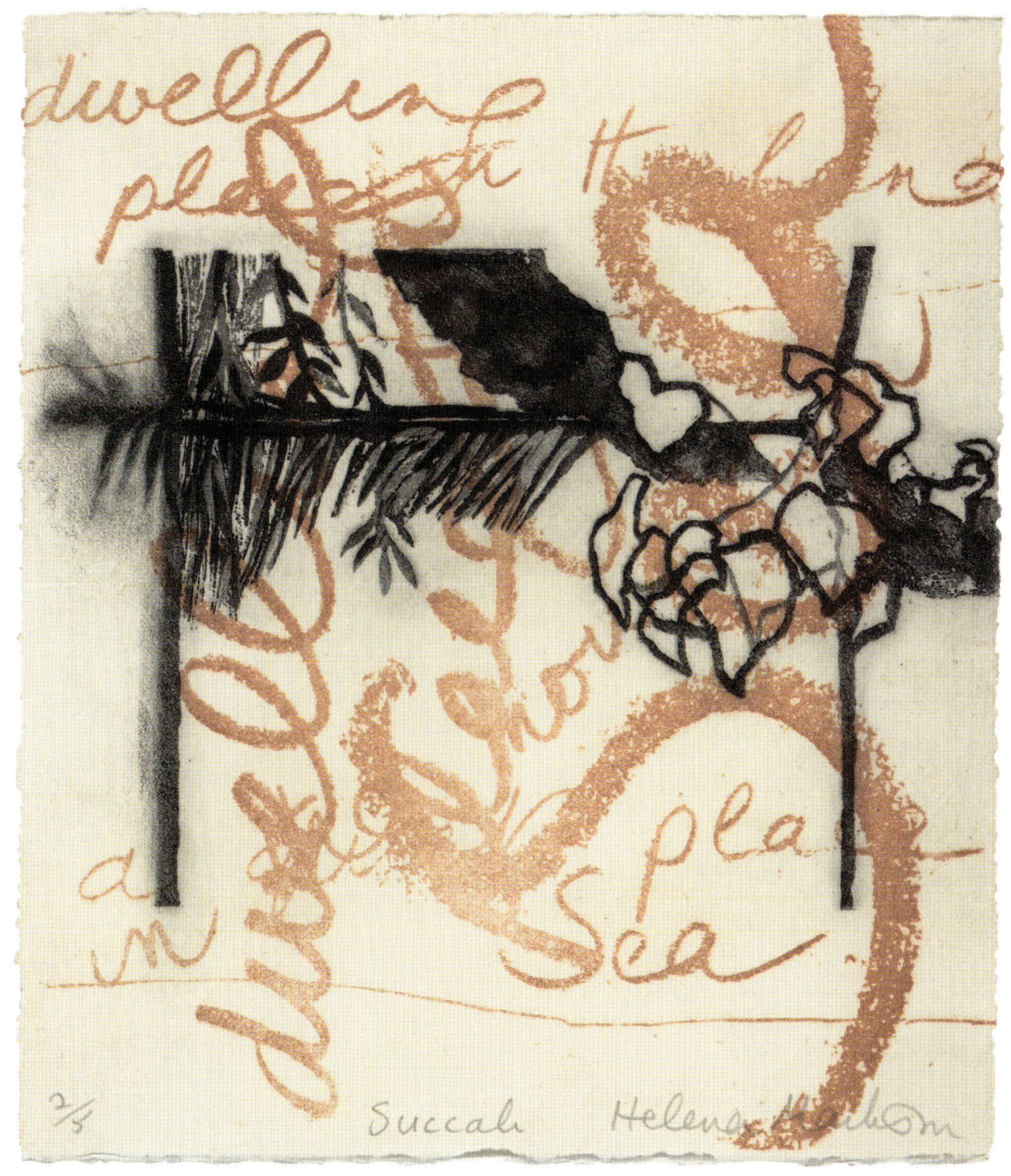


*Succah*

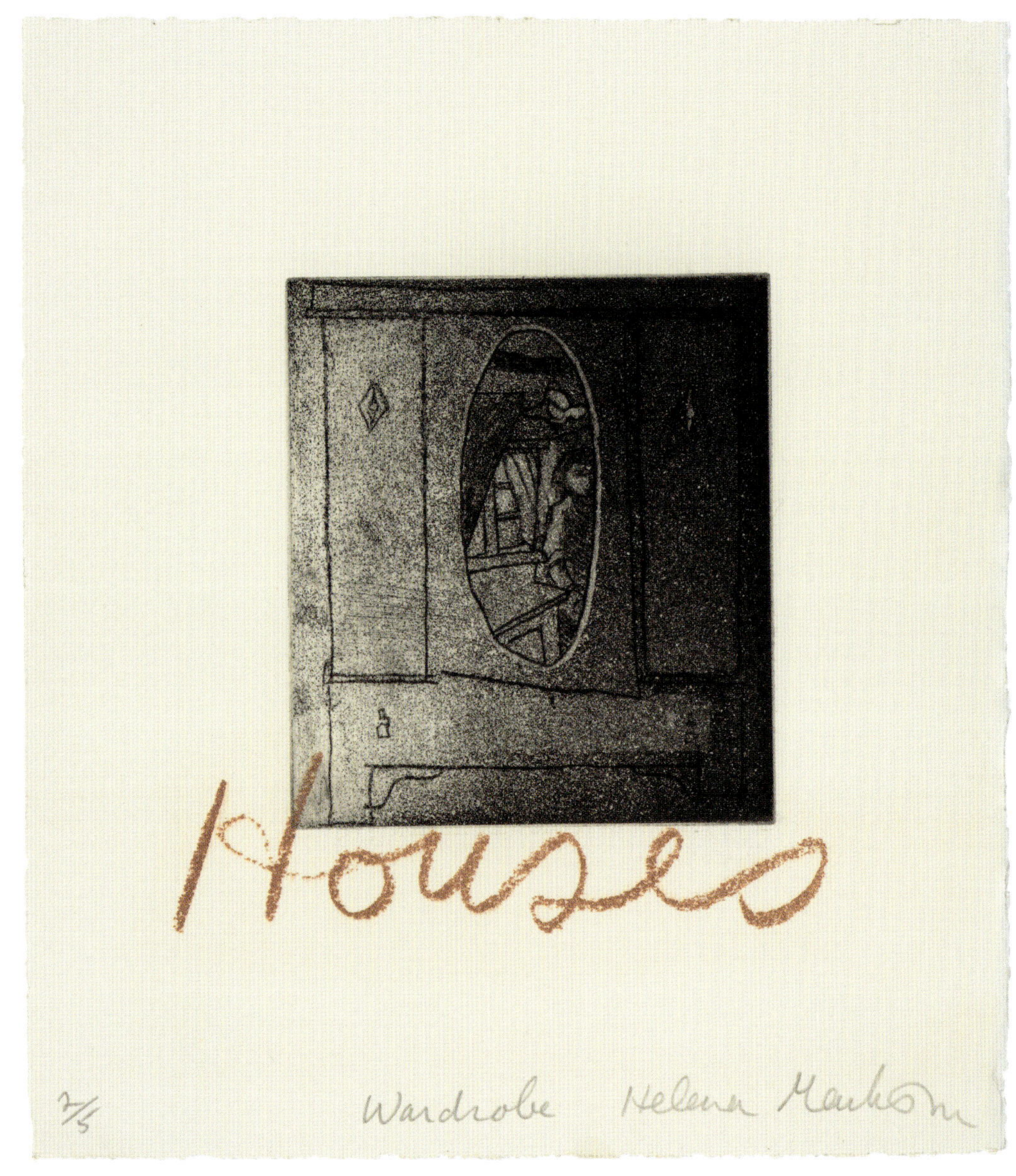

*Wardrobe*

Helena finished teaching in 2002 becoming Professor
Emeritus at the University of Haifa. By this time she had
given almost thirty-five years to teaching generations of
young students. After retirement from teaching Helena
continued to work on her own printmaking and spent
longer periods of time in England visiting her brother and
her friends. When she died in 2012 she was working on
a new series of etchings based on the Botanical Gardens
in Cambridge.

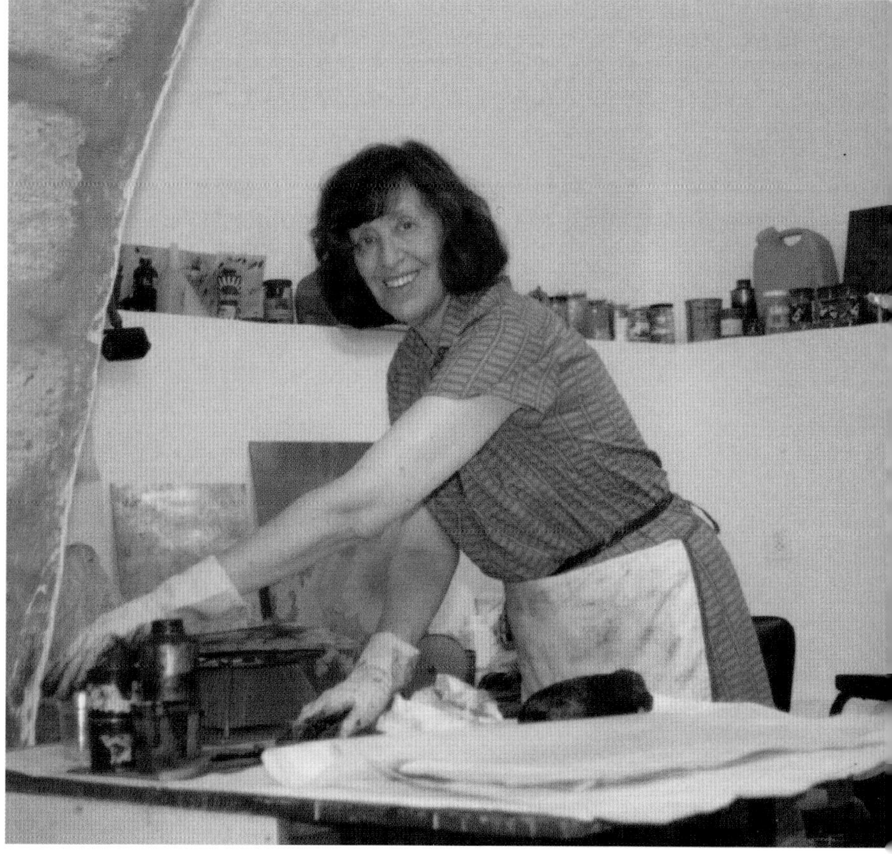

Helena Markson

Helena's many colleagues and friends remember her not only for her close friendship but also for her work and commitment to printmaking and teaching. Teaching colleagues recall how Helena would see many things in the world as though they were new to her, as if through the eyes of a child, giving her an energy and enthusiasm that pushed her to create her own work and to teach and encourage others.

*'Helena Markson was a prominent artist printmaker, and a pioneer of modern printmaking in Israel. She is well remembered for her beautiful aquatint etchings of serene landscapes of diverse places such as the slopes of Mount Carmel and the streets of Liverpool. She left the University of Haifa a beautifully equipped classic print studio. There are not many like it in Israel and none in an Israeli University.'[27]*

Helena Markson was an important influence on printmaking both in England and in Israel. She lived a life dedicated to teaching and printmaking, always so willing to share her skill and experience. She explored printmaking throughout her life and across the decades created a rich body of work by responding to and interpreting the world around her. She was influenced very personally by the places where she lived and worked, visually creating and sharing her feelings about the *persona* of the place. Her prints are now held in many collections across the world.

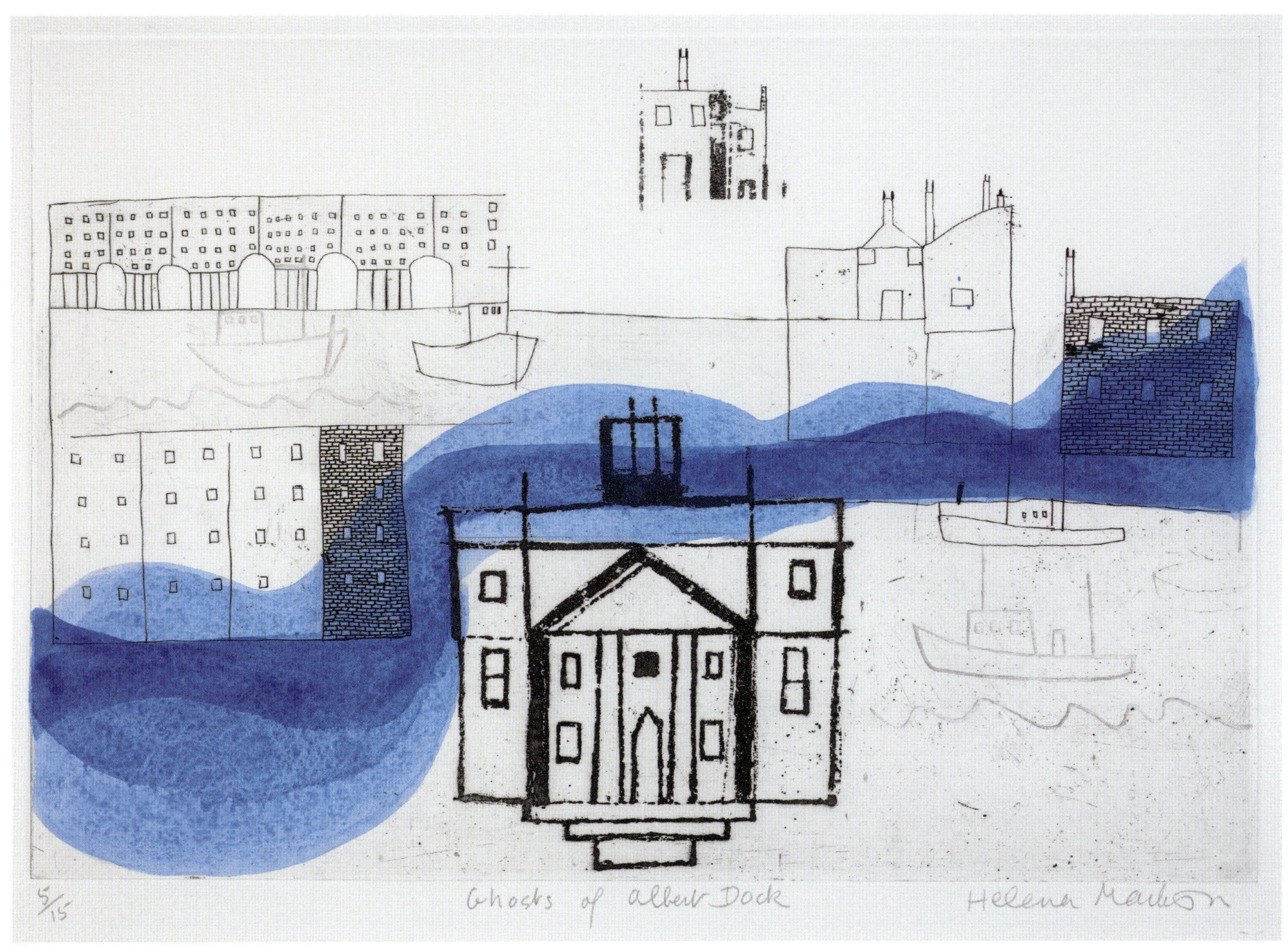


*Ghosts of Albert Dock*   2012 etching and aquatint 28cm x 40.5cm

1   Helena Markson, personal notes.

2   Merlyn Evans, Reference Letter for Helena Markson, March 1960.

3   James Burr, *Apollo Magazine*, April 1966, p. 300.

4   Robert Erskine, Introduction to 'The Graven Image' catalogue, Whitechapel Art Gallery, April–May 1959.

5   David Urwin 'Prints, Prints', *Art News and Review*, No. 8, May 1959.

6   James Burr, *Art News and Review*, Vol. XI, No. 19, 1960.

7   *Townscape* Summer Vol. 36 No. 2, 1962.

8   *Ibid*.

9   Helena Markson personal notes, October 2007.

10  *Ibid*.

11  *Ibid*.

12  Markson quote 1999 Tessa Sidey, *Editions Alecto*, Lund Humphries 2003 p. 158.

13  *Ibid*.

14  *Ibid*.

15  Sidey, *op.cit.*, p. 159.

16  *Ibid*.

17  Sidey, *op.cit.*, p. 12.

18  Sidey, *op.cit.*, p. 159.

19  *Ibid*.

20  *Ibid*.

21  *Ibid*.

22  Carel Weight, Foreword 'Pictures for Schools' exhibition catalogue, 1966.

23  Helena Markson, personal notes.

24  Aya Dinstein, 'Exhibition of Immigrant-Artists' Catalogue, June 1971.

25  Helena Markson, University of Connecticut Library, April 1985.

26  Helena Markson Introduction in exhibition catalogue, 'Helena Markson Aquatints', 1993–4 at Israel Museum, Jerusalem.

27  Prof. Avishai Ayal, Haifa University June 2013

Helena Markson specialised in colour etching and aquatint.

Both etching and aquatint come under the term of intaglio technique. Intaglio refers to all printing and printmaking techniques that involve making indents or incisions into a plate or print surface, which hold the ink when ink is applied to the surface and then wiped clean.

**ETCHING** is an intaglio printmaking technique that uses chemical action to produce incised lines in a metal printing plate, which then hold the applied ink and form the image. The plate, traditionally copper but now often zinc, is prepared with an acid-resistant ground. Lines are drawn through the ground, exposing the metal. The plate is then immersed in acid and the exposed metal is 'bitten', producing incised lines. Stronger acid and longer exposure produce more deeply bitten lines. The resist is removed and ink applied to the sunken lines, but wiped from the surface. The plate is then placed against paper and passed through a printing press with great pressure to transfer the ink from the recessed lines.

**AQUATINT** is an intaglio printmaking technique, which is used to create tonal effects rather than lines. Fine particles of acid-resistant material, such as powdered rosin, are attached to a printing plate by heating. The plate is then immersed in an acid bath, just like etching. The acid eats into the metal around the particles to produce a granular pattern of tiny indented rings. These hold sufficient ink to give the effect of an area of wash when inked and printed. Gradations of tone can be achieved by varying the length of time the plate remains in the acid; longer periods produce more deeply-bitten rings, which print darker areas of tone. It is often used in combination with other intaglio techniques.

Helena Markson used etching and aquatint to create many of her prints. She worked on copper plates using separate plates for each colour. To achieve the feel of brush marks in her prints Helena also used a form of aquatint called sugar-lift. For this the printmaker uses a solution of sugar and water (sometimes coloured with ink) which is applied to the plate with a brush. The image is drawn with the brush directly on to the plate before the acid-resistant ground is

applied. The plate is then immersed in warm water and the
sugar lifts the acid resist to expose the image. The plate is
then etched following the etching process. By combining
these processes Helena was able to achieve a painterly feel
to her prints.

Helena's notes give details about how she made her prints.
She lists the processes, number of plates and the colours,
often using three or four colours. For example:

*Pier Head*
Etching, sugar-lift aquatint, four copperplates, printed in
blue, orange, crimson red, green.

*See image page 67.*

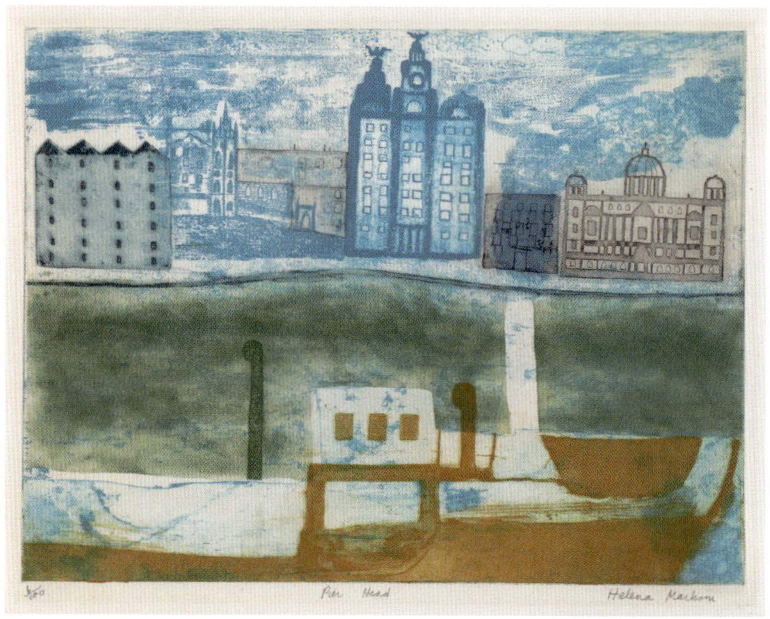

*Queen's Dock*

Etching, sugar-lift aquatint, four copperplates, printed in blue, black, purple, brick red.

*See image page 63.*

*Falconer Square*

Etching, sugar-lift aquatint, three copperplates, printed in Naples yellow, brick red, two blues wiped onto a single plate.

*See image page 81.*

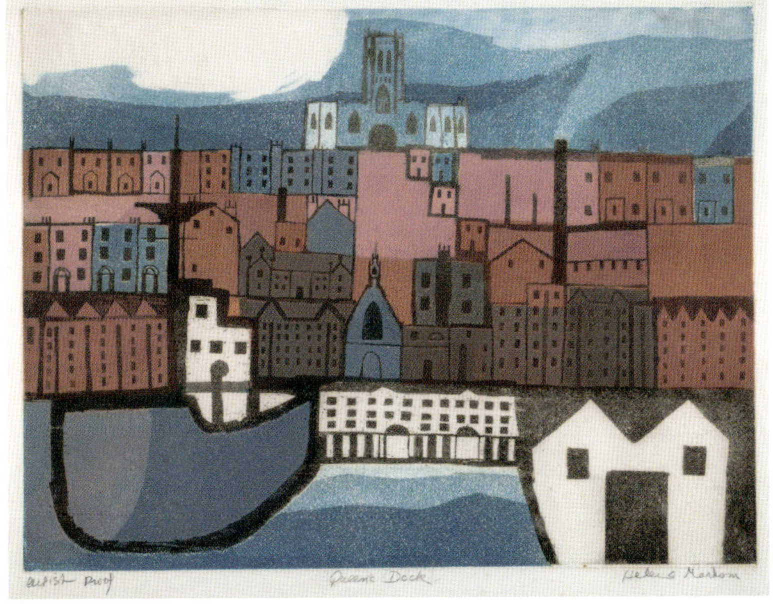

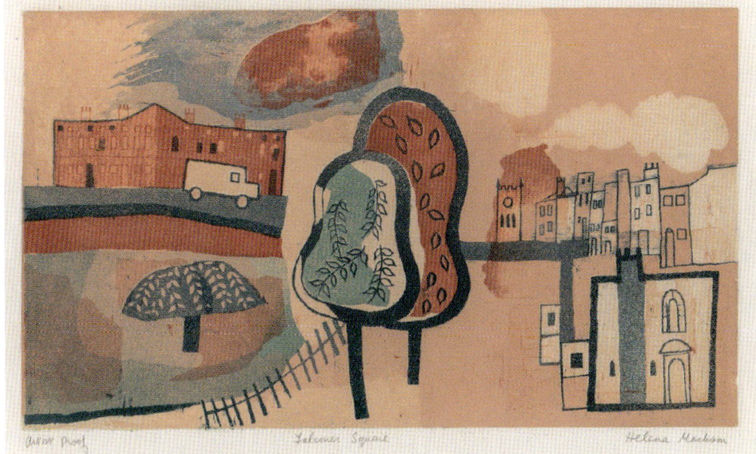

# EXHIBITIONS

**SOLO EXHIBITIONS**

| | |
|---|---|
| 1964 | London, Editions Alecto Gallery |
| 1965 | Liverpool, Walker Art Gallery |
| 1967 | Jerusalem, The Artist House |
| 1969 | Haifa, Nachmani Gallery |
| 1972 | Safed, Museum of Printing Art |
| 1983 | Jerusalem, Debel Gallery |
| 1985 | University of Connecticut, Homer Babbidge Library |
| 1994 | Jerusalem, Israel Museum |
| 1996 | Haifa, University Art Gallery |
| 1987 | University of Tennessee at Chattanooga |
| 2004 | London, Belgrave Gallery |

**GROUP EXHIBITIONS**

| | |
|---|---|
| 1956 | London St George's Gallery |
| 1959 | London Whitechapel Art Gallery, 'Graven Image' |
| 1960 | London, The Arts Council Senefelder Group |
| 1961 | Leeds City Art Gallery, Colour Lithographs |
| 1963 | London R.W.S. Gallery, 'Graven Image' |
| 1966 | Bristol Arnolfini Gallery, 'British Prints in the Sixties' |
| 1969 | London Nahmani's Gallery, 'Five Artists' |
| 1971 | Haifa, Museum of Modern Art Graphic Show |
| 1972 | Tel Aviv Museum, 'Graphic Art in Israel Today' |
| 1977 | London Tate Gallery, 'Artists at Curwen' |
| 1997 | Ljubljana Biennale International Centre for Graphic Art |
| 1997 | Haifa, University of Haifa Art in the University |
| 2000 | Jerusalem Print Workshop 'The Print and the Poem' |
| 2003–4 | Manchester, Whitworth Art Gallery and tour 'Editions Alecto – A Fury of Prints' |

Albuquerque Tamarind Institute
Carnegie Library, New York
Cunard Shipping Company
Dallas Museum of Fine Art, Texas
Haifa Museum of Modern Art
Jerusalem, Israel Museum
Leeds City Art Gallery
Liverpool Public Libraries
Museum of Modern Art, New York
National Museum of Wales, Cardiff

New York Public Library
Oregon State University, Oregon
Safed Museum of Printing Art
Sheffield City Art Gallery
Tate Gallery, London
Tel Aviv Museum
Time Magazine Building, London
UK Government Art Collection (GAC)
United Nations Buildings, New York
Walker Art Gallery, Liverpool

Emma Mason opened Emma Mason Prints in 2004.
The gallery specialises in original prints by artists working
in Britain from the post-war years to the present day.
Emma studied art history and Italian at Leicester University.
After many years working in the fruit trade as an importer
Emma changed career to set up the gallery. She has written
about post-war original prints for various publications and,
with her husband Richard, has published two books on the
printmaker Robert Tavener.

Helena Markson's archive of prints, including work for sale,
is held by Emma Mason Prints, specialist dealer and gallery.

www.emmamason.co.uk